Country Life

KU-720-396

WILDLIFE
in Towns and Cities
gardens, parks and waterways

Michael Chinery and W.G. Teagle

COUNTRY LIFE BOOKS

Acknowledgements for the field guide

I must express my gratitude to all those who have so kindly given me the benefit of their knowledge and experience, and in particular I should like to thank Peter C. Barnard, S. J. Brooks, David J. Cash, Nicholas Derry, Miss P. Gilbert, Dr Alan Harrington, A. M. Hutson, Keith H. Hyatt, Miss Paula Jenkins, Jack R. Laundon, J. R. Press and F. R. Wanless of the British Museum (Natural History), Dr Stephen Harris of the University of Bristol, David M. Kemp of Leeson House Field Studies Centre, Dr David Reid of the Royal Botanic Gardens, Kew, J. R. White of the Nature Conservancy Council, Dr R. E. Stebbings of the Institute of Terrestrial Ecology, Stanley Cramp, A. W. Jones, Mrs M. G. Parkinson, and John and Jean Bowerman. I also wish to thank Michael Chinery for his many invaluable suggestions, especially in the entomological field, and my wife Joyce for scrutinising each page as it came off the typewriter.

I accept full responsibility for any factual errors which may occur in the field guide text, and I hope readers will let me know of any they may find. There are, I know, many sins of omission; a lot of interesting detail has been left out because of lack of space.

Finally, I should like to thank the artists, Mrs Cynthia Pow, John Davis, Ian Garrard, Roger Gorringe and Ken Oliver, for their splendid co-operation, and the staff of Newnes Books for their patience and understanding.

W. G. Teagle, Swanage, 1984

Publishers' note. During the production of this book, the publishers heard of the death of the artist Ian Garrard whose work is a mainstay of this and many other publications. His personality and talent will be sadly missed.

Published by Country Life Books
an imprint of Newnes Books, a Division
of the Hamlyn Publishing Group Limited,
84–88 The Centre, Feltham, Middlesex, England

© Newnes Books, a Division of the Hamlyn Publishing Group Limited 1985

All rights reserved. No part of this publication may be reproduced, stored in a retrieval system, or transmitted, in any form or by any means, electronic, mechanical, photocopying, recording or otherwise, without the permission of the Publisher and the copyright holder.

ISBN 0 600 35674 4 (cased)
ISBN 0 600 35763 5 (softback)

Printed in Italy

Contents

Introduction
Michael Chinery

Nature in towns and cities

Towns and cities are comparatively new habitats in biological terms, a product of the evolution of man from a hunting to a settled way of life that began about 10,000 years ago. The original communities were probably no more than family groupings, but, as agricultural skills increased and food became more plentiful, individuals were freed to produce other goods for barter which led to the division of labour which is the basis of any organised community.

As settlements grew, plants and animals adapted to exploit the new habitats that were created.

Today a multitude of creatures co-exists with man in his concrete and asphalt habitat exploiting, almost every niche with as much vigour as that of any natural ecosystem.

The city as a habitat

The modern city centre is clearly further from open country than a town centre and *may* be subject to different environmental pressures, but the immense variation in urban planning and development makes it pointless to attempt to distinguish between the wildlife of towns and that of cities. The densely built-up centre, dotted with a few parks and churchyards, and the sprawling suburbs with their abundant gardens and other open spaces are typical of many British towns, but we find some marked differences when we look at towns in other parts of Europe. The relatively sterile centre is still there, often with its high-rise flats and offices, but there are commonly more open spaces close to the centre squares and parks used for recreation – and there are often more trees, especially in the warmer areas where they are planted for shade. It is in the suburbs, however, that we see the greatest differences, for gardening is not the obsession it is in Britain and we find that there is far less greenery on the outskirts of most continental European towns. Many suburban houses in France and Scandinavia, for example, have no garden at all and there is a very abrupt boundary between the town and the surrounding countryside.

The town habitat is obviously man-made, but many of its component parts are not too dissimilar from natural habitats. Where development has been carried out gradually, some of the smaller areas such as churchyards and river banks may be remnants of the original natural habitats and may support the original species.

Man-made parks and cemeteries, with their planted trees and shrubs, are not unlike woodland margins and may contain a rich

This abandoned machinery on wasteland provides shelter for pioneer plants like these spear thistles and scentless mayweed. Many pioneer plants produce thousands of flighted seeds which allow them to quickly colonise almost any piece of bare ground.

assortment of bird and insect life. Gravestones and walls of all kinds provide vertical surfaces very similar to natural rocks and cliffs, and not surprisingly they are colonised by assorted plants and animals which normally live on these rocks and cliffs. Even in the completely built-up centre of a big city the tall buildings provide nesting sites for pigeons and kestrels – birds which can survive in such places indefinitely without ever seeing a tree or any other green plant. But it is our suburban gardens, with their amazing diversity of habitat, that contribute most to the variety of our town wildlife. The value of the garden is enhanced, certainly as far as the birds are concerned, by the food that so many people deliberately put out for the animals. This brings in greater numbers of birds, in terms of species as well as individuals, and also increases their survival rate, especially during the winter months. Urban blackbirds have been shown to be in the region of 10 per cent heavier than birds living in country areas, and this is certainly due to the extra food supplies. Not all food is deliberately provided, however, for man is both wasteful and untidy and he scatters large amounts of food around his towns and cities. Urban pigeons and sparrows need look no further than the street markets for their sustenance, while foxes (in Britain) and many other animals have discovered that our dustbins are well worth investigating for an evening meal.

Our communications networks also benefit urban wildlife. Road-sides and railway banks are littered with food of various kinds,

Even though this scene (**above**) may look very polluted the water itself must be relatively clean to allow the mute swans to breed.

Industry and nature co-exist in delicate balance. The countryside forgives many of man's excesses, but sometimes pollution becomes just too much. Here, trees near a steel works have been killed by airborne pollution.

much of it fallen from lorries and wagons, and they support plenty of animal life. Railway banks are especially rich habitats because they suffer very little from human interference. Canals and rivers may be equally important and, together with roads and railways, they form major highways along which wildlife can penetrate right to town centres. Once there, the plants and animals find another welcome in the form of warmth: our homes and offices, our vehicles, and assorted machinery are continually pumping out heat and the city centre is generally several degrees warmer than the surrounding countryside. This higher temperature may be sufficient for alien plants and animals to establish themselves, but it is the inside of our buildings that are the prime targets for animal life in this context. In our factories, warehouses, and homes we produce and store an abundance of food to suit all tastes and animals from home and abroad have not been slow to take advantage of it. They can live in the most densely built-up areas, for they are completely independent of the outside environment.

We can see from this that the urban environment offers many advantages to wildlife, but it also poses many problems and, compared with the surrounding countryside, the town actually supports relatively few species. Destruction of the natural habitat during urban development clearly drives out many species which are unable to make use of the artificial environment afterwards. Apart from a few algae mosses and lichens, plant life cannot establish itself on solid concrete, although some species have a jolly good try at lifting and breaking asphalt and similar surfaces. Continuous pressure of feet and wheels in the busiest areas eliminates even the tiny mosses that might otherwise colonise minute pavement cracks, and without plants city streets can support little animal life.

Air pollution is another major problem posed by the urban environment, and one which has been responsible for the disappearance of quite a lot of species from our cities in recent decades. On the other hand, some insects have mananged to turn industrial pollution to their own advantage. Those animals that have managed to solve the problems of urban living may find one further advantage – their natural enemies may not have always managed it.

Prospects for the future

The future of our urban wildlife is in our own hands and, with the increase in the urban wildlife parks and wildlife gardens we can feel reasonably confident of its continued prosperity. But it is imperative to continue the fight against pollution and to ensure that the open spaces remain open if we are to prevent virtual sterility from descending upon our city centres. It is, however, an equally sobering thought that wildlife could take over our cities if it were given the chance. Towns and cities are artificial communities, and nature is always eager to reclaim them for herself. Neglected areas such as derelict industrial areas and disused railway yards are quickly over-run by vegetation and soon invaded by animals as large as foxes. The speed with which bombed sites were covered with plants during the Second World War provided even more dramatic proof of nature's regenerative powers, although even this example pales into insignificance when compared with the way in which tropical forests can overwhelm abandoned settlements and cause buildings to collapse.

The maintenance of urban wildlife will always involve a compromise between the requirements of man and those of nature, but if we are willing to strive for this not-too-difficult compromise the rewards are considerable. Not only will the city become a healthier and more attractive environment but city-dwellers may become more aware of the natural world around them – beyond as well as within the city limits – and do something to ensure that it is treated with more respect.

The scope of the book

The urban naturalist might not have the variety of species enjoyed by the countryman, but the various terrestrial and aquatic habitats within a typical town will yield more than enough plants and animals to keep busy.

The first part of the book consists of a number of short essays on topics of special interest to the urban naturalist. Their aim is essen-. tially to explain urban natural history, but there are also suggestions for encouraging wildlife to visit urban gardens. In this section, where plant and animal names are not accompanied by their Latin names an illustration and entry can be found in the field guide.

The second section of this book is a field guide designed to help the interested observer to identify the more common and conspicuous species that occur in towns in Northern Europe. (For the purposes of this book we have taken Northern Europe to be the area shown by the map on page 81.) They are not found in all towns or in all countries, and the normal distribution, so far as it is known, is given for each species. Because towns and cities are the foci of commerce, however, many creatures get transported from place to place – by air, land, and sea – and may well turn up well beyond their normal ranges. Such expansions are generally shortlived because relatively few individuals arrive at the same destination and they fail to establish themselves. But there are exceptions, one of the best known being the little scorpion *Euscorpius flavicaudis*, which has at least two outposts in Britain, far beyond its normal home in southern Europe.

The third section of the book is a gazetteer listing various interesting nature reserves and sites found within urban boundries where wildlife can be seen to best advantage. Of particular interest are the urban wildlife parks, created specifically to attract and conserve the plants and animals in towns and cities and to stimulate interest in them.

Urban wildlife habitats　　　W.G. Teagle

Man created towns and cities to meet the needs of mankind, but other forms of life have benefited. Each settlement is a unique complex of plant and animal habitats, for no two towns are exactly alike. The conditions which allow wildlife colonisation vary considerably from place to place, since they are not only dependent on latitude, altitude, climate and physiography, but on human attitudes and behaviour. Even within one country these factors can account for the presence of some species and the absence of others. Far greater differences can therefore be expected when comparing flora and fauna of places as far apart as Paris and Stockholm.

Streets and buildings

Few people really believe these days that towns are little more than brick-and-mortar deserts, but one must recognise that some urban habitats are in fact desolate. Roads, pavements, paths and precincts can cover a third of the urban land surface, and an equivalent area can be occupied by buildings.

Yet even in the most densely built-up parts of a city, where one is very conscious of the surrounding buildings, traffic noise, petrol fumes and crowds of people, one may still find vegetation. The air carries the seeds and spores of many plants, some of which may alight and germinate in the most inhospitable places. Cushion-forming species can survive between paving slabs, unharmed by human feet. Taller vegetation may escape being trampled when found at the foot of a wall or fence. One may look in vain for lichens on the stonework, for few of these can tolerate the sulphur dioxide in the inner city atmosphere, but ferns can sometimes gain a root-hold on shady walls, and flowering plants may become established in the mortar joints and cracks in the bricks and stones.

Many cliff-nesting birds have accepted town buildings as man-made rock-stacks. Some use roof-tops, some the ledges and ornamental features, and others the holes and crevices resulting from disrepair. Man-made structures also provide song-posts and roosting sites. Mammals have also made their home under man's roof, as have many insects.

Tree-lined streets soften the townscape, and, if laid out imaginatively, they can serve as green corridors which link the town's innermost open spaces with the suburbs and the surrounding countryside. The trees provide nesting, feeding and roosting sites for birds, and their foliage supports invertebrates, including the caterpillars of several moths.

9

Neglected cemeteries provide a sanctuary for all manner of wildlife. Many, such as this one in Albany Park London, are now managed as nature reserves.

Trees (**below**) not only make the urban landscape appear less forbidding, they also supply food, cover and breeding places for many animals.

Neglected land

Buildings may be demolished, sometimes deliberately to make room for something new, or as a result of fire, civil disorder or military conflict. Ruined buildings can also be a feature of abandoned industrial sites. If left undisturbed these places are rapidly reclaimed by nature. Following the Second World War scenes of urban destruction were widespread throughout Europe. Most of these war-damaged sites started off more or less devoid of vegetation, but the rubble was soon covered with prolific annual plants which arose

This derelict canal site is in the first stages of plant colonisation. Before long, if the site is left, shrubby plants like buddleia, bramble and silver birch may move in.

from wind-borne seeds. These attracted pollinating insects and seed-eating and insectivorous birds. Other plants grew from seeds deposited in bird droppings or from the remains of office workers' picnic lunches. The City of London bomb sites acquired hayfield plants from the shovelfuls of horse manure thrown there by street cleaners. Many of the plant colonists were species of foreign origin. Today, although the extent of the dereliction is infinitely less, the general sequence of colonisation is the same.

Disused railway property, derelict dockyards, and overgrown allotments, churchyards and cemeteries are other examples of neglected areas that can become havens for wildlife. Any site, if left long enough, can become clothed with trees and bushes, and the greater the diversity of vegetation, the wider the range of animal life it can accommodate. Some of the abandoned industrial sites in Britain have pools and marshes as well as rough grassland, scrub and woodland. They are among the richest of all urban habitats, and several of them have been recognised by the Nature Conservancy Council as Sites of Special Scientific Interest (SSSIs).

Watercourses

It was to meet the needs of industry that Britain developed its network of canals, mainly between the middle of the 18th century and the first quarter of the 19th century. Unlike the inland water-ways of Continental Europe, they lost their economic importance

11

with the coming of the railways. Some have disappeared altogether, others have been restored and are mainly used by pleasure craft. All surviving canals are of interest to naturalists, for, like the railway banks and some of the tree-lined roads, they link the town with the country. Their banks often display the attractive waterside flowers which are usually destroyed when river banks are modified in the interests of flood prevention and which cannot grow on the concrete shores of the average park lake. Their sluggish waters encourage the spread of aquatic plants and invertebrates which are unable to become established in other urban watercourses and, unless hopelessly polluted, they are inhabited by several species of fish.

Urban streams, rivers and estuaries have all been used as rubbish tips and open sewers in their time. The insanitary condition of one of Europe's major rivers at the end of the 18th century provoked this outburst from Samuel Taylor Coleridge:

> The River Rhine, it is well known,
> Doth wash your city of Cologne;
> But tell me, Nymphs, what power divine
> Shall henceforth wash the River Rhine?

Today the river is still heavily polluted – with chemical effluents. Just over a decade ago the Mersey was aptly described as 'a massive unflushed lavatory', and in the late 1950s the tidal waters of the Thames were too foul for fish life.

Over the past few years there have been encouraging improvements. Recent efforts to combat water pollution have enabled fish to return to some urban rivers. The supreme example is the transformation of the Thames, which is once again clean enough for salmon to have been caught from it. Its restoration is one of the most remarkable conservation achievements of this century.

Waste disposal

In mediaeval times household waste and human excrement lay in the streets, to be scavenged by kites, ravens and domestic pigs. Irresponsible townsfolk still dump their household rubbish on vacant sites or leave it to pollute streams, and even more regrettable is the action of a municipal cleansing department when it uses town refuse to fill in a biologically interesting quarry, marsh or flooded gravel pit as a cheap alternative to incineration.

Refuse tips are usually situated on the urban fringes. Unsightly and malodorous they may be, but they are not barren of wildlife. They support myriads of invertebrates, the plants of disturbed ground, gardeners' rejects, rats, foxes, avian scavengers like the starlings, gulls and crows, and flocks of finches attracted by the

Refuse tips attract a wide range of scavenging animals all jostling for a share of the abundant supplies of rotting food. These gulls probably spend most of the year inland at tips, migrating to the coast to breed.

seeding vegetation. The warmth created by the putrefaction of organic waste makes it possible for house crickets to inhabit the rubbish mounds. These insects are caught by the bats that haunt the tips at twilight.

Many coastal towns are guilty of discharging untreated sewage into the sea, but safer and more sophisticated methods of disposal are employed inland. The modern sewage purification works, with their percolating filters, attract a variety of birds, although not as wide a range as the old-fashioned sewage farms that preceded them. Sewage works are usually situated on the fringes of the built-up area or even beyond them. They cannot perhaps be legitimately classified as urban habitats, but abandoned sites may become surrounded by suburbia and retain, for a while, their man-made marshland and their attraction for wetland birds.

Reservoirs

Drinking water reservoirs may also lie well beyond the towns they serve, but some of the older ones are now surrounded by houses. In Britain many of these man-made lakes are stocked with fish for anglers and most of them have become important refuges for thousands of wintering duck.

Town-dwellers' growing awareness of the need for conservation has led to volunteer groups actively creating urban wildlife habitats. Here, a small pond is being built and saplings planted with room for grassland and other habitats, yet to be laid, in the foreground.

The feeder reservoirs that were built to supply Britain's canals can be of even greater interest to the general naturalist, for they not only have open water to attract wildfowl, but marginal growth that provides nesting sites for smaller birds. They also cater for the needs of amphibians and a wide range of aquatic invertebrates. Several of these old reservoirs are now encapsulated within the built-up area and are managed, together with their green surroundings, as nature reserves and recreation centres.

Gardens and parks

Private and public gardens can be regarded as the urban equivalent of one of the richest of all rural habitats – the woodland edge. Provided that those who care for them can appreciate the importance of working *with* nature instead of against it, gardens can play a valuable part in the conservation of plants and animals in built-up areas. Different species are likely to be encountered in Continental gardens from those we know in Britain and Ireland. The grey squirrel does not occur and familiar birds like the robin and the dunnock may only be occasional shy visitors. Townsfolk in other European countries may entertain birds not established in the British Isles, like the icterine warbler and the serin. Continental gardens also reflect different tastes and attitudes, with some more devoted to fruit and vegetable growing than the cultivation of flowers. Some

Europeans favour extreme formality, while others, like the Swedes, may prefer gardens to look like an extension of the countryside. The manicured lawn is nowhere more the indispensable feature it is in Britain.

Public open spaces should be the richest of urban wildlife habitats, and there are certainly some that do come up to the naturalists' expectations – wild places that have preserved something of their character even though they have been enclosed by the urban sprawl. In England these range from small commons like that of Barnes in South London to the vast expanse of Sutton Park in the West Midlands. Many Continental towns have their woods and forests.

Urban conservationists should resist any efforts that are made to tame these valuable remnants of wilderness. All too many town parks consist mainly of what has been described as 'urban savannah' – flat expanses of mown grass with isolated standard trees. It is true that many of them also have formal gardens, tidy shrubberies and concrete pools or lakes, but these only reinforce the impression that these are places where wild nature has been subdued rather than encouraged. That birds and mammals have learned to exploit this environment is a tribute to their adaptability. The degree to which they are able to do so depends, however, on the behaviour of the visiting public. It is not everywhere that wild birds are bold enough to feed from human hands, or that nest-boxes and trees can escape being destroyed by vandals.

Changing attitudes

At one time wildlife was ruthlessly exploited and cruelly treated throughout Europe. Today it is threatened more by environmental pollution and loss of habitat than by human hostility. More people are interested in the conservation of nature and natural resources, and more town-dwellers are aware of the wildlife around them. Many are joining organisations which can save biologically interesting sites under threat, present scientific evidence to official bodies concerned with town-planning, parks administration, land drainage and outdoor education, and find volunteers to help create and manage urban nature reserves.

Ecologically designed landscapes which reflect the most pleasant features of the Dutch countryside have become an accepted part of town life in parts of The Netherlands. They have shown that there is an alternative to concrete ponds and urban savannah, and it is cheering to know that local authorities in other countries are following the Dutch example. The final outcome should not only be an environment favourable to wildlife, but a much more pleasant habitat for man.

Birds in towns and cities

J. Denis Summers-Smith

Some birds have always found towns and cities appealing places in which to make a living. The grains which early man specialised in growing must have been an attraction to granivorous species, such as sparrows and pigeons. Food given to domesticated animals also attracted wild birds. As man's habits changed so the birds which were becoming dependent upon him changed their habits to suit. As towns increased in size domesticated animals were withdrawn to farms on their outskirts, only to be replaced in time with horses which provided birds with oats spilled from their nose bags and seed passed through in their droppings. Mediaeval towns and cities had no rubbish collection service or inadequate sewage disposal; this also provided food for scavenging birds. The replacement of the horse by the internal combustion engine and the improvements in sanitation and rubbish clearance reduced the quantity of food to be found within the town. But the scavengers can still forage on the rubbish tips on the urban fringes.

More recently the increasing attention to the social amenity of clean air and the creation of smokeless zones has led to an increasing insect population that has allowed the colonisation, or perhaps recolonisation, of the urban environment by aerial insect feeders such as swifts and house martins. Also, changing attitudes to birds have allowed a whole range of birds previously caught for the pot or cage, or hunted as a pastime, to penetrate the cities.

Man's buildings also provide safe nesting places: holes in thatch and under eaves for birds such as sparrows and starlings; ledges for cliff nesters such as feral rock pigeons and kestrels; and rooftops for herring gulls. Ledges also provide good roosting places with protection from the elements and the advantage in temperate latitude cities of a slightly higher temperature through waste heat, when compared with the surrounding countryside.

Another important feature of towns which provides a different habitat for bird life are public parks and squares with their trees, flower beds and grass; and in the less intensively built-up surrounding suburbs, this is continued in the increasing space given over to gardens and playing fields that give a connecting corridor between the central parks and the open countryside. These areas provide a refuge for an avifauna not completely adapted to the built-up environment, but increasingly attracted by deliberate feeding or the unintentional provision of scraps from luncheon packages and open air restaurants. The wide range of birds willing to accept such

Buildings provide ideal artificial rock faces upon which seabirds, such as these kittiwakes (**right**), can nest.

Today, town pigeons (**below**) are so much a part of our towns and cities that it is little realised that they are descended from rock doves, domesticated over 6,500 years ago.

'unnatural' foods as bread and cooked meat testifies to their capacity to adapt to new opportunities.

The truly urban birds – pigeons and sparrows

There are two bird species which have the town as their predominant habitat and can properly be described as urban birds: the town pigeon and the house sparrow. It is interesting to consider how this association has evolved.

The town pigeon is a descendant of the rock dove that, as it name implies, is a bird of rocky cliffs, widely distributed over North Africa, Europe and Asia as far east as India. Its evolution as a town bird has been from the progeny of escaped domesticated birds, a process that is still going on. The domestication of rock doves dates back at least 6,500 years and the bird has become associated with man for a variety of reasons. Firstly, as a sacred bird in early cultures in the Middle East; secondly, as a messenger and source of food in the Roman Empire; and today for racing and showing. Domestic ation has led to the selection of a very large number of distinctive varieties; Darwin estimated more than 100 breeds. Many of the feral pigeons resemble the ancestral rock dove, but dark-plumaged birds predominate in towns, suggesting some form of industrial melanism. The feral stock is still being added to by escaped birds shown by the increasing range of plumage variations found in city flocks.

The wild rock dove nests in cavities in cliffs and moves to the open country to feed on seeds, particularly cultivated cereals when available. Town pigeons are to be found mainly in the squares and parks in the centre of large towns, but they also occur in docks and industrial areas, and even in the most closely built-up areas. This is related without doubt to the availability of large buildings and structures that simulate the cliffs used by their ancestors for nesting, usually the older public buildings, bridges and cranes with their nooks and crannies. The availability of food is also important in attracting town pigeons. This is now commonly bread, though in docks they can still find spilled grain and in the town centres street markets provide a source of vegetable food.

In Continental Europe, wild rock doves occur only as far north as the Pyrenees and the Alps, though off the coast they spread up to the Faeroes, 400 kilometres north of the British Isles. The northern limit of the town pigeon extends almost as far as there are towns. The little evidence that is available suggests that the birds are very sedentary, seldom moving more than a few kilometres. Urban dens ities can be very high with up to 50 birds per square kilometre recorded and more in some places such as Leicester Square in London. Numbers were much reduced in British cities during the Second World War with bread rationing, but built up again when bread became more available.

The house sparrow is the most closely associated with man of all wild birds, nesting in holes in houses or in the close vicinity and feeding on grain ripening in the fields, in stackyards or when it is put out as animal food. In town centres sparrows subsist on scraps of food discarded or deliberately put out by man, supplemented by seeds, fruit and invertebrates as available. They can properly be described as omnivorous.

The house sparrow's adaptation to the built-up environment is quite extraordinary; not only is it present in parks and open squares, but also under cover in such places as railway stations and factories with easy access through open ends and large doors, and some even live in totally enclosed areas. These birds appear to spend all their lives indoors as many of the buildings in which they are found are air conditioned so that there is no ready access to the outside. The fact that it is now predominantly a town bird is illustrated by censuses that have shown a density of 2·5 to 5 birds per hectare in towns with less than 1·5 birds per hectare in more rural areas.

A noticeable feature of house sparrows is that they are particularly wary when compared with other small birds like robins and thrushes that certainly in Britain can be much more confiding. Being so close to man, who is still a potential predator, wariness has a selective advantage that would be much less significant in birds that are basically woodland and woodland edge species. This is not to

House sparrows are true town-dwellers, cheekily picking up a meal wherever they can. There are over twice as many house sparrows resident in urban areas as in rural ones.

say that sparrows cannot be tamed; the birds in St. James's Park in London, after much feeding from friendly visitors, have become so tame that they will readily perch on hands to obtain food. This, however, remains an exception and generally sparrows are rather distrustful of man.

In the United Kingdom the tree sparrow, a close relative of the house sparrow, is not generally recognised as a town bird, though at times it penetrates into larger gardens on the outskirts, being much more a bird of open farmland where there are scattered hedgerow trees. In many parts of Northern Europe, however, the tree sparrow is to be found in towns behaving like a house sparrow

Birds of parks and gardens

As already described, a number of woodland edge birds have readily adapted to urban life in town parks and gardens. Several thrushes are well established as urban birds. The blackbird is the most successful of these and, though basically a woodland floor species, can now be found in parts of towns where trees are completely missing, provided there is some ground where it can find invertebrate food. Song thrushes are less common, but nonetheless very familiar town birds. Both species can become very tame, the song thrush particularly so, as it attends closely the gardener exposing earthworms as he turns over the soil. These species are early nesters and lack of concealed sites before the foliage is fully developed means that many early nests succumb to domestic cats, though later they are more successful and obviously raise enough young to maintain the urban population.

Thrushes are related to robins and black redstarts. The former of these is perhaps the most conspicuous garden bird in Britain, though in continental Europe it tends to be much more of a woodland species. In Northern Europe the black redstart is a more familiar urban bird, though it does not really replace the robin, being more associated with buildings and ruins than gardens; in Germany it is called the Hausrotschwanz (house redtail).

Tits are another group of woodland species that are a familiar sight in parks and gardens, particularly the great tit and blue tit. These birds raise large broods of young on small caterpillars, mostly the larvae of the winter moth, but these are not available in sufficient numbers in most towns to support large breeding populations, and the tits tend to disappear to more favourable localities to breed in the spring. Apart from this they are frequent garden visitors, appreciating the nuts and fat that are often provided. Although at any one time only a few birds may be present, ringing has shown that large numbers are involved and the urban populations probably make a circuit of the gardens where food is regularly put out.

The finches are another family of birds which have readily taken to the urban habitat. Chaffinches, greenfinches, goldfinches and bullfinches are all familiar garden birds, while serins are increasingly seen in towns in Continental Europe. Greenfinches are adept at hanging on to suspended nut feeders and compete with tits at this source of food. This habit has been copied by chaffinches, though they are much less well adapted to feeding in this way, and are more at home on the ground where they collect the pieces of nut chipped off by the other species.

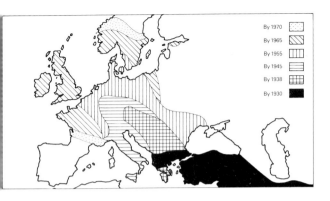

By 1970	(dotted)
By 1965	(diagonal hatch)
By 1955	(vertical hatch)
By 1945	(horizontal lines)
By 1938	(cross hatch)
By 1930	(solid black)

Over the past 50 years the collared dove has spread all the way across Europe due, it is thought, to them learning to feed upon man's grain supplies (see page 23).

The starling is another species that has adapted well to urban life. It originally nested in holes in trees, frequently old woodpecker holes, and fed in the surrounding grassland. It now nests in holes in houses and feeds on lawns and playing fields. Except when breeding, it is a communal rooster. Large roosts are commonly found in trees in the centre of towns and when the leaves fall in the autumn the birds move to the ledges on large buildings, which provide a safer and more sheltered site.

Water birds

Mallard are found on almost any stretch of water in towns. Elsewhere they are understandably wary as they are liable to be shot, but on park lakes they become extremely familiar where bread is provided. They even occasionally nest in window boxes in town centres and cause traffic problems when they lead their young to the nearest water. Coots and moorhens require a little more cover, but readily turn up if there are islands and marginal vegetation. The moorhen, although normally a very shy bird, again becomes very tame in these surroundings. Gulls are attracted to the rubbish tips in towns for feeding and resort to the larger stretches of water for bathing. Black-headed gulls are commonly found at park lakes, where they join mallards and moorhens in competition for bread.

Birds of prey

While not a significant habitat for avian predators, the increasing numbers of prey species attracts birds of prey into towns. The kestrel is the most important of these; in the open country it feeds

In winter, stretches of urban water may be less likely to freeze over than rural rivers and ponds, a factor which may have attracted these birds onto this reservoir.

Kestrels are now a common sight hovering and diving for small rodents at the side of our main roads and motorways. Some are so familiar with the roar of lorries and cars that they perch on flyovers waiting for prey to break cover.

mainly on small mammals, supplemented by smaller numbers of birds and insects, but in the towns birds become the major item of their diet. Sparrowhawks, now making something of a recovery after the very low numbers associated with pesticide poisoning, are increasingly seen in town suburbs and at bird tables where the concentration of small birds provides an attractive source of food. Tawny owls are also found in town parks and find sparrow roosts an easy feeding ground.

Some recent changes

The following examples are given to show the dynamism of bird life. The collared dove is an Asian species that until the end of the last century was found no further west than Asia Minor. At the beginning of this century it spread into the Balkans and from there moved rapidly throughout Europe, reaching Britain and Scandinavia in the early 1950s. In Europe it is primarily associated with built-up areas, occurring in large numbers near grain silos and breeding in the larger gardens and parks with suitable trees. It is now an important element in the urban avifauna.

Another less spectacular penetration of the urban environment has been by the magpie. In Britain the spread into towns coincided with the increase in numbers that occurred as the control measures that were carried out in the name of game preservation were relaxed during the Second World War, the birds first spreading into the suburbs and then more recently into the city centres, provided there are suitable trees for nesting.

In the past 40–50 years, there has been a dramatic increase in the use of rooftops as nest sites by large gulls.

Birds living in cities are exposed to artificial lighting and some have quickly made use of this in gardens illuminated by street lights. Robins sing through the winter and start singing earlier in the morning than their cousins in the country. Both town pigeons and house sparrows continue feeding by artificial light and sparrows have been seen catching moths at lights in the small hours of the morning to feed their young.

It can be seen from this brief survey how the city has provided a range of habitats that in turn give it a varied and interesting bird life. A great attraction to the bird watcher is that many of these species have become so accustomed to man in the urban environment that they are much more approachable and easier to observe. The rapid changes in distribution and behaviour that occur in birds are becoming increasingly clear and nowhere is there a greater opportunity for this to be observed than in our towns and cities.

Urban Mammals

Stephen Harris

Ever since man ceased to be a nomad, he has shared the area around his settlements with a variety of urban mammals. As long ago as 6,000 BC, commensal house mice were living in a Neolithic urban community in Turkey, and there were house mouse infestations in early Egyptian towns. In fact, it seems probable that it was the development of large cities in the Classical world that encouraged the spread of commensal house mice in the western Mediterranean area, and thence to the rest of Europe.

Today, many city dwellers view the presence of most wild mammals in their city with pleasure, since conflict between human and wild residents is generally limited. However, this has not always been the case. For instance, in 1166 a rabid wolf is reported to have entered the town of Carmarthen in Wales and bitten twenty two people, most of whom subsequently died. Wolves still enter isolated towns and villages in Russia to scavenge during hard winters, and there are several apparently authentic reports of snow bound villages being besieged by hungry wolves. In Britain our commonest urban carnivore is the fox, which is little larger than the average domestic cat, and there have been no authenticated cases of foxes attacking even very small children.

Foxes

Although foxes are common in most English towns and cities from Nottingham southwards, and in parts of Glasgow and Edinburgh in Scotland, they are generally much rarer in Continental Europe. They do occur in Copenhagen and Stockholm and as the current outbreak of rabies spreads across France, rabid foxes have even been seen in gardens on the outskirts of Paris.

The appearance of foxes in British urban areas is a comparatively recent phenomenon. Prior to the Second World War foxes could be seen on some of the large open spaces in cities such as London and Bristol, but sightings away from open areas were few. The rapid spread of the fox in the post-war era has been documented most thoroughly in London; here foxes were common in the south and east suburbs in the early 1950s, and by 1965 had colonised much of south London. They were then to be found within ten kilometres of the city centre. Foxes were rarer on the north side of the river. The spread has continued, although at a slower rate, and in the early 1970s foxes were even seen occasionally in the city centre.

Even in those cities where urban foxes are present they tend to be confined to certain parts of the city. This patchy distribution

One reason for the increase in the number of foxes found in towns and cities has been the fact that they have mastered the art of scavenging from domestic dustbins.

occurs because town foxes have very specific habitat requirements. They are most numerous in urban areas that consist largely or exclusively of privately-owned residential properties, particularly those built in the inter-war years. Modern housing estates, industrial areas and residential developments consisting largely of council-rented properties all contain fewer or no foxes. It is this habitat preference that explains the rarity of foxes in the industrial towns of northern England and Wales, whilst the commuter and dormitory towns of southern England contain large numbers of foxes. In fact in the most suitable areas urban fox densities may be up to five times those seen in the surrounding countryside.

Badgers

Foxes are relatively recent and very successful colonists of urban areas; in contrast the badgers are generally less successful relict populations that have managed to survive urban encroachment. Comparatively few towns and cities in Britain have urban badger populations; those that do include parts of south and west London, a few towns on the south coast and in Essex, Edinburgh, Bath, Cheltenham and Bristol, which has a particularly thriving badger population. They are also found in parts of Copenhagen. Badgers are most likely to have survived in cities where areas of rough land have been left undeveloped or retained as natural parkland, but setts are sometimes dug into the foundations of buildings or in small gardens. Today parts of Bristol contain between ten and twenty adult badgers per square kilometre, a density that rivals some of those in the most favourable rural habitats.

Although urban badgers may be quite numerous, they are only rarely seen. Compared with rural badgers, they emerge later each night, often not leaving the sett until well after dark, and tend to stay in the sett area until the traffic on the surrounding roads has subsided. In rural areas badgers specialise in feeding on earthworms, whilst in urban areas they are less specific in their feeding habits, taking a wide range of food items. Fruit provides most of the food in the late summer and autumn, whilst scavenging is more important in the winter and spring and predation on invertebrates (mainly beetles) in the summer. To find this variety of food the badgers may travel several kilometres in a night, criss-crossing their home range, which is often less than half a square kilometre in total area.

Rats and mice

Many species of small mammals live in urban areas, and, of those, three introduced species of rodent seem to be particularly well adapted to coexist with man. Until recently it was thought that the black or ship rat did not arrive in Britain until the 11th or 12th centuries, introduced from the Middle East by the returning Crusaders. However, recent discoveries of ship rat remains in Roman deposits from London and York suggest that it actually arrived several centuries earlier. Essentially an animal of warmer climates, it is probable that the ship rat was mainly associated with the warmth and shelter provided by buildings and was always rare away from urban areas. In the British Isles, Denmark and Fenno-Scandia, the ship rat is now largely confined to commercial premises in and around ports; elsewhere in Europe it is a more common urban species, usually in the upper storeys of buildings. This decline was linked with the arrival and spread of the brown or common rat, which probably arrived in England in 1728, and most of the rest of Europe by the end of the century. Unlike the ship rat, the common rat has not remained confined to buildings, but has also colonised a wide range of rural habitats.

In urban areas large colonies of common rats can sometimes be found in sewers and on rubbish tips but generally the number of rats is low. Recent surveys in some British towns have shown that only 3 per cent of urban premises are infested with rats, and that most (80 per cent) of the rat infestations are confined to the outside of buildings. In these situations the number of rats is low and unlike the large infestations that can occur in rural areas, the typical urban rat population consists of small scattered groups. One survey found

Black rats are still closely associated with ships and seaports betraying their other name, ship rat. This black rat is looking for food amongst the flotsam on the silted bank of the river Thames.

House mice are truly commensal with man, finding a home in a wide range of urban habitats. As well as eating almost anything, they are prolific breeders and may produce between five and ten litters each year.

that the average size of an urban rat colony is only 2·2 individuals; about a third of these are single male rats, with the rest of the colonies consisting of a family group of one or two adult rats with young.

In contrast to rats, house mice tend to live mainly within buildings, both commercial and domestic. In more open situations such as gardens, allotments, derelict land and railway embankments house mice are rare; this may be because they are unable to compete successfully with wood mice, which are widely distributed in such habitats. Certainly in rural areas in Britain free-living house mice are more common on islands such as Skomer, where wood mice are absent. On the island of St. Kilda, off west Scotland, where both species were present, the house mouse became extinct within two years of the human evacuation of the island and the loss of its commensal niche.

The house mouse is found living commensally with man over virtually all of the tropical and temperate areas of the world. In Northern Europe it is resident in a wide range of urban habitats, from lofts, attics and cellars in houses to cold stores where the temperature is well below zero. If sufficient food is available urban house mice can breed throughout the year irrespective of the temperature, producing between five and ten litters of young, and so may attain very high densities. In such situations the house mouse colony has a complex social structure and each mouse has a very small home range, sometimes only a few square metres, which overlaps with home ranges of neighbouring mice.

Two other species of rodent, the wood mouse and the short-tailed field vole, are common in urban areas. The former is an adaptable species found in areas of natural cover such as that afforded by railway embankments and wasteland, but is also common in gardens and allotments, where it may damage garden crops. Wood mice will also enter houses, particularly in winter, but in occupied buildings seem to compete less well with house mice. The field vole lives in areas of short grassland, and so is well adapted to exploiting urban habitats; it is to be found throughout most smaller cities and to within a short distance of the centre of larger cities. Field voles are most common on allotments, wasteland, grassy embankments and neglected gardens, and form an important food item for urban raptors and foxes.

Squirrels

The red squirrel is the native species of Northern Europe, and on the Continent is still common in parks and gardens. The same was true in Britain until the grey squirrel was introduced from North America at the turn of the century. The grey squirrel is better adapted to living in mixed deciduous and more open habitats than the red squirrel, and today is a common resident in parks and mature gardens in many urban areas throughout Britain and Ireland. Often grey squirrels will enter the roof spaces of houses, where they will spend the winter and breed during the summer. They can cause a considerable amount of damage; like rats they will gnaw lead pipes and electricity cables, and have even damaged roof beams sufficiently for the roof to collapse.

In parks grey squirrel numbers may equal those seen in natural deciduous woodland; these high densities can survive only because of the additional food supplied by local residents. Despite this supplementary feeding, the squirrels may cause considerable damage to flower beds and ornamental trees, and nut-bearing trees such as oaks may be devastated so no mature fruits are produced.

Hedgehogs

A survey in Britain of city dwellers' attitudes to their wild neighbours would probably indicate that the hedgehog is our most popular urban mammal. Hedgehogs are widespread in gardens, allotments, parks and golf courses. In fact hedgehogs are particularly common on the outskirts of urban areas and commuter dormitory districts, and the analysis of road death records suggests that there are more hedgehogs in towns and villages than in the surrounding rural areas, even after allowing for the greater amount of traffic in suburban areas and hence the increased chance of a hedgehog being run over. Urban areas may be particularly suitable for hedgehogs because they provide a wide range of sites for them to build both their summer and winter nests, and also offer a variety of food sources. Besides the scraps specifically put out for them by householders, urban hedgehogs feed on beetles, earwigs, slugs, snails, noctuid moth caterpillars and earthworms, the last two being collected from the surface of lawns on wet nights. The hedgehogs have overlapping home ranges, so that several may come to a single garden to feed.

One possible factor contributing to the success of hedgehogs in an urban area is the milder winter climate. In a city the frost-free period may be up to six weeks longer than that in the surrounding rural area, and this extra time may enable late-born litters of young-

Long Pampas grass

Hedge bottom

Compost bin

Behind shed next to hedge

Holes in shed

Heap of leaves   Logs

Here are a few suggestions for possible hedgehog hibernation sites. Above all, if you find a hibernating hedgehog in your garden: DO NOT DISTURB!

sters to put on enough weight to survive the winter. Only when a hedgehog has attained a weight of about 400 grammes will it have accumulated enough fat to last it through hibernation.

Bats

Many species of bat will roost in buildings in rural areas, but the most common ones in urban areas are the pipistrelle and the brown long-eared bat. Less frequent are the Leisler's bat, although it has been found in Hyde Park close to central London, the noctule, which sometimes roosts in suburban trees, the serotine (*Eptesicus serotinus*), which may be found hunting insects over sewage farms and similar sites, and Daubenton's bat (*Myotis daubentoni*), which will hunt insects over park ponds and suburban canals. Even quite rare species of bat may be found in urban areas; greater horseshoe bats roost in buildings in parts of southern England and Wales, and in parts of central Europe the mouse-eared bat, a species now practically extinct in Britain, is relatively common in some cities. A survey of bat roosts in British buildings found that most colonies are in buildings less than 60 years old, and a third are in buildings less than fifteen years old; one bat colony even moved into a house before the builder had finished. Bats gain access to their roosts through broken tiles, between warped boards, under lead flashings and through small holes in the walls. Most colonies are in confined spaces such as behind tiles or weatherboards, and this may help the bats to conserve heat when they cluster together.

In recent years bats appear to have undergone a serious decline in Britain, and this is still continuing. Reasons for this are uncertain, but human attitudes to bats may be a contributory factor. Colonies in buildings have been destroyed by pest control companies,

Like all other bats, these long-eared bats, roosting in eaves of a house, are protected by law. They are much maligned creatures which do no harm, and have fascinating life-styles catching insects on the wing with the aid of their echo-locating squeaks.

blocked in or out by the householder who objects to their presence, or killed by the chemicals used for remedial timber treatment. These chemicals have been demonstrated to have serious effects on bats for years after their application.

Other occasional visitors

Besides the mammals that regularly inhabit our urban areas, several other species can be seen occasionally. Moles are most common in undisturbed pasture, and do occur in lawns on the rural fringes of cities. Rabbits will penetrate far into some cities, digging burrows in natural parkland, railway embankments and undisturbed areas of waste land and factories. Similar habitats will also contain common shrews (*Sorex araneus*), which can be found quite close to the city centre, whereas pygmy shrews (*Sorex minutus*) are most common on the fringes of the city. In small towns in parts of Hertfordshire and Buckinghamshire in Britain and in south and central Europe, the edible dormouse (*Glis glis*) will live in roof spaces, where it damages stored fruit crops and causes similar problems to the grey squirrel. On the Continent the beech or stone marten (*Martes foina*) is a common urban mammal; it also lives in the attics of houses.

Occasionally, surprisingly large wild mammals enter urban areas. Both muntjac (*Muntiacus reevesi*) and roe deer (*Capreolus capreolus*) are currently expanding their range in rural areas of Britain and dispersing animals will penetrate far into a city, following corridors of natural vegetation along railway embankments and river valleys.

Pet dogs and cats

Despite the variety of our urban wildlife, the most conspicuous mammals living in our cities are undoubtedly pet dogs and cats. The impact of these animals on the urban ecosystem has not yet been studied in detail, but it must be considerable. It has been estimated that each year 60 per cent of all birds that visit gardens in Britain are killed by pet cats. Also, these pets cause more problems than most of our wild mammals. Stray dogs and cats cause numerous road accidents, foul pavements and public areas, and possibly also spread parasitic worms such as *Toxocara* to humans. Stray cat colonies are common on many city sites such as factories, hospitals, waste land and sometimes in residential areas throughout much of Northern Europe. These colonies may number several hundred cats in dockland habitats, but the average size is fifteen to twenty animals. Stray dogs are a feature of many British cities, but in Europe they are tolerated less due to the ever present threat of rabies. Even in Britain more local authorities are now employing dog wardens to remove stray animals.

Introduced plants

John Dony

The truly native flora of Britain and Northern Europe is limited mainly to those plants which grow regularly in their woods, mires, virgin pastures and other natural habitats. This often leaves some doubt with regard to the origin of other plants that occur in man-made surroundings, frequently together with the native species. Plant introduction is by no means new. Some species that were at one time frequent but are now seen no longer were no doubt introductions in their day. Given time there is always a struggle for the native vegetation to become dominant. With improved communications, the world is becoming smaller, giving scope for a greater movement of plants.

Derelict ground

Where buildings await demolition or have recently been demolished, the waste land in the vicinity will readily become colonised by plants which are already growing nearby. These will, in the main, be garden plants, most of which will have been selected for their ability to survive in the climatic conditions of the neighbourhood. Michaelmas daisies (*Aster* spp.), native mainly in North America, Japanese knotweed and Russian-vine (*Bilderdykia aubertii*), a native of China notwithstanding its English name, may take control but the Butterfly-bush, also originally from China, will soon appear if near at hand. Damp north- or west-facing walls will also provide niches not only for native ferns but also for more tender species normally grown indoors such as *Pteris cretica* and *Cyrtomium falcatum*.

In the meantime any bare ground, however small in area, will be colonised by Oxford ragwort with the assistance of its wind-borne seeds. It gained its English name because for a long time Oxford was the only place where one could be sure of seeing it as it had been brought there by University botanists in the 18th century from volcanically formed soils in Italy. In the early years of the present century it began to spread from Oxford, slowly at first but eventually reaching London along the railway lines. It thrived on the bombed sites during the Second World War, and has spread over most of Britain. It spread in much the same way in Northern Europe. It is not an unattractive species, its increase assisted by its flowering almost throughout the year so adding colour to otherwise drab surroundings. Another early invader will be the stickly groundsel, also from southern Europe, which began to increase at about the

Oxford ragwort (**above**), introduced from Italy in the 18th century, produces masses of wind-blown seeds. Their spread has closely followed the growth of the railway network, the seeds being sucked along the track by passing trains.

Of the plants colonising this patch of wasteland (**above right**), the most obvious is the butterfly bush with its purple panicles of flowers. This shrub originally came from China.

Rosebay willow herb (**right**) is extremely common and is one of the first colonisers of disturbed ground. Eighty years ago this plant was confined to a few local patches.

same time as the Oxford ragwort. Considering how often the two species grow together in their new surroundings it is not surprising that they have hybridised.

Another wind-borne intruder will most certainly be the colourful rosebay willowherb which a hundred years ago was known in Britain mainly as a garden plant. Sir Edward Salisbury recalled that it was rare in Hertfordshire in the First World War period and at that time I knew only one site in which it was growing wild in adjacent Bedfordshire. It was soon to spread rapidly, there being a possibility that this was a newcomer a more robust strain from North America indistinguishable from the European plants. There may be doubt with regard to this but none with the more modest American willowherb (*Epilobium adenocaulon*) which was almost certainly introduced to Britain by Canadian troop movements during the First World War. It is also an early colonist of bare ground. Yet another may be the Canadian fleabane (*Conyza canadensis*) which, with its small, colourless flowers and fluffy heads of seeds, is less attractive than the other species. Although known on this side of the Atlantic for about 300 years for some unknown reason it has only increased in numbers in recent years.

Two additional early colonists of the open areas have a similar history except that they may be dispersed mainly by their fruits sticking to clothing. These are the gallant soldier (*Galinsoga parviflora*) and shaggy soldier (*G. ciliata*), natives of South and Central America. The former has been in Britain for over a hundred years, having been introduced in the first place, no doubt accidentally, into Kew Gardens, from where it escaped. The 'Kew Weed', as it was often known, has since spread over much of Britain and the Continent to become a weed in sandy fields as much as in towns. By contrast the shaggy soldier is a relative newcomer, met more often in built-up areas. They are both comparatively small, having little claim to be considered attractive.

Most of these relatively recent invaders of the waste places are from North America which has a climate similar to that of Northern Europe, but some of them appear to have become cosmopolitan and can be seen in any large city growing alongside other plants of European origin. They play an important part in the initial colonisation of bare earth to such an extent that one wonders what took place before they arrived. Plant colonisation was no doubt a much slower process.

Less certain is the appearance of plants introduced with bird-seed mixtures of foreign origin. The mixture itself is mainly composed of grass seeds, some of the species becoming quite attractive when fully grown, such as millet (*Panicum miliaceum*), the bristle-grasses

(*Setaria viridis*, *S. italica* and *S. lutescens*), canary-grasses (*Phalaris canariensis* and *P. minor*), the cockspurs (*Echinochloa crus-galli*, *E. colonum* and *E. utilis*), finger-grass (*Digitaria sanguinalis*) and darnel (*Lolium temulentum*) – this last, by the way, was a curse to farmers until about a hundred years ago as its large seeds were difficult to separate from the wheat grain. It has now become extinct as a weed of arable land.

The bird-seed mixtures may contain some impurities which it is suggested are rejected by the cage-birds, so providing an excellent opportunity for alien plant species to appear when waste from the bird cages and aviaries is thrown away. Among these are gold-of-pleasure (*Camelina sativa*) which does not belie its English name, likewise apple of Peru (*Nicandra physalodes*). Others include niger (*Guizotia abyssinica*) and *Salvia reflexa*, which has small lilac flowers, while hemp (*Cannabis sativa*) attracts considerable attention wherever it happens to occur. Perhaps the most interesting species is the false thorow-wax (*Bupleurum lancifolium*) which is so similar to the genuine thorow-wax (*B. rotundifolium*) that it is often mistaken for it. The latter was at one time a weed of arable fields, for the same reason as darnel, but as such is to be seen no longer. The bird-seed aliens cannot be considered to be important as they are not permanent but they have attracted much attention. Dr. J. L. Mason, who has made a study of them, estimated that about 30 species have been introduced into Britain as ingredients of bird-seed mixtures and probably another 400 species as impurites in the mixture.

Railway embankments and abandoned tracks

Wasteland adjacent to railways is a home for many introduced plants, providing a well-drained habitat with a high sulphur content in its often shallow soils. It has in the past been the main agency for the increase of Oxford ragwort and sticky groundsel. Mention may also be made of bladder-senna (*Colutea arborescens*), a shrub with large yellow pea-like flowers which, in Britain at least, is limited in the wild to railway banks and is especially frequent in the London area. Its large seeds have no obvious means of dispersal but it has been suggested that new plants arise from seeds buried by small animals. During the Second World War when labour became scarce in Britain, the maintenance of the permanent ways was abandoned for a time. They rapidly became colonised far inland by plants normally seen only on the coast, such as Danish scurvy-grass (*Cochlearia danica*) and sea mouse-ear (*Cerastium diffusum*). A recently dismantled railway track even within a town is always worth examining for the unexpected plants it may reveal. Railway banks, especially those south- or west-facing, readily become colonised by hawkweeds (*Hieracium* spp.) and mouse-ear hawkweeds (*Pilosella* spp.), some of which are of alien or garden origin.

Grass seed

Grassing with imported grass-seed is being done increasingly on new playing fields, newly created golf courses, amenity areas within towns and the wide verges of new roads and motorways. The suppliers may guarantee a more than 99 per cent purity of the seed, usually strains of rye-grass (*Lolium* spp.), fescues (*Festuca* spp.) and other perennial grasses, but there is always the possibility of other, alien, species arriving as impurities. These may include crimson clover (*Trifolium incarnatum*), flower-of-the-hour (*Hibiscus trionum*), a most attractive species, and *Downingia elegans*, a small plant with bright blue flowers allied to the lobelias. In addition there are a number of alien grass species introduced with the imported seed. It is not in these newly created grassy areas but in lawns and other similar established sites that in the last 50 years slender speedwell, a native of the Near East, has appeared – to the despair of many gardeners. It very rarely sets viable seed in Northern Europe but spreads almost entirely from fragments that break off from parent plants and readily root.

Industrial colonisers

Most built-up areas will support some industries, many of which use imported raw materials, providing another possibility for plant introduction.

The most striking example is the processing of raw wool which may come from almost any quarter of the globe. In the first instance the wool must be cleaned to remove grease and dirt. This is done by passing it through steam chambers and sulphuric acid baths which remove fruits that have clung to the wool by means of burs and seeds that are glutinous, sticking to the greasy wool. In addition there is also a degree of waste. The cleaned wool is then combed to separate the longer strands from the shorter – the tops from the noils – eventually leaving what is little more than wool dust with additional seed content. The waste ground around the mills will provide still more plant introductions.

Water aliens

Most of the introduced plants so far considered here are of temporary duration when they occur in Northern Europe away from their natural surroundings, but an exception must be made for others to be seen growing by watersides or submerged in water.

Every built-up area has its open water be it river or canal or at the very least lakes in public parks. Where the shores are muddy, they provide space for new plants to come in or those already there to increase. An example of the latter is to be seen with the sweet-flag (*Acorus calamus*) a native of Asia Minor which was introduced into Northern Europe about 400 years ago, its iris-like leaves being strewn in passages of large houses and in aisles of churches: when crushed the leaves gave off a sweet scent that was thought to be some protection from plague. A peculiarity of the species is that it does not set viable seed in its new surroundings but nevertheless it is a familiar sight by many a lake or riverside. The simple reason for this is that over a long period new plants have been formed from the rhizomes of others already there. By contrast, the balsams have an efficient method of propagation by means of an explosive mechanism in their fruits which expels the seeds some distance. The most attractive species is without doubt the orange balsam (*Impatiens capensis*) from North America which was introduced in the middle years of the 19th century, soon spreading rapidly along

The beautiful Indian balsam or policeman's helmet was introduced into Europe from the Himalayas. It is now found in profusion along many of our urban waterways.

some English waterways but apparently missing others completely. The Indian balsam, or policeman's helmet, more spectacular than beautiful, is a more recent introduction which has become dominant on some canal and river banks mainly in industrial areas. Colourful when viewed from a distance, close to hand it gives off a most unpleasant odour.

It is in the water itself that the most interesting of all invaders are to be seen. Outflows of warm water into canals may allow some aquatics to survive that otherwise could not do so. Such are the large-flowered water-thyme (*Egeria densa*) which has only its relatively large white flowers showing above the surface of the water and tape-grass (*Vallisneria spiralis*), whose slender flower-stalks eventually forms spirals within the water. More successful examples of colonisation are provided by the waterweeds (*Elodea* spp.), one of which, the Canadian waterweed, was introduced to European waterways about 150 years ago after which it spread rapidly, soon choking some water-courses. Eventually it assumed more modest proportions but it is still common. Within the last 20 years two closely allied species have arrived: Nuttall's waterweed (*Elodea nuttallii*) and *E. ernstaei*, the former spreading almost as rapidly as the Canadian waterweed did earlier. In the meantime yet another more robust species appeared, the curly water-thyme (*Lagarosiphon major*), of South African origin. This has snake-like submerged leafy branches which, like the waterweeds, have small infertile flowers floating on thread-like stems on the surface. These aquatic species all increase in number by the rooting of fragments which break from parent plants and the only possible source for the occurrence of these aquatic species is their use in aquaria.

Still more plants of alien origin are to be found floating on the surface of the water, the most interesting being the water fern (*Azolla filiculoides*), yet another native of North America which arrived in Northern Europe about a hundred years ago, taking about another 30 more years to reach Britain. Plants are usually not more than three centimetres in diameter, dark green in colour, becoming reddish at maturity and spreading either by spores or by parts breaking away to form new plants. It has a tendency to increase very rapidly, becoming the dominant plant for a short while, only to disappear as quickly as it came, often following a spell of cold weather.

In Britain at least the number of species of introduced plants that can be seen outnumber those that are native, but with regard to the number of individual plants the reverse is still fortunately maintained. The naturalised and alien flora is best studied in urban surroundings but by no means limited to them.

Greenhouse natural history   Alan Toogood

For at least two centuries greenhouses and conservatories have been popular in towns and cities, not only in botanic gardens, but also in many private gardens, and their popularity is steadily increasing.

These artificial environments have enabled an increased range of flora and fauna, particularly tropical and sub-tropical insects, to become established in Britain and Northern Europe. Various European insects, particularly those from warmer climates, have also become established in these favourable micro-climates. The relatively higher temperatures of greenhouses favour animals from warmer climates and encourage all-year-round activity.

How insects were introduced

Many of the tropical and sub-tropical insects were originally introduced to Europe on plants collected for botanic gardens and nurseries by plant hunters of the past, long before there was strict control on importation of plant material. Because they were accidentally introduced so long ago, and in some cases have spread worldwide, the true origins of many tropical insects are not known. Insects are spread not only by man, but also by wind (e.g. aphids are carried long distances), flight and ocean currents. In the last instance eggs, larvae and adults can be carried on floating debris. Each year the Gulf Stream transports thousands of tropical insects to Europe but it is generally too cold for these to survive.

Like many other garden creatures such as woodlice, centipedes and snails, this zebra spider (*Salticus scenicus*) may also make its home in the more favourable micro-climate of the greenhouse.

Insects from warm climates

Cockroaches Of the insects which have their origins in the tropics, or at least warmer climates, and are now resident in Britain and Northern Europe, the cockroaches are among the most interesting. These insects are almost all tropical, but in recent times several species have been spread around the world on ships, of which they are regular inhabitants. They are very common in urban areas, inhabiting not only greenhouses but also sheds, outhouses and any other warm building they can get into. They inhabit damp places and are found in organic matter and among all kinds of plants.

Cockroaches are fast runners, with long legs and antennae, and are nocturnal. Two of the most common in towns and cities are the flightless Oriental or common cockroach and the American cockroach (*Periplaneta americana*). Under glass cockroaches breed continuously if conditions are warm, and they will feed on seeds, seedlings, leaves, stems, flowers (e.g. orchids and chrysanthemums), and the aerial roots of orchids.

Whitefly The glasshouse whitefly (*Trialeurodes vaporariorum*) is thought to originate from Central America or Brazil, but this is not certain. In any case it is now distributed worldwide and thrives outdoors in the Channel Islands. It feeds by sucking the sap of almost all plants and is common on pelargoniums, fuchsias and begonias.

The adults are about 1·25mm long, like little white moths, and the nymphs, called 'scales', are oval, flat and transparent. Both produce sticky honeydew, on which grow sooty moulds. Generally, reproduction is parthenogenetic (the eggs are not fertilised) and breeding is continuous in warm conditions, with a cycle of three to four weeks in summer. Adults and nymphs are generally found on the underside of leaves.

Scales There are several scale insects found under glass. Scale insects are sap suckers; the females are motionless, covered with a protective scale, and produce honeydew. They include the tropical soft scale (*Coccus hesperidum*) which is found throughout warm and temperate zones.

The soft scale is oval and flat, coloured yellow to brown. It is translucent, 4mm long, and is found on the underside of leaves. The nymphs of this and the other species (called crawlers) move over leaves to find a feeding place where they stay put and, soon after, the protective scale is formed. Host plants include: citrus, oleander, stephanotis, azalea, ferns, ficus and hibiscus.

The fluted scale (*Icerya purchasi*) is a native of Australia but is found in many parts of the world, and is a serious pest of citrus trees. It is now biologically controlled in many countries with the aid of an Australian ladybird (*Rodolia cardinalis*). The female fluted scale is oval, 3mm long, orange brown, and the rear-end is pushed up by the wax-covered egg-sac. Host plants also include acacia trees.

Mealy-bugs are related to scale insects and both nymphs and adults are sap suckers. Several are found under glass in Britain and Northern Europe, including the citrus mealy-bug (*Planococcus citri*) which is found naturally on citrus trees in the tropics and sub-tropics. The vine mealy-bug (*Pseudococcus obscurus*) is also common under glass. In general, these insects are covered with white wax, are soft, oval, flattish, and about 4mm long. Reproduction is continuous under warm glass, and host plants include orchids, palms, cacti, asparagus ferns and gardenia (citrus mealybug), and vines, ferns, azalea and pelargoniums (vine mealy-bug).

The American cockroach is found in warm kitchens as well as greenhouses.

Greenhouse whitefly are often first noticed as a little cloud of white specks rising from plants if their leaves are disturbed.

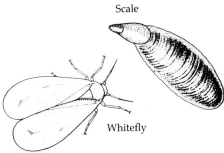

Scale

Whitefly

Mealy-bugs (**above**) are scale insects. Only the females have legs and can move. Mealy-bugs are extremely difficult to erradicate once established.

This arum aphid, with its parthenogenically produced offspring, is feeding on a cyclamen.

Pharaoh's ant is an imported species and its spread is nearly worldwide. It is found in buildings throughout Europe.

Stick insects are sometimes found in greenhouses in towns and cities, but they are more common in greenhouses in botanical gardens, no doubt having escaped or been released from captivity. They are popular 'pets' with some people.

Stick insects occur mainly in tropical forests, but several live in temperate regions. They feed on the foliage of various trees and shrubs. They are elongated insects, with long legs and antennae, move very little and resemble twigs (a form of camouflage which protects them from enemies). Several species have become established in Britain and Northern Europe: the prickly stick insect (*Acanthoxyla prasina*) from New Zealand, the smooth stick insect (*Clitarchus hookeri*) also from New Zealand, both established in a few warmer parts, and the laboratory stick insect (*Carausius morosus*) the one commonly kept in captivity. They will feed on many tropical plants in a warm greenhouse, including members of the Gesneriaceae family.

Insects from cool climates
Crickets Among insects from temperate or cooler areas, the crickets are among the best known and some have become quite 'domesticated', living in kitchens, bakeries and the like in rural and urban areas. This is certainly true of the house cricket. It originates from North Africa but is very widespread in Northern Europe. It lives on plant material and can be found

outdoors in warm weather, in rubbish tips, etc. The house cricket is 19mm long, grey-brown, with long hind legs but it cannot jump a long way. It is nocturnal, and at night makes a shrill chirping sound by rubbing its front wings together. Under glass it will gnaw stems, foliage, flowers, and the aerial roots of orchids, although it is not yet ranked as a serious pest,

The greenhouse camel cricket (*Tachycines asynamorus*), also widely distributed in European greenhouses, originated in Asia. It is a strange-looking creature with a humped back, and it is wingless. The antennae are extremely long, and the long palps look like legs.

A particularly fascinating species is the European mole cricket (*Gryllotalpa gryllotalpa*) found in Europe and the Channel Islands but now rare in Britain. It lives in burrows in moist soil and eats plants, worms and insects. It is remarkable because it resembles a mole in that it possesses front legs which are formed for digging through the soil. It sometimes flies, and is nocturnal. Under glass it will gnaw roots, and stems at or below soil level, but is not considered a serious pest.

Aphids   Quite a few species of aphid are found under glass, including the fern aphid (*Idiopterus nephrelepidis*) probably introduced but now widespread over Britain and Northern Europe. This small aphid is deep green to black with whitish legs, and like other species it exudes honeydew upon which grow sooty moulds. Host plants are ferns, like *Nephrolepis*, *Polypodium* and *Pteris*. The sap-sucking action of this insect causes the fronds to curl.

One of the most common and widespread aphids under glass is the mottled arum aphid (*Aulacorthum circumflexum*), yellow-green with dark markings. It reproduces entirely by parthenogenesis and feeds on many plants such as arum lilies, cyclamen, begonias, azaleas, chrysanthemums, ferns, orchids and members of the Liliaceae.

Carnation tortrix moth   A native of southern Europe, the carnation tortrix moth (*Cacoecimorpha pronubana*) is now widely established under glass in southern England, France and parts of Germany. It is adapting to cooler conditions and is spreading north. The caterpillars feed on many plants, including carnations, acacia, *Chorizema* and *Grevillea*. They are up to 20mm long, yellow-green to olive-green, and bind leaves together with silk and feed inside; or roll up tips of leaves. They drop from plants on silk threads when disturbed. The adults are nocturnal, and have greyish-brown forewings, orange hindwings and a wing span of about 16mm. Two generations are produced each year.

Biological control of greenhouse insect pests

Some insects and other creatures have been introduced intentionally to Britain and Northern Europe; those which are used for biological control of greenhouse pests. For instance, the Australian ladybird (*Cryptolaemus montrouzieri*) black, with a reddish thorax, is used to control mealybugs; and the Chilean predatory mite *Phystoseiulus persimilis* feeds on glasshouse red spider mites.

The parasitic wasp, *Encarsia formosa*, is found in Britain, probably imported with plants, and is thought to be of tropical origin. It is a pin-head size insect, with yellow abdomen and dark head and thorax and parasites whitefly nymphs. An egg is laid in each whitefly nymph which develops into a larvae and devours its host. These three introductions are now common in greenhouses in botanic gardens and those of commercial growers.

Other creatures found under glass

Glasshouse millipede (*Oxidus gracilis*) is a tropical species, but widely distributed in temperate regions. It inhabits damp situations and lives in soil and leaf litter, feeding on dead or decaying plant material, and also on live plants under glass.

This species is flattened, reddish brown, about 19mm long with a segmented body and 32 pairs of legs. It is one of the flat millipedes and is slow moving. Under glass it feeds on seedlings, and the roots and stems of a wide variety of plants.

Mites The greenhouse red spider mites are of tropical origin and are serious pests throughout the world. They relish hot dry conditions. The two species found under glass are *Tetranychus urticae* and *T. cinnabarinus*, and the former is also found out of doors on weeds and cultivated plants.

These are sap-sucking creatures whose feeding results in fine, pale speckling on the upper surfaces of leaves. They can just be seen with the naked eye and are found on the underside of leaves. The females are red. There may be many generations per year if conditions are sufficiently warm, and these mites produce fine silk webs enabling them to swing or glide from one part of a plant to another. Host plants include citrus, carnation, chrysanthemums, hydrangeas and many others.

Weeds found under glass

Generally very few weeds are found under glass, but nevertheless garden weeds can spring up in soil beds, pots and other containers. Seeds may be blown in by the wind, or carried in on gardeners' boots. Gardeners usually partially sterilise soil and compost to kill weed seeds, by means of heat.

Green algae are found under glass (and outdoors coating trees, fences, walls and so on) where there are moist conditions. Probably the most common alga is *Pleurococcus vulgaris*, a single-celled plant, which appears as a powdery soft coating on virtually everything: pots, trays, soil, staging, paths, glass, and between glass overlaps.

This alga is not harmful to other plants, but as far as the gardener is concerned it is unsightly. Therefore greenhouses and conservatories are regularly cleaned to remove it, together with plant containers and staging.

Mother of thousands or mind-your-own-business (*Helxine/Soleirolia soleirolii*) is an exotic perennial plant which can become a weed in greenhouses. It is a native of Sardinia and Corsica, which grows naturally in cool, moist, often shady places and favours a moist atmosphere: this is why it can rapidly become established under glass.

Mosses are also found under glass where they grow on the surface of soil and compost, relishing the moist humid conditions. Mosses do not have true roots. They are anchored to the soil by hairs or rhizoids which have the same function as root hairs in the higher plants.

Various species may be found under glass, like *Brachythecium rutabulum*, which occurs naturally in grassland and is also found in lawns. Grasslands are also the natural habitat of *Leptobryum pyriforme*, which commonly grows in pots and soil borders. The distinctive spore capsules are red-brown and carried on long orange-red stalks. Again the mosses are not harmful to other plants, but they could swamp and smother very slow-growing seedlings. Gardeners, therefore, generally scrape moss off the surface of soil.

Liverworts The most common species under glass is *Marchantia polymorpha*, whose natural habitats are wet places, marshy areas and banks of streams. As with mosses, it does not harm plants, but may smother seedlings, and is generally scraped away.

The origins of household insects

Michael Chinery

Millions of pounds are spent every year on moth-proofers and other insecticides to control clothes moths, carpet beetles, woodworm, and many other insects that invade our homes and other buildings. Virtually no home, however new, is without some insect life. Many of these unwelcome guests, like the midges that come in through the door and then spend all of their time trying to escape through the window, do no harm. Others, however, pose real threats to our homes and, despite the application of numerous insecticidal dusts and aerosols, cause an immense amount of damage. All our food-stuffs and furnishings are at risk, and so are the floorboards and other timbers with which our houses are constructed. Even our own bodies are not immune from irritating pests like fleas and bed-bugs. The insect world knows virtually no boundaries when it comes to feeding, with almost every natural organic material being devoured by at least one species. It is interesting to list just a few of the more unusual food materials used by insects: fabrics and building timbers have already been mentioned, and to these we can add leather, cork, dried tobacco, flour and other dried cereal products, paper, beeswax, and animal flesh – both fresh and decaying. From this short list you can see why insects cause so much damage in our homes, and also in other buildings such as warehouses, granaries, and flour mills.

It is certain that this horde of household insects were around long before man came on the scene, but where did they live before we started to build houses for them to invade? The bees, wasps, and ants that nest in our buildings merely find them convenient and often warmer and drier alternatives to their natural nesting sites, but in other respects their lives are just the some as they have always been. Fleas and bed-bugs have also experienced few changes in their life-style, having lived by sucking our blood ever since our ancestors started to live in caves and other permanent homes. It is no surprise that they moved into houses with us, although it must be said that these insects are much less common today as a result of higher standards of hygiene.

But what about the clothes moths and carpet beetles and other fabric pests? They have not always had cosy wardrobes of clothes or deep-pile carpets in which to set up home. To answer the question of their origin, we must look more closely at the materials that these insects eat – or, more accurately, at the materials that their larvae eat. These materials consist largely of dry animal fibres –

woollen fabrics and furs – which are not common in the wild, especially in the relatively moist climates of western Europe: but they do occur in the nests of birds and rodents, and this is where most of our household fabric pests probably originated.

Investigations in several places, notably the former Pest Infestation Laboratory at Slough, near London, have revealed an amazing number of insect species living in old birds' nests. All the familiar pests, such as the clothes moths, have been found, together with many completely harmless species. It must be remembered that, in their natural habitats, all of these insects perform a useful scavenging role and that they did not become pests until man started to make use of dried hairs and other natural fibres.

Insects found in birds' nests

Fleas are found in the nests of several species, but do not include the human fleas. This is not to say that they will not bite you, however, for they certainly will if you give them the chance. Bird fleas are rarely troublesome in the house, although short-lived plagues may occur when the insects leave disturbed nests. The majority of household fleas come from pet cats and dogs.

Moths The most abundant insect in the house sparrow nest is generally the larva of the case-bearing clothes moth (*Tinea pellionella*). There may be more than a thousand of these larvae in a single nest, each living in a portable silken case. The species is even more common in the nests of jackdaws and town pigeons. The larvae pupate in their cases and the adults emerge from June to October. It is but a short flight from nests on and around the houses to our clothes cupboards and carpets, where they can continue to breed throughout the year. The case-bearing clothes moth likes a relatively high humidity and has declined as a household pest in recent years through the increased incidence of central heating. The common clothes moth is a much more serious household pest, but rarely occurs in birds' nests. It prefers higher temperatures and lower humidities than its case-bearing cousin and probably originated in a warmer climate.

The larvae of the brown house moth are often as common as those of the case-bearing clothes moth and sometimes very much more abundant, especially in nests on and around houses. Few nests escape the attentions of this abundant scavenger, but it is absent from the very driest ones. The larvae are fat and white and reach a length of about 2·5cm. They feed on a wide variety of both plant and animal material and damage foodstuffs as well as fabrics, although, like the case-bearing clothes moth, this species is a major problem only in damper homes. The larvae of the white-shouldered house moth are very similar, but are slightly smaller and rather less common, both in nests and in houses.

Beetles of numerous kinds breed in birds' nests. The mealworm beetle (*Tenebrio molitor*) is far from the commonest, but its golden yellow larva, so loved by the robin, occurs in quite a high proportion of sparrow and pigeon nests. Although cereal products are its main foods, the mealworm is truly omnivorous.

The varied carpet beetle is a very serious pest of clothing and other household fabrics as well as carpets. Its larva, known as a 'woolly bear', is also abundant in the nests of house sparrows and house martins, although rarely found in the nests of other species. The adults fly well and readily invade houses to lay their eggs, and it is the resulting larvae that cause the damage. Many larvae reared in nests also invade the house when approaching maturity. Compared with the irregular, silk-shrouded holes caused by clothes moth larvae, the feeding holes of the woolly bears are very clear. As well as woollens and other animal fibres, the larvae eat cottons – although these have no food value for them – and can live quite happily on flour and other cereal products. Dried meat is very acceptable and the larvae commonly damage entomological collections, although less frequently than the closely related museum beetle (*Anthrenus museorum*). The adult beetles can be found indoors at all times of year, but are most common in spring and early summer, at which time they can also be found out of doors on the flowers of hogweed and other umbellifers. The varied carpet beetle is very much an insect of the suburbs in Britain: in rural areas it is largely replaced by the museum beetle and the equally similar dark carpet beetle (*A. fuscus*), while in heavily built-up areas it is probably absent because there are few flowers on which the adults can feed. The species is confined largely to the southern counties in Britain. Its country cousins extend far to the north, but are much less often seen in houses.

The fur beetle is a close relative of the carpet beetle and is another common inhabitant of birds' nests, particularly those of house sparrows and jackdaws. The adult is black with two small white spots on its back. It is about 5mm long and, when resting, could easily be mistaken for a small seed. It is mature in the spring and often found on flowers. The bristly larva eats a wide range of foods, including cereal products and all kinds of wool-based fabrics. Feathers and dried meat are also acceptable. The insects commonly breed in the fluff and other debris that accumulates between and underneath floor-boards. In such situations, the insects can also do severe damage to carpets. Although widely distributed, the fur beetle is not a major pest.

Silverfish are one of the most familiar household insects, hiding in crevices by day and roaming the house at night in search of starch-rich foods. Spilled flour, book-binding paste and other glues, and even paper itself are eaten. Stamp collectors should keep an eye open for this insect, although damage is generally slight in really dry conditions. The insects require a fairly high humidity, which explains their liking for kitchens and bathrooms. Silverfish turn up occasionally in birds' nests on and around houses, and are sometimes very common in pigeons' nests where they seem to survive on a diet of solid guano. Like so many 'domestic' insects, the silverfish has been carried all over the world in our foodstuffs and other materials and we do not know where it originated. The fact that it is rarely found out of doors in Northern Europe suggests a tropical or sub-tropical origin, and it may be that, as far as European populations are concerned, the insects have gone from houses into birds' nests and not vice-versa.

Other sources of household insects

The nests of various rodents, especially rats and mice, contain an assortment of insects similar to that found in birds' nests, although the proportions may differ just as they do between the nests of different bird species. This variation is due largely to the differences in composition and humidity of the nests. Abandoned wasp nests provide yet more breeding sites for domestic pests, many household infestations of carpet beetles and fur beetles having been traced to old nests in the roof space. The wasps' droppings, dead larvae, and even the papery fabric of the nest itself are consumed after the wasp colony has disintegrated in the autumn. Scores of beetle species have been found in these old nests, together with various flies and moth larvae. These scavengers, several of which can be a nuisance in the house, do not take very long to reduce the wasp nest to a pile of dust.

Ants

One other group of insects that often takes up residence in our houses are the ants. Pharaoh's ant can be a real problem, but the others – mostly the common black ant – do their foraging out of doors as a rule: unless they find a convenient corridor leading to the pantry!

Destroyers of food – stored product pests

In purely economic terms, the insects that destroy our foods are much more important than those which attack household fabrics. The most serious are those that attack grain and various cereal products, and it has been estimated that something like 5 per cent of the world's production is destroyed by these insects each year. Some of the losses occur in the fields, especially in tropical areas, but in Europe most of the damage occurs after harvest. The insects involved are thus known as stored-product pests. Granaries, flour-mills, and warehouses are the main buildings affected, with only minor damage occurring in houses. We have already met some of these domestic species. A great many more occur in mills and granaries, with beetles and moths causing the most damage. The grain weevil (*Sitophilus granarius*) is one of the main culprits. It prefers whole grains – especially wheat, barley, and maize – and is therefore not likely to establish itself in many houses, although it will also tackle biscuits and pasta products such as spaghetti. Buildings around granaries may be invaded, but the weevil cannot fly and does not travel far. Although distributed all over the world in grain stores, it is rarely found out of doors and seems to be entirely dependent on man. It almost certainly originated in sub-tropical areas, where it fed on the grain in the wild, but has since transferred its attentions to our stores.

The Australian spider beetle (*Ptinus tectus*), introduced to Europe at the beginning of the 20th Century, is now very well established in mills and grain stores and also quite common in houses. It is one of several rather similar beetles with long legs and a marked constriction in front of the elytra (wing cases). This gives them a spider-like appearance. Most of these beetles are truly omnivorous and, as well as grain, they will eat dried meat and animal droppings, skins, and fabrics. The Australian spider beetle often breeds in birds' nests.

Dried fruit, chocolate, nuts, and cereal products are attacked by several species of small moths, most of which came originally from warmer climates but are now well established in food factories and warehouses. The Mediterranean flour moth (*Ephestia kuehniella*) is a very common example. It is a dull greyish brown with a wingspan of about 2cm and, despite its name, it came originally from India. As with all the moths, it is actually the larvae that do the damage. They are pinkish white and they spin copious amounts of silk as they feed. The silk binds the food together and can cause problems in food processing machinery. These moths are not serious pests in houses, however, although they can fly quite well and regularly turn up in houses close to mills and granaries.

The meal moth (*Pyralis farinalis*) is a pretty insect with yellow and purplish brown wings. It sometimes comes to lighted windows at night, possibly having grown up in neighbouring nests where its yellowish larva lives in a silken tube and feeds on debris of all

Silverfish (**above**) are often seen darting across the floor. Their slippery silver scales make them hard to catch.

The presence of death-watch beetle may only become apparent when the adult beetles (**above**) emerge from their large 'worm holes'. They may also make their presence known when the beetles 'tap' against wood as a mating call in spring.

kinds. Cereal products are the main foods of this species, however, and it is not a serious domestic pest. Flour mills and granaries are the main homes of this moth.

Wood borers

Floor-boards, rafters, and other building timbers are regularly attacked by wood-boring beetles, and many pieces of fine furniture have been destroyed by these insects. It is not difficult to explain the origin of these pests, for they teem in the woods around us and play a major role in the breaking down of dead stumps and fallen branches. Best known of the many species is the furniture beetle, also and perhaps more accurately known as the common house borer – because it attacks far more than just furniture. Woodworm is the insect's more popular name, although this refers more properly to the larva. The species is native to most parts of Europe, where there are very few buildings without it, and it has been taken by man to almost all other temperate regions of the world. It will attack almost any kind of timber. The adult beetle lays her eggs in cracks and on rough surfaces, and the resulting larvae tunnel their way into the wood. They feed on the timber for two or more years, their development being quicker in slightly damp wood. Pupation takes place in the wood, and the adults then leave through the familiar neat exit holes which are 1·5–2mm in diameter. You can see the beetles, often on window panes, from May to July. Although the exit holes indicate that the adults have escaped and that the timber has already been damaged, it is well worth filling the holes in furniture and polishing over the filling. Apart from enhancing the appearance of the furniture, this stops the adults from laying more eggs in the holes. Heavy infestations will reduce the timber to powder in a few years and, contrary to popular belief, the timber does not have to be old before it is attacked: 'worm-holes' do not imply that a piece of furniture is antique!

The infamous death-watch beetle (*Xestobium rufovillosum*) is much larger than the furniture beetle and its exit holes are 3–5mm across. This pest occurs mainly in oak, and requires a certain degree of moisture and fungal decay before it can establish itself. It is thus generally found only in the older houses. Churches and other historic buildings are particularly at risk from this beetle.

As a final example of 'domestic' wood borers, I have choosen the woodwasp or horntail. The female is a fearsome-looking insect with her long ovipositor, although she is quite harmless: the ovipostor has no sting and is used to drill into coniferous trunks and to lay the eggs there. The woodwasp is really an insect of the coniferous forests and plantations, but it is occurring with increasing frequency in a suburban areas and in new housing developments. The larvae take several years to mature in the timber and those that survive the sawmill and subsequent building operations may continue to develop in new buildings. The adults then emerge from floor-boards and other timbers and often cause unnecessary panic. Their occurrence in suburban areas is probably due to the popularity of home extensions and sun-lounges. The insects are unlikely to be numerous enough to do any serious damage, and once they have emerged there will be no further infestation, for the female lays her eggs only in timber still clad with bark.

Prevention is better than cure

We cannot discuss here the various ways of controlling household pests, except to emphasise that prevention is better than cure. Clothes and other fabrics can be treated with moth-proofers to repel the insects, while timbers can be treated with many proprietary materials to kill existing wood borers and to deter others from taking up residence. Spring-cleaning and regular sweeping to remove accumulations of dust will keep down populations of carpet beetles and similar pests, and the removal of *old* nests of birds and wasps will obviously do away with many potential pests. The true urban naturalist, however, will probably feel that any advantage in this direction is outweighed by the reduction in bird life. I, for one, would rather have house martins and a few house moths than no martins – and probably still a few house moths!

Industrial melanism: evolution in action

Michael Tweedie

People have been collecting butterflies and moths for over 250 years, and the peppered moth (*Biston betularia*) received both its English and Latin names soon after the middle of the 18th century. This is a fairly large moth with a looper type of caterpillar and normally has white wings which are speckled or 'peppered' with black. In the middle of the 19th century collectors were surprised to hear of the capture in Manchester, England of a specimen in which the wings were black. By 1864 the majority of the moths taken near Manchester were black and this form rapidly displaced the normal speckled form in industrialised urban areas. In the unspoiled countryside the speckled form continued to predominate. In Europe the same phenomenon was observed, but it was in England that the effect was greatest and here that most research has been done.

It was in the early 1800s that the effects of the Industrial Revolution, with the burning of coal on a large scale, began to become apparent. Sulphur dioxide in the air killed practically all the lichens growing on the trunks and branches of trees, and the bare bark was stained black by soot dissolved in falling rain.

Black varieties of animals which are normally coloured otherwise are known as melanics. The correspondence, in both timing and localisation, between the black peppered moths and the onset of industrial pollution made it clear that the two must be connected, and this was the beginning of the story of industrial melanism. Most of the examples of it have been observed among moths, and over a hundred British and Northern European species show signs of colour darkening induced by the industrial environment. Nevertheless, the peppered moth was the earliest recorded melanic and has remained both the most easily recognised example and the most suitable for research into the phenomenon.

Research into industrial melanism in the peppered moth

In the first half of the present century there was some unconvincing experimental work, and much speculation, as to how melanism was brought about by smoke pollution. It was pointed out by some entomologists that black moths might be better concealed on blackened bark, and breeding in captivity seemed to show that the black variety was hardier than the normal one. No attempt was made to provide a firm biological basis for these assumptions.

In the mid-1950s the late Dr H. B. D. Kettlewell started on an intensive study of the ecology, distribution and genetics of the

Smoke billowing from factory chimneys, forming a black pall across the countryside is the image most often evoked by the Industrial Revolution. Successive Clean Air Acts have greatly reduced this type of airborne pollution, perhaps reducing the opportunity for melanics to survive in the future.

peppered moth in Britain. His experiments required the breeding of huge numbers of the moths from stock collected from all over the country. In what was perhaps the most important experiment he chose two areas of woodland of contrasting type, both well populated with birds. One of them was a heavily polluted wood near industrial Birmingham, Sutton Park, the other a wood in Dorset in which were no signs of pollution, the trees being well coated with lichen. The experiments were carried out in May and June, when the peppered moth flies naturally in the wild. Both woods contained wild populations, and in the soot-blackened Birmingham wood 90 per cent of the wild moths were black; in the Dorset locality 95 per cent were speckled and only 5 per cent black.

In 1953 some hundreds of bred male moths were released in the Birmingham wood over a period of eleven days. Each moth had a coloured dot of paint on the underside of one wing. The moths were placed on tree trunks, one moth to a tree, and the numbers of black and speckled ones so released was recorded. Each night traps were set to capture the moths and a careful record was kept of the recaptured marked ones. It was found that 27·5 per cent of the black ones released were retaken but only 13 per cent of the speckled ones, indicating that in polluted and blackened surroundings the survival rate of the black moths was over twice as high as that of the speckled ones. Later the experiment was repeated in the wood in Dorset, and the results were almost exactly reversed, with the speckled moths enjoying a survival rate double that of the others.

Two methods were used to recapture the male moths. One was with the use of traps with mercury vapour light bulbs, which attract almost all night-flying moths. The other consisted of muslin cages hung up all round the experimental area, each containing a newly hatched female. Virgin female moths emit a specific scent or pheromone which powerfully attracts males of their own species, and the moths could be netted as they fluttered round the cages trying to get in. This is, of course, the reason why only males were marked and released, but it is also true that male moths fly more actively than females and are more likely to be caught in light traps. Naturally many male moths of the wild population were caught, but could be distinguished by the absence of the spot of paint. The males are easily distinguished from the females by their feathery antennae.

It seemed reasonable to suppose that the different survival rates were caused by birds, hunting by day as the predator's sense of sight was obviously involved. In collaboration with Professor N. Tinbergen, Dr Kettlewell devised another sort of experiment to test this supposition. A birdwatcher's hide was erected near a suitable tree and equal numbers of black and speckled moths were placed on the bark; they are inactive by day and can easily be persuaded to sit and remain in any required position. Day after day repetition of watching and filming from the hide showed that in the polluted wood redstarts ate 43 speckled moths and only 15 black ones; dunnocks and robins also took considerably more speckled moths. In the Dorset wood five species of birds were seen to take 164 black moths and 26 speckled ones. Here the birds were the spotted flycatcher, robin, yellowhammer, song thrush and nuthatch. All found the black moths more readily than the well concealed speckled ones. The flycatchers and yellowhammers hunted by hovering up and down the trunk, and they found very few speckled moths. The nuthatches, running up and down on the bark found a number of camouflaged moths, but even they took more black than speckled ones.

Breeding experiments revealed that there are two distinct forms of the black moth. The more frequent one has the wings quite black and is known as form *carbonaria*. The other, equally well concealed

The normal peppered moth (top) and melanic form (below) shows how, in areas of little pollution, the normal form blends with the lichen-covered tree trunk and is less susceptible to predation by birds.

on polluted bark, is black with faint white speckling and is called *insularia*; it is less common than *carbonaria* and has a different distribution.

Between 1952 and 1970 Dr Kettlewell enlisted the help of collectors all over Britain to survey the distribution of the typical and the two black forms, and a map was produced based on over 30,000 records from 83 localities. An interesting feature is the predominance of *carbonaria* not only in the industrial areas of London and the Midlands but to the east of them as well. This is accounted for by supposing that the dominant westerly winds blow the smoke and polluted air to the east forming a 'pollution shadow', and it is a fact that lichen is absent or very sparse on the trees in eastern England. In East Anglia, however, although the trees are bare of lichen their bark is not stained with soot because the wind does not carry this so far as the sulphur dioxide gas. The black moths are conspicuous on the pale bark and yet they predominate. It is thought that this is due to the heterozygous form of *carbonaria* (see box, over) being more hardy in the presence of polluted larval food than either the

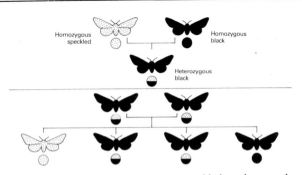

Homozygous speckled
Homozygous black
Heterozygous black

The upper diagram shows a homozygous speckled moth crossed with a homozygous black (melanic) moth: all the offspring are heterozygous black (melanic). In the lower diagram two heterozygous black moths (melanic) are crossed. The offspring are a quarter homozygous speckled, a quarter homozygous black (melanic) and a half heterozygous black (melanic). The circles under each moth indicate its genetic condition.

Genetics of the peppered moth
It is well known that characters, such as wing colour in moths, are conveyed from parents to offspring by genes derived from each parent. In respect of its colouration a peppered moth can exist in one of three conditions. A speckled moth possesses a gene determining this appearance from both parents, and is termed homozygous for this colour. Similarly a *carbonaria* moth may be homozygous for black colouration, but a proportion of the population will have a 'black' gene from one parent and a 'speckled' one from the other, and such individuals are termed heterozygous. One would expect them to be intermediate in appearance, but they are in fact black, because black is dominant over speckled. Both *carbonaria* and *insularia* 'off black' are dominant over the speckled form; *carbonaria* is dominant over *insularia*.

black or speckled homozygous forms. The 'off-black' *insularia* form largely replaces *carbonaria* in South Wales, Gloucester and the Severn valley. Only Devon and Cornwall and northern Scotland are wholly free of either melanic form.

The conclusion that Dr Kettlewell reached was that industrial melanism in moths is produced by natural selection as a result of predation by birds in a rapidly changing environment. His work is of great importance because it demonstrates evolutionary change taking place quickly enough to be observed and recorded, and it is still the only well documented example of this. In natural conditions environmental change is always too slow for evolution to have been observed during the century or so that has passed since it was established as the basis of biology.

Other moths which show industrial melanism

Among other moths which show industrial melanism *Apocheima pilosaria*, which has the rather cumbersome English name pale brindled beauty, has been closely studied. It differs from the peppered moth in several respects. It is on the wing from January to March, and only the male can fly, the female being completely wingless. Also, *pilosaria* has a completely different resting posture, with the forewings covering the hind wings. It suffers the same sort of predation as the peppered moth, but does not have to contend with the summer migrants such as flycatchers and redstarts. Possibly insectivorous birds hunt more eagerly in the winter when food is scarce; but on the other hand they have young to feed in the summer. The main melanic form of *pilosaria* has been named *monacharia* and has black fore-wings and grey hind-wings. There are other genetically distinct melanic forms, recognisable in males but not in the wingless females, which are either grey or black. Melanism in *pilosaria* has a more westerly distribution than in the peppered moth. It is concentrated in the Midlands and South Wales and occurs in central Scotland. In the 'pollution shadow' in East Anglia, where most peppered moths are black, typical *pilosaria* predominates, probably because pollution there does not blacken the trees.

The scalloped hazel (*Gonodontis bidentata*) shows industrial melanism clearly and its black form is appropriately named *nigra*. This is not distributed evenly over the polluted areas, as the *carbonaria* and *insularia* forms of the peppered moth are, but is patchy in distribution, abundant in some urban areas, absent in others where the typical form occurs. This seems to be due to the curiously feeble flight of the moth; although both sexes are winged they never fly far. Release and recapture experiments have shown that they seldom fly more than 150 metres from the point of release, while peppered moths will fly a kilometre or so. The larva of *bidentata* feeds on the leaves of a variety of trees and bushes, and in urban surroundings subsists mainly on privet.

The three moths so far discussed all belong to the family Geometridae. The green-brindled crescent (*Allophyes oxyacanthae*) belongs to the Noctuidae, and is typically brown delicately marked with green, but a plain dark brown form called *capucina* occurs occasionally wherever the moth is found. In polluted areas, where other species are represented by melanic forms, *capucina* predominates by up to 90 per cent over the typical *oxyacanthae*. This moth flies in the autumn and its larva feeds on blackthorn and other kinds of *Prunus*.

Predominant melanism occurs under natural as well as polluted conditions. On peaty moors the soil colour is dark, and moth species are often represented by melanic forms in moorland regions. In the Shetland Islands this kind of melanism is illustrated by the ingrailed clay (*Diarsia mendica*) and the autumnal rustic (*Paradiarsia glareosa*) Natural melanics are also found in pine forests, obviously evolved to match the dark coloured pine bark.

Other invertebrates which show industrial melanism

Most known cases of insect industrial melanism are found among moths, but one, of a quite unusual type, have been observed in the two-spot ladybird (*Adalia bipunctata*). Typically it is red with a pair of black spots, but there are melanic forms in which the red is partly or almost wholly replaced by black leaving some small red spots. These melanic forms predominate in the industrial Midlands and on Merseyside. In the latter area and also around Glasgow they may account for over 90 per cent of the population. Ladybirds, however, do not benefit by concealment; their bright red coloration is a warning that they are ill-tasting to the point of being inedible. An inexperienced bird that pecks one will remember its distinctive appearance and never touch another. It is true that black sometimes serves as an 'aposematic' or warning colour in other beetles, but this gives no explanation of black ladybirds in soot-polluted surroundings. It seems that the explanation does not involve protection from predators at all, but is provided by the lack or weakness of sunlight in areas that are mantled by smoke. Ladybirds are sun-loving insects and need to be warmed by the sun to maintain full activity. A black surface absorbs heat more readily than a pale one of any colour, so that black mutants have an advantage in a gloomy environment.

Two kinds of spiders have been found to have developed industrial melanic forms. One of these is the little zebra spider (*Salticus scenicus*), of which a black form was found in Manchester. Birds hunt and eat spiders, but this species is so active and restless by day that camouflage, which always depends on immobility, would not seem likely to protect it. It could well be that the sunlight factor, suggested to explain ladybird melanism, also operates in the case of the spider. The same argument applies to a wolf spider (*Arctosa perita*), of which a black form has been found on coal tips.

The institution of 'smokeless zones' has already caused a perceptible diminution in the numbers and range of black peppered moths, and a more pronounced one in the ladybird. When we at last cease to burn fossil fuels to provide heat and power industrial melanism will become a thing of the past.

Lichens and air pollution   Francis Rose

There are over 1400 species of lichens found in Britain (there are no precise figures for Northern Europe) and more than 18,000 species world-wide. They are found in every environment except in deserts, for although they can stand long periods of drought they need a stable substrate on which to grow. They are very slow growing and long-lived. They are found on tree bark, on the trunk, branches and twigs, where they do no harm to the tree. Many grow on the ground, in such places as heaths, where the white or grey bushy *Cladonia* spp. may be common. Others grow on rocks or on man-made substrates such as walls or roofs, and they are even found on such things as old boots, pieces of plastic, or bones if they lie undisturbed. The world-wide distribution, not only of lichens as a whole, but of some individual species, suggests that the lichens are a very ancient group, but they have left no fossil record as they decay too readily. Some lichen species, however, are as exacting in their habitat needs as are some rare flowering plants, and are confined to special ecological niches.

The decline of the lichens

Old records, and specimens preserved in herbaria from the 18th and early 19th centuries, tell us that many species of lichens were once common everywhere, on all sorts of substrates. For example, one large foliose lichen, *Lobaria scrobiculata*, is known to have grown even on the thatch of cottage roofs in Suffolk in the 18th century. This species has now become very rare in most of Britain, except in the remoter parts of Scotland, and is now extinct east of Exmoor and Dartmoor in England, as it is now over much of lowland Europe. Thus, if one did not know its history, one would think from its present distribution and habitats that it was an 'oceanic' species that could live only on older trees in the humid oak forests of extreme western Britain and Ireland.

Old descriptions, and old paintings, make it clear that trees every-where (except perhaps in the centres of the only quite small towns that then existed) were so covered with lichens of many species that little bare bark was visible. Compare this situation with the largely bare bark of most trees today, not only in our built-up areas but for miles out into the country around towns and cities.

Air pollution and lichens

These changes are due almost entirely to man's environmental pollution. Pollution of the air, caused by the burning of fossil fuels such as coal that contain sulphur, has been with us for a long time

This lush growth of *Parmelia* and *Usnea* spp. lichens is only found in areas with little aerial pollution.

on a small scale. Even in the later Middle Ages, there were Royal edicts against the burning of 'sea-coal' (i.e. mined coal brought by sea, as opposed to charcoal) in London fireplaces, because of the already unpleasant level of smoke produced. It was, however, the Industrial Revolution which began in England in the late 18th century, coupled with the great growth of large towns, that really got air pollution going.

Already in 1859, L. H. Grindon noticed that lichens were declining in South Lancashire and W. Nylander noticed similar changes in the lichens in the Paris parks. These changes were attributed to the effect of the visible pollutant-particulate smoke from chimneys.

It is now known, however, that it is not the visible smoke particles themselves that harm lichens, serious though these may be in providing 'condensation nuclei' on which droplets of polluted water may condense to form smogs, so bad both for human lungs and for visibility. There is no correlation between smoke concentrations as such and lichen damage. The correlation is rather with the concentration in the air of the unseen but highly toxic gas, sulphur dioxide (SO_2). Most lichens are extremely sensitive to this gas, far more so than most other plants. It affects both their photosynthesis and respiration levels. One reason why lichens are so sensitive to sulphur dioxide is their perennial nature. Many trees and herbs lose their leaves in winter, when pollution levels tend to be highest through use of more fuel for heating. A second reason is that, unlike higher plants, they have no protective waterproof skin or cuticle, with breathing pores or stomata that control access of water (and dissolved substances); they have evolved to absorb water and nutri-ents quickly over their whole surface when moisture is available; and in polluted air they absorb all the toxic substances as well. A third reason is that, unlike the mostly less sensitive mosses, the proportion of chlorophyll per unit volume of thallus is low, as only the algal cells contain it. In mosses, nearly all cells contain abundant chlorophyll, so any damaging effects are less rapidly fatal.

What is even more interesting is that lichens vary to an extraordinary degree in their sensitivity to sulphur dioxide. Such species as the large beard-lichen (*Usnea articulata*) are destroyed by sulphur dioxide levels as low as 25 micrograms per cubic metre of air over even a short period of time. One lichen (*Lecanora conizaeoides*) even appears to have a considerable sulphur requirement, and flourishes on trees and woodwork as near to the centre of London as Hyde Park. This lichen, which forms a green-grey powdery crust of relatively unwettable nature, bears tiny (c. 0·5 – 1mm wide) disc-like fruits like minute greengage-jam tarts. It was unknown to occur anywhere in the world before about 1855, when it was found in the space of ten years or so to occur in Leicestershire, near London and in the Paris parks. Was it a new genetic mutant of some related species, taking advantage of rising pollutant levels by natural selection? Or did it perhaps exist before this in some volcanic region of Europe, where natural sulphur dioxide pollution from vents in a volcanic cone was normal? We do not know, but since that time it has spread over Europe to become the commonest lichen over vast lowland areas around large cities and industrial regions, on trees, unpainted woodwork, and on sandstone walls, tolerating up to about 150 micrograms of sulphur dioxide per cubic metre of air.

In between these two extremes, there is a whole range of lichens of various tolerances to different concentrations of sulphur dioxide in the atmosphere.

As a result of this, lichen 'zones' can be recognised around our cities and industrial areas. These zones are not normally circular, but due to wind, tend to be shaped like an ellipse, with the main pollution source nearer one end of the ellipse, and its long axis extending outwards along the direction of the prevailing wind flow. Thus pollution from the London area extends much farther out into Essex to the north-east, than it does to the south or south-west, because the prevailing south-west wind tends to move the polluted air in this direction.

Topography also modifies the shape of pollution patterns. A pollution-producing city or industrial area in a narrow valley will often produce a narrow, elongated pollution zone, the high ground on either side preventing the polluted air from moving freely sideways.

It has proved possible, by correlation with chemical analysis of air collected by instruments, to put definite values on the pollution levels indicated by particular epiphytic lichens, or more accurately,

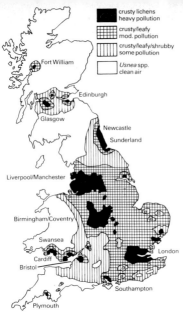

crusty lichens
heavy pollution

crusty/leafy
mod. pollution

crusty/leafy/shrubby
some pollution

Usnea spp.
clean air

Lichens absorb nutrients directly from their surface, and are therefore particularly sensitive to airborne pollution. Only a few, like this bright yellow lichen, *Xanthoria sp.*, (**right**) can live around cities with heavy air pollution.

Power station chimneys pour sulphur dioxide, from the combustion of coal, into the atmosphere (**far right**). The CEGB still disputes that this contributes to acid rain.

Some species of lichen are more tolerant of atmospheric pollution than others. This map shows zones where certain lichens grow and others do not as a reflection of the pollution level. The zones indicating most pollution occur around large industrial areas and cities and are affected by the direction of the prevailing winds and other factors such as topography. (Adapted from ACE survey map)

by particular groups of epiphytic lichens. To take an example from work in the London area, grey foliose lichens first appear to the south of London about 15 miles from the centre; these include such species as the hollow, convex-lobed *Hypogymnia physodes*, and the flat *Parmelia sulcata* with an obvious network of cracks or reticulations on its thallus. At this distance, instrumental analysis indicates that sulphur dioxide levels are about 70 micrograms per cubic metre of air. (These are the mean levels for the period October to March when pollution is always higher.) At 20 to 24 miles from the centre of London to the south and south-west, the flat, greenish-yellow foliose lichen *Parmelia caperata* starts to appear on the bases of more sheltered trees. This has been shown to indicate that sulphur dioxide levels are then down to only about 50 micrograms per cubic metre, which this species will just tolerate. Other, more sensitive species appear further out still.

These facts suggest that lichens could be used as an economical way of estimating air pollution by sulphur dioxide. The most useful lichens for this work are epiphytic species, growing on trees with bark that is naturally weakly acid. Lichens of course also occur on

lkaline substrates in and around towns, such as limestone walls, gravestones, mortar, and asbestos cement tiles. The calcium carbonate in limestone tends to neutralise the toxic acid gases, so that lichens can exist much nearer to pollution sources on limestone or mortar than on trees, where there is no 'buffering' effect. However, an interesting phenomenon was recorded by J. R. Laundon in his studies of lichens in London, where many lichens were found on tombstones in old churchyards as near to central London as Hampstead, but many of these species only occurred on tombstones erected before *c.* 1820. Further out, they occurred progressively on younger and younger dated gravestones. This suggests that some lichens can survive quite high levels of sulphur dioxide pollution on calcareous substrates but cannot colonise *new* substrates at current levels. The date is significant, and indicates a time when the area first changed from a rural environment to a polluted suburban one.

Asbestos-cement is a remarkable substrate for lichens; it may be extremely alkaline, as high as pH 11, and M. R. D. Seaward has shown that the lichen *Lecanora muralis* (which forms buff-coloured flat rosettes 2–4cm wide) can grow on asbestos-cement tiles as near to the centre of Leeds as 1·5 miles, while it only appears first on sandstone at over 5·5 miles from the city centre. Forms of pollution other than from oxides of sulphur, such as toxic metals, agricultural chemicals, and fluorides, also damage lichens, but these appear less relevant to the urban environment.

Recent changes in pollution patterns

Over the last 20–25 years, there have been many changes in urban pollution patterns and in those of Britain and Europe generally. At one time, most sulphur dioxide pollution was due to domestic coal fires, or to numerous low factory chimneys with coal-fired furnaces. Since then, more and more houses have gone over to other forms of heating such as electricity, gas, or central heating using fairly sulphur-free grades of oil. The main sources of pollution now in Britain are the tall chimneys of the Central Electricity Generating Board, although the Board still deny this, from large power stations burning coal or oil relatively rich in sulphur. Clean Air Acts eliminated much particulate smoke, though as we have seen, the smoke itself has little effect on lichens; as apparently have the emissions of carbon monoxide and lead from motor cars, harmful to humans though these things are. Pollution levels in our cities and major industrial areas have fallen considerably. One result is that the relatively sensitive lichens *Parmelia caperata* and *Usnea subfloridana* are now starting to recolonise trees in the damper open spaces of London suburbs and parts of Cheshire south of Manchester.

There is, however, a very serious side to the new patterns. The tall chimneys of our power stations certainly tend to carry away much of the sulphur dioxide from our cities; but pollution levels have risen over much of the English Midlands and over the European northern plain from northern France to Poland. There is good evidence that the pH of tree barks over wide areas of Northern Europe is falling to such an extent that quite different lichen species more typical of the naturally acid bark of pines and spruce are replacing the normal lichen floras on oak, ash and other broad leaved trees. What seems to be happening is that the sulphur dioxide from power stations in industrial regions of Europe including particularly Britain, is now carried up so high by the immensely tall chimneys (some are 200 metres tall) that it not only travels vast distances before descending, but also has time to oxidise to sulphuric acid. Some of this probably ends up in the rain which is acidifying lakes in Scandinavia with such serious results, but much also acidifies the rainfall nearer home. Rainfall has become steadily more acid over the last 150 years, and the process has greatly accelerated in the last 20 years or so. This acid rain seems to be the factor that is acidifying the bark of broad-leaved trees over much of Britain except the extreme west and south, and causing these great changes in the lichen flora. Until some remedial action (such as 'scrubbing' flue gases) is taken, the outlook not only for lichens, but for our forests, our soils, and the fish in our rivers and lakes, is rather dark.

Wildlife gardening and conservation

Michael Chinery

For the man in the street, who comes to town perhaps only to do the weekly shopping, the town garden might be nothing more than an untidy shrubbery or flower bed around the car park, for this is often the only sign of horticulture on show. But anyone who has flown over a town, or even looked down on one from a church tower, will know that a considerable acreage of greenery is tucked away behind the rows of shops and houses. There are trees and shrubberies, carefully tended lawns, and brightly coloured flower beds. Each garden may be just a small and isolated oasis amid the bricks and mortar, but added together they form an extensive nature reserve where far more than the ubiquitous pigeon and house sparrow can make their homes.

In the suburban areas the garden habitat positively explodes. Gardens here are generally larger and often spread out in front of the houses where, on view to neighbours and to the public, they tend to become show-pieces. Most wildlife habitats are threatened by increasing human population and activity and are disappearing at an alarming rate, but the garden habitat is unique in thriving on increasing human numbers and expanding with the population. It is the one habitat not under threat and, as long as we can resist the temptation to poison or otherwise destroy everything that we do not recognize, our gardens can support a very large proportion of the wildlife being evicted from elsewhere. I even suggest that it is our duty to look upon our gardens as nature reserves and to encourage wildlife into them. With a few exceptions, this can be done without detriment to either the beauty or the productivity of the garden: increased wildlife activity may even increase productivity in some instances, and surely no one can deny that the butterflies and birds add beauty to the garden.

Until now I have spoken of the garden as a single habitat, but it is actually an intricate mosaic of many different habitats, all with something valuable to offer wildlife in the form of food or shelter. Look at almost any town garden and you will find most if not all of the following habitats: walls, fences, sheds, paths, cultivated ground, and compost heaps. All provide living space for plants and animals, and the plants – the uninvited weeds as well as the purposely planted lawns and hedges, trees, and other plants – provide yet more homes as well as food for animal life. The more habitats there are in your garden, and the greater variety of plant life you can provide, the greater the variety of wildlife that will

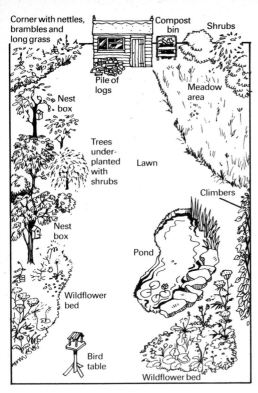

Corner with nettles, brambles and long grass

Compost bin

Shrubs

Pile of logs

Nest box

Meadow area

Trees under-planted with shrubs

Lawn

Climbers

Nest box

Pond

Wildflower bed

Bird table

Wildflower bed

Planning a garden for wildlife is worth a little thought so that you attract and provide a home for as many plants and animals as possible. This generalised plan (**left**) will give you some ideas which can be adapted to suit your own garden.

For a real cabaret, try growing a few teasels in your garden: goldfinches (**right**) will repay you with their acrobatic antics as they try to remove the developing seeds almost before the flowers have faded. These beautiful birds will also tear dandelion and plantain heads to shreds to get at the soft, young seeds.

move in. Diversity should thus be the central theme and watchword for the conservation-minded gardener. But do not expect all your visitors to stay put: wildlife is extremely mobile and, while we erect fences and hedges against our neighbours, the wild animals use these same structures as highways to move from one garden to another. It is thus the whole network of urban gardens that acts as the nature reserve, so do not worry if you can not fit all the desirable habitats into your own backyard.

Many plants and animals move in without any invitation. There can be few gardens, for example, without house sparrows, even if the birds do not actually take up residence, and equally few that are not visited by marauding mice at night. Insects drift in and out of every garden, and even the most tireless gardener can not boast of an entirely weed-free plot. But the conservationist, or wildlife gardener, is not satisfied with just the casual visitor and actively encourages wildlife to visit and settle in the garden by careful planning – and, contrary to some people's ideas, a wildlife garden *does* need planning and a good deal of hard work. A wildlife garden is

not a garden that has run wild. That should allay the fears of any non-conservationist neighbours! Wildlife gardening is all about putting in the right kinds of plants and managing them in the right way. You remain in control, although there is much to be said for not being too tidy, but the wildlife still finds a home and gives a great deal of pleasure to you and, hopefully, to your neighbours. There is an additional bonus: a well-balanced mixture of wildlife tends to keep itself in check and you will find that far less time and expense are involved in pest control.

Attracting birds to your garden

Birds are certainly the most popular of our wild animals, probably because they are largely diurnal and relatively easy to watch and identify, and bird gardening is undoubtedly the most widely practised form of wildlife gardening. Most households throw out some kind of food for the birds, even if it involves no more than shaking the crumbs from the table cloth, and the birds quickly learn when food is likely to appear. They may arrive spot on meal-times, indicating some very efficient internal clocks, or they may swoop down expectantly every time the door is opened – a good example of learning by association. House sparrows and starlings will forage in the starkest backyard if there is any chance of food, and they may be joined by the town pigeon if the yard is not too enclosed, but there is a limit to the number of species that will forage among bare bricks and mortar no matter how much food you put out for them. The first essential if you want to attract a wider variety of birds to your garden is to make it interesting to them, and this generally means planting trees or shrubs to give them cover and perching places. If the plants can provide fruits and seeds as well, so much the better, and in Britain I would always recommend native species wherever possible because these generally support more insect life – providing even more food for the birds and increasing the diversity of the garden community still further. Even a single potted shrub on a patio might encourage a blackbird or a blue tit to join the sparrows, and if you can provide a really dense clump of greenery you will be richly rewarded with robins, chaffinches, greenfinches, dunnocks, and many other species. Of course, the location of your garden is not without influence: suburban gardens and gardens in small towns relatively close to open country inevitably get more species, but birds are extremely mobile, especially during the spring and autumn migration periods, and any interesting-looking oasis in the town may bring them down, if only for a fleeting visit.

The shrubs to plant will depend to a large extent on the space available and on the type of soil in your garden: try field maple, blackthorn, hawthorn, birches, oaks, wayfaring tree, guelder rose, spindle, rowan, cherry (preferably the wild species not the double flowered non-fruiting varieties) and other native species.

Do not just stick your shrubs in without thinking. Think about their appearance in years to come and try to create a wild atmosphere – perhaps that of a woodland glade. By planting species of different heights, you can create a two layered 'woodland' in your garden. But remember that a 'wild garden' still needs to be managed if it is to look attractive. Neglect leads to a garden running wild not a wild garden!

Many people are loath to plant ivy, in the belief that it is a noxious parasite. It can definitely be invasive, but where space is no problem its evergreen foliage provides year-round cover and is a very useful addition to the bird garden. It is certainly not a true parasite – if it were, it would not be able to live happily on inanimate walls – but when growing on trees it does compete with them for water and minerals, and if it is too vigorous it can deprive the trees of a certain amount of light and carbon dioxide. But these are not good enough reasons for banning the ivy from your garden. As well as the year-round cover provided by the leaves, the flowers provide abundant nectar for insects in late autumn and the berries attract many birds in the spring. The yew and the holly are other useful evergreens, but they are rather slow-growing and have the added disadvantage of being dioecious, meaning that male and female flowers grow on separate trees. As only the female trees bear the bird-attracting fruits, and then only when there is a pollinating male fairly close at hand, the unlucky gardener can end up with just a mass of barren foliage. The best way to overcome such disappointments is to take cuttings from known female trees. Holly rarely roots satisfactorily from cuttings, but you can try grafting female shoots on to young saplings or you can buy one of the new bisexual cultivars which carry flowers of both sexes. Coniferous trees range from the rather stark, candle-like exotic cypresses to the rather more interesting Scots pine and Norway spruce – perhaps a transplanted Christmas tree if you can find one with roots! These trees are favourites of goldcrests, coal tits, crossbills and siskins.

Wild and cultivated herbaceous plants, from the humble dandelion to the stately hollyhock, also attract seed-eating birds.

Most of the plants mentioned so far can be obtained from the ever increasing number of garden centres, but it is cheaper and usually more fun to swap and barter with friends. Remember that it is illegal to dig up wild plants without the land-owner's permission, so do not be tempted to collect your shrubs from the wild, even if you might theoretically be doing good by thinning out some overcrowded saplings in the woods.

Feeding the birds

By planting the right mixture of shrubs and other plants, you can assure your feathered guests of fresh food for much of the year, but if you want to keep them around you during the winter months you must provide them with additional food – and the wider the choice of menu you provide the wider the range of avian clientele you will build up in your garden.

Most kinds of kitchen scraps are suitable for the birds – bacon rind and other fat, pastry off-cuts, bread crusts, cake and biscuit crumbs (the birds will not mind how stale they are), cheese, and cooked potato all go down very well. Put an extra potato in the saucepan each day especially for the birds. Throw your apple cores out for the birds as well. But, nutritious as your table and kitchen scraps may be, they are not as good as the birds' natural foods. It is difficult to provide large quantities of insects for the insectivorous species, although your resident robin will love you all the more if you can serve up a few mealworms from time to time: your local pet shop may be able to supply them. Fishermen's maggots – bought by weight from the tackle shop if you do not fancy breeding them yourself – are apparently less tasty, but I find that the starlings eat them readily enough. If you are continually frustrated by the starlings pushing the smaller birds aside on the bird table, try serving maggots as a first course: the starlings *might* fill themselves up and leave the other birds to dine in peace on the delicacies of the second course.

As far as the vegetarian birds are concerned, you can not go wrong with the seed mixtures specially formulated for wild birds. These mixtures contain a wide variety of seeds, suitable for many species, and are not expensive if bought in bulk from specialist suppliers. These seed mixtures contain many small seeds attractive to the slender-beaked birds as well as to the specialist seed-eaters, but it is a good idea to cater for the softer-beaked birds with some crushed seed or raw oatmeal. Peanuts, of course, need no introduction to the bird-gardener: served with or without their shells, they are a first-rate source of energy for all kinds of birds, but do not put out salted nuts, or any other salty food, for salt is bad for all our garden birds. Sunflower seeds are eagerly taken by many birds, especially the greenfinches, and are easily obtained: why not grow your own and enjoy the brilliant flowers as well as the antics of the birds pecking at the ripening seeds? Coconut is another favourite, but it *must* be fresh: desiccated coconut swells up when eaten and does no good at all to tiny stomachs. Simply saw a fresh coconut in half and hang each half up like a bell. The tits will be especially grateful. Fruit is always acceptable, even when past its best in our eyes: apples are great favourites with blackbirds and starlings and are quickly reduced to empty skins in the winter. If you are feeling generous, put out a handful of sultanas or other dried fruit from time to time.

As long as they get a meal, the birds do not really mind how it is served and are quite happy to forage for scraps on the ground. Some species, like the dunnock, prefer to feed on the ground. But the enthusiastic bird-gardener goes to considerable lengths to present the food in a variety of interesting ways – interesting to both bird and bird-watcher – and is usually handsomely rewarded. The central feature, as in most dining rooms, is the table. You will find an amazing array of bird tables in pet shops and garden centres. Some are good and some are bad, while many seem designed more to show off the carpenter's skill than to attract birds. A good range of tables and other feeding devices can be obtained from the Royal

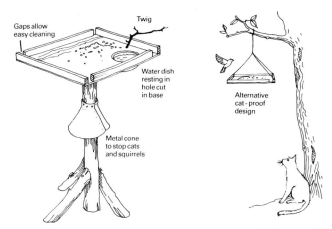

Gaps allow easy cleaning

Twig

Water dish resting in hole cut in base

Metal cone to stop cats and squirrels

Alternative cat-proof design

A bird table need not be a little Swiss chalet on a post! In fact, probably the simpler the table the more birds you will attract. Make sure the table is well away from any trees or shrubs which might enable cats to get in amongst the diners.

Society for the Protection of Birds, but you do not need to be a do-it-yourself expert to make a perfectly satisfactory bird table yourself. It is basically nothing more than a wooden platform, at least 60cm square for the best results, fixed to a post about two metres high. At this height, it is out of the reach of cats – a problem in urban and rural gardens alike – as long as the post is smooth and unclimb-able. There should be a rim around the edge of the table to prevent the food from blowing away too easily, but leave a couple of gaps so that the rain can drain away. A roof is not necessary, although some people find that a fairly low roof does discourage the starlings – for a short while anyway!

The lawn is the traditional place for the bird table, but do not put it more than two or three yards from some bushes or other cover, for many of our smaller birds are distinctly agoraphobic. If you have no lawn, you can fix the table to a tree or a wall, or even to a window-sill, but remember the cat problem. You might prefer to hang the table like a tray from a slender branch or from a wire stretched across the garden above head-height: This will certainly solve the cat problem, but it does not deter that other scourge of the bird-gardener, the grey squirrel. Apart from completely enclosing your bird-table in a steel-mesh cage, there seems to be no answer to this menace and you might as well make the best of it. There is no denying that it is an attractive animal, and one can not help admiring its tightrope skills as it scampers along the wire to reach a hanging tray. Its dexterity in hauling up a hanging coconut is also to be admired, but the fact remains that it is a pest.

Kitchen or table scraps can be put loose on the bird table, but a more interesting way of serving this food is in the form of a 'bird pudding' served in half a coconut shell hung upside down like a bell. It used to be said that only the tits would be able to get at the mixture. They are certainly the only common garden birds that can cling upside-down on the shells for any length of time, but birds do not take long to learn new tricks and the house sparrows can cling to the rim of the shell quite long enough to get a good beakful of pudding. Dunnocks patrol the ground beneath waiting for the inevitable crumbs to fall, while my resident robin has learnt to hover long enough under the shell to get a beakful. An enterprising song thrush used to feed regularly from one pudding-filled shell by darting vertically up at it and grabbing a beakful – a sort of kingfisher dive in reverse.

Another idea for feeding is the 'pudding stick'. It is loved by tits and, if you are lucky enough to have them in the area, woodpeckers and nuthatches. Greenfinches and house sparrows also manage to cling on, wings flapping furiously, while they dig out the goodies, but the stick seems to defeat the starlings – much to the delight of many bird-gardeners. Starlings certainly have big appetites and tend to shove smaller birds out of the way, but they do not really deserve the contempt poured upon them: their plumage is really quite beautiful and their mealtime antics are most amusing.

Peanuts are usually sold in small polythene nets for hanging on trees or on the bird table, but the material is easily damaged by beaks and claws and it is better to serve the nuts in a purpose made wire cage. Scraps of meat and fat can also be put in the cage so that they have to be pecked at: served loose on the bird table, they are carried away and eaten elsewhere unless finely chopped. And while talking of meat, do not forget to hang up the bones from the weekend joint so that the birds can peck them clean!

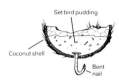 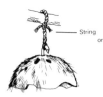

Bird pudding and the pudding stick
An interesting way of serving bird food is in the form of a 'pudding'. Add your kitchen scraps, together with some oatmeal, or other cereal, and a handful of dried fruit, to some melted fat in a basin. Pack it into a coconut shell as it begins to solidify. When the mixture is well set, hang the shell up in the garden and watch the fun. The 'pudding stick' is simply a small log or piece of timber with the holes stuffed with pudding.

If you have a bird table you may find it easier to turn out the bird pudding onto the top. Here, a great tit (left) and blue tit tuck into the feast.

There are many other ways of serving up the birds' food, and every gardener has his or her favourite system, but the really important thing is regularity. Once you start to feed the birds in the winter they will rely on you and will wait for the food each day: if it does not arrive they might not leave themselves enough time to go off and search elsewhere, and this could be disastrous in really cold weather. The time of day is not that important, but early morning is good because the birds can usually use a good breakfast after a cold night. And good news for all those starling-haters – the starlings are generally late arrivals in the garden after their communal roosting and the smaller birds can feed in peace. Water is all too often forgotten by the gardener, but the birds need it and will appreciate a few shallow dishes – especially in very cold weather when natural water is frozen over. Refill the dishes regularly to keep them as ice-free as possible.

Bread and similar materials can be put out throughout the year in small quantities to keep the house sparrows happy, but other forms of feeding should be reduced as the breeding season approaches, for many of the foods are harmful to nestlings. If you stop the feeding gradually, the birds will get into the habit of searching for natural foods and will have no difficulty in finding enough insects to keep the nestlings happy. Put out small quantities of food, preferably not fatty materials, during the summer to remind the birds of your existence, and they should come flocking back in the autumn.

Many of the birds that visit your garden during the winter to feed will move off to search for breeding sites in the spring, but you might be able to persuade some to stay by providing them with suitable nesting sites. Shrubs and hedges and climbers on the walls are fine for thrushes and blackbirds, and also for dunnocks, but the tits nest in holes. They will make use of nestboxes instead of natural tree holes, and this is one very important way in which the town gardener can help the bird population, for the number of old trees with suitable nesting holes is very limited in the urban environment.

As with bird tables, there are many nest-box designs. Two simple designs for a tit box are shown here. The exact size of the box does not matter, but the size of the entrance hole is important – no more than 2·75cm diameter if you want to prevent the house sparrows from squatting. Do not worry about any deficiencies in your carpentry skills: a bit of ventilation is good for the birds, but any large gaps are easily plugged with mastic. Make sure there is a small drainage hole in the bottom. Take care to choose a good site for the box. It should be at least two metres from the ground to avoid the cat problem, and must not be placed anywhere that is exposed to the full sun or to regular strong winds. You can fix the box to a wall or to a tree, but always make sure that the entrance hole is protected from rain. Screws are better than nails for fixing the box to a tree, for it can then be taken down more easily – not in the breeding season – if repairs are necessary at any time.

Most birds are territorial. The size of the territory depends on the availability of food supplies, but it is rare to find more than two or three pairs of blue tits to the acre in the breeding season. Of course, you might be lucky enough to get a pair on each side of your garden, with a territorial boundary down the middle, and there is nothing to prevent a great tit from sharing with a blue tit.

The open-fronted nest-box is ideal for robins and blackbirds, and may even entice a spotted flycatcher to nest in your garden. Unlike the tit-boxes, the open-fronted types must be given a certain amount of cover. Put them in the forks of trees and shrubs, or amongst the ivy and other creepers on the wall. All boxes should be in position well before the nesting season – preferably by late autumn – so that the birds can get used to them. Do try the traditional old kettle or saucepan in the hedge: robins really do build in such places. And if you have an old garden wall, especially one with a good coat of vegetation, try taking out a brick or stone here and there – wrens and flycatchers could very well make use of the cavity.

For your own amusement as well as the birds' comfort, provide them with furnishings as well as homes. Polythene nut bags stuffed with various materials and scattered round the garden, fixed to the

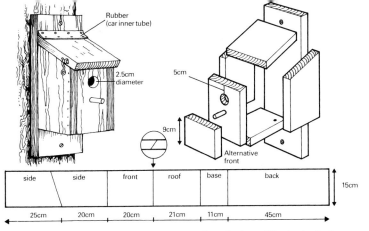

side	side	front	roof	base	back	
25cm	20cm	20cm	21cm	11cm	45cm	15cm

Different bird species prefer different nest box designs. The basic design, shown here, which may be modified to accommodate other birds, is built for 'small hole nesters', such as sparrows, tits and wrens. When you fix the box on the tree make sure it is in a position which will not let rain in through the entrance hole.

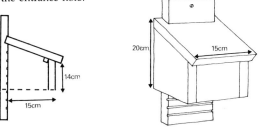

This bat box design will accommodate most species. It should be attached in a warm dry place which has open access to the outside, perhaps in the roof of a shed or garage.

ground or hung from trees, will provide a lot of fun. String, cotton, strips of brown paper, feathers, straw, and the sweepings from the local hairdresser's floor can all be put out for nesting material. Wool is excellent, but avoid brightly coloured pieces which might make the nests too conspicuous to cats and other predators.

Before leaving the subject of nest-boxes, a word about bats is in order. These fascinating mammals have declined drastically in recent years, largely through loss of habitat, so you might like to put up one or two bat boxes under the eaves or on a tall tree. Many bats roost in buildings, new as well as old, but older houses allow plenty of access to the roof space. The really dedicated bat-fan might consider making a few small openings under the eaves. A few bats will do no harm and will repay your hospitality by keeping your roof space free from woodworm and other unwelcome insects.

Butterfly gardening

Attracting butterflies to your garden is all about growing the right kinds of flowers to interest them. The urban garden can never compete with the open countryside and will never pull in more than a few of our native butterflies, but you can contribute significantly to butterfly well-being by judicious planting. Remember that several of our species are migratory and might well drop in to enjoy a feast in your garden even if they do not stay very long. The red admiral and the painted lady are well known migrants and not uncommon visitors to gardens right in the middle of town, together with the large white. The latter is attractive in the flower garden but less welcome among the cabbages. Other butterflies that you can expect in the urban garden include the peacock, small tortoiseshell, brimstone (*Gonepteryx rhamni*), comma, holly blue, and small white. If there are railway embankments and similar areas in the vicinity, look out also for the small copper (*Lycaena phlaeas*) and the occasional orange-tip (*Anthocharis cardamines*) and meadow brown (*Maniola jurtina*). Many moths will also appreciate your flower garden, with the migratory humming-bird hawkmoth (*Macroglossum stellatarum*) being one of the most conspicuous because of its day-flying habits.

Butterflies are attracted to flowers by the colour and scent, but

The ice-plant (*Sedum spectabile*) is a wonderful source of nectar for late-flying butterflies, such as this comma, before they go into hibernation in September.

they actually feed on the nectar. You should therefore plant nectar-rich flowers, and this often means the old-fashioned 'cottage-garden' flowers. Today's cultivated varieties have been produced to bring colour into the garden, and they certainly do that, but the large and colourful blooms have often been produced at the expense of nectar and the flowers are of no interest to the butterflies.

The value of ivy as a nectar source has already been mentioned. It also serves as a food plant of the holly blue butterfly and is worth planting by a wall just for that. It is often forgotten that nectar-rich flowers are not the butterflies' only requirements: in the caterpillar stage they are leaf-eaters and most species have distinct preferences in their diet. Peacocks, small tortoiseshells, and red admirals – three of our most colourful garden butterflies – all feed on stinging nettles in the larval stage, and if you are really going to encourage these species you ought to grow nettles as well. The average gardener might draw the line at this, but many gardens have the odd corner where a clump of nettles could be allowed to flourish. It is often said that small clumps are of no value and that the butterflies need extensive nettle beds in which to breed, but they *do* use small patches when they find them and a small clump is certainly better than no clump at all. Other insects will also make their homes in the nettles, and if you allow a few docks and dead-nettles to remain as well many moth species will benefit. It all comes down to the business of not being *too* tidy if you want to attract and conserve insects in your garden. A patch of long grass might encourage the caterpillars of the meadow brown, as well as providing seeds for the birds later on, and do not be too keen to trim the hedge: let caterpillars keep some of the foliage in trim for you. Some of these caterpillars will end up as bird food – not a bad thing for bird conservation – but some will mature into butterflies and moths to add even more interest to the garden.

Avoid the temptation to buy in butterflies from dealers in an attempt to beautify your garden. They might stay around for a while, but most of them usually disappear quite quickly and, unless the right kinds of food plants are available in the area, you are doing nothing for the conservation of the species.

Wasps and bees

Every gardener knows the value of bees in pollinating crops and other flowers, but few appreciate the value of wasps. Even fewer would consider inviting them into the garden, but this is a worth-while project in the interests of conservation and it can also provide the gardener with fascinating viewing. I am not talking about the familiar social wasps which make a nuisance of themselves in the autumn, although they do a tremendous amount of good by gobbling up thousands of insect pests in spring and summer, but about the numerous solitary species. These are generally a bit smaller than the social wasps and, instead of building up large colonies, each female builds a small nest of her own. She stocks it with paralysed flies, aphids, or other insects and lays one or more eggs before sealing up the nest and leaving her offspring to demolish the larder. Many of these solitary wasps nest in the ground, but others prefer hollow stems, dead wood, or holes in walls. Old garden walls with soft mortar are ideal nesting sites, but you can provide artificial homes by leaving a few logs around the garden and even drilling small holes in them – anything from 2mm to 10mm across. Short canes, dead hogweed stems, or even small bundles of drinking straws glued under window-sills may also attract the wasps, and if they take up residence you can watch them coming in with prey, homing in on the entrance hole with amazing accuracy.

The majority of gardeners probably recognise only two kinds of bees – honey bees and bumble bees – but there are actually hundreds of different kinds. Most of them are solitary creatures like the wasps described above, and you can attract them to your garden with a wide variety of flowers and perhaps encourage them to stay in artificial homes like those provided for the wasps. Most of them prefer to nest in the ground, however, and often choose lawns and well-trodden paths. Bumble bees generally nest on or under the

A loose stack of logs in a corner of the garden will provide a warm, dry place for hedgehogs to hibernate in and a home for beetles, insects and fungi.

Creating a wildlife garden does not mean letting your garden go wild. Here, a pond has been carefully placed, and planted with wild flowers and water plants to encourage newts and frogs as well as a wide range of insects.

ground, several species seeking out old mouse holes in which to build their nests. They are not too keen on artificial homes, but can sometimes be persuaded to build in an up-turned flower pot which has been partly filled with the bedding from a pet mouse's cage. Give the pot some kind of covering to keep out the rain. In addition to helping the urban bee population, you will get considerable enjoyment out of watching the pollen-laden bees returning to the nest and knowing that they have been busy on some of your flowers.

The garden pond

Nothing beats a pond for attracting the widest possible range of wildlife into a garden. It provides water for birds and other animals to drink, and a home for countless insects and other small animals. With the loss of so many ponds from the countryside, largely through changes in agricultural practice, the garden pond is becoming a major sanctuary for frogs and newts – even in the middle of towns. These rather quaint animals actually spend only

79

a relatively short time in the water each year, and outside the breeding season they may wander considerable distances over land. So do not be surprised to find them invading a newly made pond. In fact, you need not introduce anything apart from a few water plants to your pond: all the animal life will arrive under its own steam or by hitching lifts on other animals. The eggs of water snails, fishes, and many other creatures have all been shown to be carried in the mud attached to birds' feet.

The garden pond does not have to be big to be useful: a newt colony bred for many years in a pond no more than 60cm square in my own garden. But it must be at least 45cm deep, and preferably a bit more, to prevent the water from freezing solid in the winter. The method of construction is a matter of personal choice. Many people prefer the pre-formed fibreglass pond, which is merely dropped into a hole of similar shape. It can be filled immediately and truly fulfils its claim to be an instant pond. The only disadvantage is that you have to have what size and shape you can get. For a greater choice, I recommend the flexible pond liner. Thick black polythene can be used, but purpose-made liners are worth the extra money. Dig a hole of any shape you like and place the liner in position over it – make sure you buy a liner big enough to cover your excavations! As you fill the pond, the liner takes the shape of the hole. It is a good idea to line the hole first with soft sand or peat, or even a layer of newspaper, to prevent any possibility of a sharp stone piercing the liner. Surround the pond with flagstones, turf, or rockery stone. The wildlife will not mind whether you create a formal or informal pond, but do provide a shallow area where frogs can spawn. A sloping margin at one end will allow newts to get in and out easily. This will also enable birds to drink and bathe and inquisitive hedgehogs to escape if they fall in.

Water lilies, yellow flags, and all the usual pond plants can be added to the pond. Those which root on the bottom are best planted in polythene baskets – which normally come with the plants if you buy them from the garden centre. Lilies can be put in the deepest part of the pond, with the others on shallow shelves around the edges. It is a good idea to drop the edge of the pond at one end so that excess water drains away to form a boggy patch where you can plant marsh marigolds (*Caltha palustris*) and other semi-aquatic species and form yet another habitat in your garden. Always try to use rainwater for topping up your pond in hot weather. Tap water contains more minerals and usually leads to an excessive growth of algae in the pond. This does not necessarily do any harm, but you will not be able to watch the many amusing dramas that go on under the water's surface.

Field Guide

Abbreviations and symbols used in the field guide. Some abbreviations are explained on the pages on which they occur. Abbreviations used when describing the distribution of a species:

B	Britain (England, Scotland and Wales)	Ir	Ireland
		LC	Low Countries (Belgium and The Netherlands)
Be	Belgium		
D	Denmark	Ne	The Netherlands
En	England	No	Norway
ex	except	Sca	Scandinavia (Denmark, Norway, Sweden, Finland and Iceland)
F	France		
Fi	Finland		
FS	Fenno-Scandia (Finland, Norway and Sweden)	Sco	Scotland
		T	throughout Northern Europe
G	Germany		
Ic	Iceland	Wa	Wales
		C.	central

Other abbreviations used

		E.	east
acc	of accidental occurrence	imm	immature
agg	aggregate. Placed after a scientific name, e.g. *Rubus fruticosus*, to indicate that a number of microspecies are grouped together under that name	juv	juvenile
		N.	north
		S.	south
		sp.	species (singular)
		spp.	species (plural)
		W.	west

For the purposes of this book, Northern Europe is the area designated in this map.

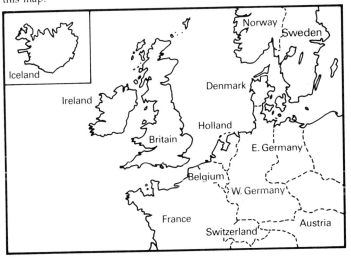

Trees   Large Broad-Leaved Trees

Deciduous trees reaching a height of 30m or more.

London Plane *Platanus* × *hispanica*   Platanaceae
Generally considered a hybrid between **Oriental plane** *P. orientalis* (which has more deeply cut leaves) and **American plane** *P. occidentalis*. Has glossy, five-lobed leaves and globular brown fruits. The flaking bark gives the trunk a characteristic appearance. Widely planted in streets, parks and squares, except in the north. It probably originated in S. Europe and therefore grows best where summers are warm. The late appearance of the leaves and the ease with which they are cleansed by rain are advantageous in polluted atmospheres. Also in the tree's favour is the fact that the root system can function under pavements and in compacted soil.

Sycamore *Acer pseudoplatanus*   Aceraceae
The 'Plane' in Scotland. Has dark, five-lobed, red-stalked leaves (sometimes with black blotches caused by the fungus *Rhytisma acerinum*), pendulous flowers in April, and two-winged fruits.

An extensively planted native of S. and C. Europe, frequently naturalised. It has long been established in Britain, but the date of introduction is unknown. Seeds are wind-dispersed, the seedlings appearing in profusion on any open ground. In unmanaged places the sycamore becomes the dominant tree and is regarded as a 'weed'.

Common Lime *Tilia* × *europaea*   Tiliaceae
A hybrid between **large-leaved lime** *T. platyphyllos* and **small-leaved lime** *T. cordata*, both of which are planted in towns, but less often. Can reach 40m but is often severely pollarded. Leaves may be covered with red 'nail-galls' caused by an eriophyid mite. Fragrant flowers attract bees. Trunk often disfigured by sprouting bosses.

Widely distributed except in the N., limes are frequently used as avenue and boulevard trees (e.g. Unter den Linden, Berlin). They can meet with disapproval, for they attract lime aphids *Eucallipterus tiliae*, which shower everything beneath with sticky honeydew. **Silver limes** *T. tomentosa* and silver pendent limes *T. petiolaris* are also planted.

Horse Chestnut *Aesculus hippocastanum*   Hippocastanaceae
Well known for its sticky buds, each with a horseshoe-shaped leaf scar below it, and its fruit, the spiny green cases enclosing the 'conkers' with which British children engage in harmless duelling. An unmistakable tree in spring with its white candle-like inflorescences. The red flowered *Aesculus* × *carnea* is smaller, with non-sticky buds and less spiny fruit. A native of the Balkans, widely planted in gardens, parks and squares, except in the N.

Copper Beech *Fagus sylvatica* 'purpurea'   Fagaceae
The name covers several cultivated dark-leaved forms of the **common beech** *Fagus sylvatica*, a fine tree which many fortunate towns have inherited from an age when the air was cleaner. (Beeches are hard to establish when atmospheric pollution is particularly bad.) Copper varieties have the smooth grey bark of the typical beech and produce similar fruits (mast), consisting of one or two nuts in a woody, spiny case formed by bracts. They differ only in the colour of their foliage. Widely, perhaps excessively, planted in parks, gardens, churchyards and cemeteries.

London Plane

Sycamore

flowers fruits

fruits

Horse Chestnut

uit

conker

flowers

ommon Lime

uits

Copper Beech

English Elm

fruits

fruits

Wych Elm

Trees Elms and Black Poplars

Elms (Ulmaceae) are tall deciduous trees with toothed leaves which often feel rough and have one side of the blade shorter than the other. The flowers appear before the leaves. They have no petals, but their red stamens render them clearly visible, even at a distance. The fruits are wind-dispersed, assisted by the membraneous wing surrounding the seed. Since 1971 millions of British elms have died through Dutch elm disease. This is caused by a fungus *Ceratocystis ulmi*, which damages the tree's conductive tissue; dead foliage in July is evidence of its lethal activity. The spores are carried by elm bark beetles *Scolytus* spp. Identification of elms is often difficult. Hybrids are frequent, although it is only the wych elm that commonly sets seed!

English Elm *Ulmus procera*
Up to *c*. 30m, but now mainly known in Britain from the suckers which arose before disease killed the parent trees. Mature trees have massive branches, the upper ones spreading to form the crown. Leaves asymmetrical, 4·5 – 9cm. Probably introduced into England at an early date; certainly an introduction in other parts of Britain and Ireland. Once a common feature of older parks and gardens, sometimes as the relics of a vanished hedgerow.

Wych Elm *Ulmus glabra*
Up to *c*. 40m, with a broad, spreading silhouette. Large (8–18cm), rough leaves, in which the longer side almost conceals the stalk. Rarely produces suckers. Wych elms are found in parks, gardens and churchyards, and several cultivars are planted. 'Lutescens', occurs as street tree. T, ex Ic and western F

84

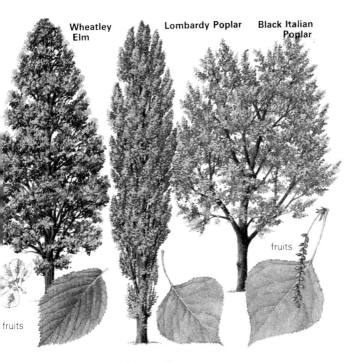

Wheatley
Elm

Lombardy Poplar

Black Italian
Poplar

fruits

fruits

Wheatley, Guernsey or Jersey Elm

variety (*sarniensis*) of the **smooth-leaved elm** *Ulmus carpinifolia*. Normally under 30m, neat and conical. Leaves of *c*. 7cm, shiny above. Smooth-leaved elms have a mainly southerly distribution; absent from Sca and rarely planted in Ir or N. of Edinburgh. Wheatley elms are especially common in the English Midlands, in parks and streets, and alongside bypasses.

Poplars are deciduous trees of the willow family (Salicaceae), but have broadbladed, long-stemmed leaves. Their flowers, in pendulous catkins, appear before the foliage, males and females on different trees. The commonest urban poplars are varieties and hybrids of the **black poplar** *Populus nigra*.

Lombardy Poplar *Populus nigra* var. *italica*

Up to 35m, spire-shaped; the average person's idea of a poplar. Introduced from N. Italy. Extensively planted, often in lines, sometimes to screen factory buildings or along park boundaries.

Black Italian Poplar *Populus* × *euramericana*

(= × *canadensis*) 'serotina'

The commonest of several cultivars resulting from hybridisation between *P. nigra* and American spp. Up to *c*. 40m, with a straight, stout, un-bossed, grey trunk, deeply scored with parallel fissures, and lacking lower branches. The uppermost branches are nearly vertical.

This tree's rapid growth and its ability to tolerate the urban atmosphere account for its frequent occurrence in parks, beside railways and around industrial sites. Its roots can damage buildings if it is planted too near them.

Trees Ornamental Species

The following are decorative deciduous trees of parks and gardens, some which are also planted in suburban roads. They are relatively small and the fore unlikely to cause offence by overshadowing the houses. Some of the produce attractively coloured fruit, which is eaten by birds.

Rowan or Mountain Ash *Sorbus aucuparia*   Rosaceae
Can reach 20m but is usually much smaller. A slender-trunked tree w sharply inclined branches. Pinnate leaves with toothed leaflets. Flowers May, the fruit ripening in August.

A very hardy tree, widely planted but also surviving as a wild tree in urb woodland and occasionally bird-sown. The berries are soon taken by thrush (especially mistle thrushes) and starlings. T.

Swedish Whitebeam *Sorbus intermedia*   Rosaceae
Can reach 15m but usually much smaller. Leaves toothed towards the tip a lobed towards the base; grey and woolly underneath. Flowers in May, t fruits ripening in September.

A native of S. Sweden and the Baltic islands, including Bornholm (Denmar naturalised in other parts of Denmark and in N. Germany, and often plante elsewhere in streets and parks – quite commonly in Britain. It is tolerant air pollution. The fruits are eaten by thrushes and woodpigeons, and the see can be bird-sown.

Purple Crab *Malus* × *purpurea*   Rosaceae
Up to 7·5m. A hybrid of horticultural origin frequently planted for its reddis purple blossom in late April and early May. Flowers appear before the purpl flushed leaves are fully expanded. Small purple apples are produced in la summer.

Pissard's Plum or Purple-leaved Cherry Plum *Prunus cerasifera* 'Atropurpurea' (= *Prunus pissardii*)   Rosaceae
Up to 5·4m. Valued for the early appearance of its white blosso (February–March); less so perhaps for the dark purplish foliage which follow it. Commonly planted, sometimes in streets, and also used for hedging. Th pink flower-buds may be eaten by bullfinches.

Japanese Cherry *Prunus serrulata* 'Kanzan'   Rosaceae
7·5–9m. A showy cultivar which has been extensively, perhaps excessivel planted in parks, roads and gardens. In April the stiffly ascending branche are heavily laden with massed bunches of large, pink, semi-double flower In autumn the leaves turn from green to gold, pink and sometimes re Colourful it may be, but it is of little ecological value!

Common Laburnum *Laburnum anagyroides*   Leguminosae
3–7m. A native of C. and S. Europe, much admired for its cascades of yello 'pea flowers' (April–June) but almost as poisonous as the yew (p. 95). ALL i parts are highly toxic and not just the seeds in the 'pea-pods' that are so ofte eaten by children, sometimes with fatal results. Fish can also be killed by th tree's debris falling into a garden pond. Laburnums seed very readily.

Voss's laburnum *L.* × *watereri*, a hybrid between the common specie and the **Scotch** or **alpine laburnum** *L. alpina*, is now more often planted. too is poisonous, but its fruit is poorly developed and therefore attracts les interest.

Rowan
flowers
fruits

flowers
fruits
Swedish Whitebeam

Purple Crab

Pissard's Plum

Common Laburnum

flowers
fruit

Japanese Cherry 'Kanzan'

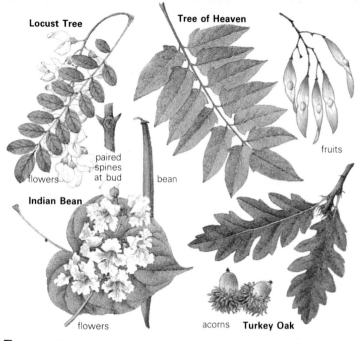

Locust Tree

Tree of Heaven

paired spines at bud

flowers

bean

fruits

Indian Bean

flowers

acorns **Turkey Oak**

Trees Mainly Exotic Species

Only one of the following is native to the area covered by this book. The others are 'exotic' in the true sense of the word, i.e. 'from outside'.

Locust Tree or False Acacia *Robinia pseudoacacia* Leguminosae

Up to 27m. A deciduous tree with deeply furrowed bark, spiny shoots and pinnate leaves. Pendulous sprays of white 'pea-flowers' in June and long narrow seed pods. A pollution-tolerant native of N. America, commonly planted in parks and gardens, except in the N.; often established on railway banks. It freely produces spiny suckers and is naturalised over much of Europe, being especially common in France.

Indian Bean *Catalpa bignonioides* Bignoniaceae

Up to 18m; grows best where summers are hot. A spreading deciduous tree with large heart-shaped leaves, and, in July, conical flower clusters that are rather suggestive of those of horse chestnut (p. 82) when seen at a distance. The fruits, long, slim pods, remain dangling on the tree all winter.

A native of N. America, frequently planted in parks, but not in the N. It is well represented in London.

Tree of Heaven *Ailanthus altissima* Simaroubaceae

Sometimes over 20m. A hardy, pollution-tolerant, rather ash-like deciduous tree with large pinnate leaves and pale streaks on the bark. Greenish flowers in July and winged fruits in autumn.

A native of China, commonly planted in gardens, parks, streets and squares,

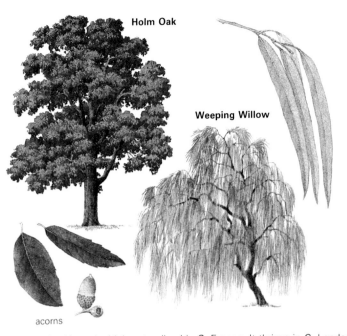

Holm Oak

Weeping Willow

acorns

except in the N., and widely naturalised in C. Europe. It thrives in C. London and sets seed readily, often colonising railway banks.

Holm Oak *Quercus ilex* Fagaceae

Up to 30m but usually less. A broad-crowned evergreen not immediately recognisable as an oak unless one notices the woolly-cupped acorns. Leaves very variable in shape – those on basal shoots can be spiny (holm = holly); densely woolly underneath.

The holm oak is essentially a Mediterranean tree but its natural range does extend up the Biscay coast as far as Brittany. Planted in parks and gardens, especially in coastal areas, but not in the N., not even Scotland. Naturalised in places in S. England, sometimes from forgotten acorns buried by jays.

Turkey Oak *Quercus cerris* Fagaceae

35m or more. A deciduous tree with ascending branches, distinguished by its deeply cut leaves, shaggy acorn cups and, from all other European oaks, by the long narrow appendages (stipules) round the buds.

A native of S. and SC. Europe and SW. Asia, widely introduced further N. and frequently naturalised. In Britain it is less common N. of the English Midlands, but it occurs in the Edinburgh area.

'Weeping willows' *Salix* spp. Salicaceae

Recognisable as a group by their narrow leaves and curtains of long branches, and included here because one of them, the brown-twigged *S. babylonica*, is probably Chinese.

Some hybrids and cultivars have the same weeping habit, however, and the yellow-twigged *S. alba* 'Tristis' (*c.* 20m) is now more usually planted.

Trees and Shrubs   More Exotic Species

Garden Privet *Ligustrum ovalifolium*   Oleaceae
Up to 5m, but usually clipped to under 2m. A partially deciduous, smoke
tolerant Japanese shrub, mainly used for park and garden hedging, muc
more frequently than the European species *L. vulgare*, which has narrowe
leaves. Also a constituent of 19th century park shrubberies, along with othe
oriental bushes. Flowers June–July, with a heavy, sickly-sweet perfume
Poisonous black berries produced on unclipped bushes, September–Octobe
Has been extensively planted, except in the N.

Japanese Spindle *Euonymus japonicus*   Celastraceae
3–4·5m. An evergreen shrub or small tree with glossy, leathery, toothe
leaves, often planted to fulfil the same functions as privet. It forms a dens
hedge when clipped, and its ability to tolerate salty air ensures its popularit
in coastal towns, especially in S. England. Its European range is restricte
however, by its inability to withstand cold, dry conditions.

Snowberry *Symphoricarpos albus* (= *S. rivularis*)   Caprifoliaceae
1–3m. A deciduous shrub, most noticeable from September onwards, whe
bearing its white berries. Flowers in March–July, bell-shaped, in small pin
clusters. Leaves variable in shape, but mainly oval.
  A native of western N. America, commonly planted in parks and gardens
sometimes as a hedge. It spreads by suckers – the berries are usually ignore
by birds – and it can form dense thickets. T, ex Ic and Fi.

Firethorn *Pyracantha coccinea*   Rosaceae
2m or more. A hardy, spiny, evergreen tree or shrub, one of several member
of this genus which are grown for their dense clusters of white flowers an
bunches of attractive fruit. Leaves usually toothed, unlike those c
Cotoneaster. A native of S. Europe, flowering in June. The bright berries ca
last until March, providing food for birds, including waxwings (p. 176) whe
these appear. The plant is occasionally bird-sown. B. Ir and F.

Cotoneasters *Cotoneaster* spp.   Rosaceae
The genus *Cotoneaster* includes a few trees, but most of its members ar
shrubs, some deciduous, others evergreen. Unlike the *Pyracantha* spp. the
are without thorns. Many species and hybrids are grown in gardens for th
sake of their red berries, and several of them are bird-sown.
  Wallspray *Cotoneaster horizontalis*, a native of China, is one of the mor
easily recognised deciduous shrubs, with the herring-bone arrangement of it
branches, which are closely beaded with berries in autumn. The flowers attrac
nectar-seeking wasps in spring; the berries provide food for blackbirds an
other thrushes, and wintering blackcaps. Young plants often become estab
lished under places where birds habitually perch, especially walls. **Rockspra**
C. microphyllos, a Himalayan species, is also bird-sown, and the semi-ever
green **Khasia berry** *C. simonsii* of Assam is naturalised in many places.

Rhododendron *Rhododendron ponticum*   Ericaceae
Up to 6m. The rhododendron most often planted. An evergreen shrub or tre
with glossy, dark green leaves. Purple flowers in June.
  A native of Iberia and Asia Minor which, on becoming naturalised in a 'wild
urban park, can obliterate the native ground flora. B, Ir, western F.

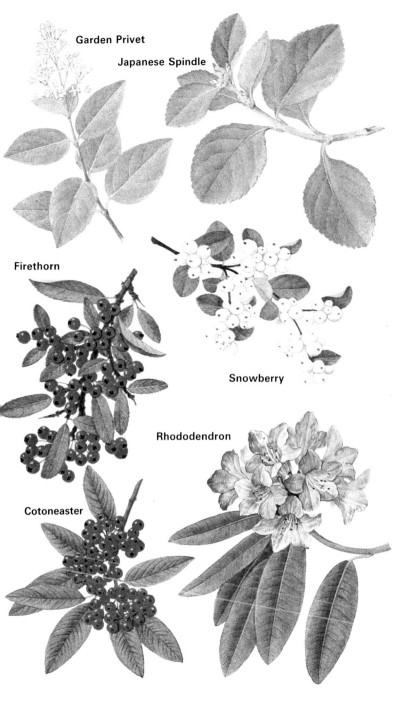

Garden Privet

Japanese Spindle

Firethorn

Snowberry

Rhododendron

Cotoneaster

Trees and Shrubs Waste Ground Colonists

Two of the following species are deliberately planted in parks and gardens, but they are also quick to join the others as invaders of vacant land.

Silver Birch *Betula pendula* Betulaceae

Up to 30m. A graceful deciduous tree well known for its attractive bark, which becomes silvery white with age, with contrasting black diamond-shaped patches.

The popularity of this fast-growing European native as a park, garden and street tree partly accounts for its abundance as a colonist of railway banks and almost any piece of urban land left vacant for a longish time. Its wind-borne seeds set very readily. It has formed woodland on English town commons that are no longer used for grazing, and its spread sometimes has to be controlled. T, ex Ic.

Elder *Sambucus nigra* Caprifoliaceae

Up to 10m. An untidy deciduous shrub rather than a tree, best known for its creamy flower-heads (June–July) and its black berries.

Elders are characteristic plants of disturbed ground, their seeds widely distributed by birds. Roosting starlings which have gorged themselves on berries will stain pavements with their purple droppings and dense elder thickets can develop under roosting trees, as in St. James's Park, London. T, ex Ic.

The **red-berried elder** *S. racemosa* is not native to B or Ir but occurs naturally throughout the E. part of the area covered by this book (G, D, Sw, southern No and eastern F). It is a waste-ground plant in Berlin.

'Pussy willows' *Salix* spp. Salicaceae

The name is loosely given to members of the complex group of smaller, broad-leaved willows that produce silver-haired catkins. In March and April the pollen-gilded flowers not only attract bees and moths but 'palm' collectors seeking material for Easter decorations. The leaves are the food of many moth larvae. **Goat willow** or **great sallow** *S. caprea* up (to 16m) is one of the commonest urban species. It occurs naturally in the wilder open spaces and its wind-borne seeds enable it to spread further afield. T, ex Ic.

Butterfly Bush or Buddleia *Buddleja davidii* Buddlejaceae

1–5m. The familiar butterfly attractant, a sprawling garden shrub, deciduous but rarely completely leafless. Flowers June–October, the main butterfly season.

A Chinese plant brought to Europe *c.* 1890. No longer confined to gardens, its tiny, wind-dispersed seeds having widely established it on rubbly wasteland and crumbling walls. Wartime devastation certainly helped it to spread. B (mainly S. England), Ir (rare), F, LC, G.

Bramble *Rubus fruticosus* agg. Rosaceae

The familiar, scrambling, semi-evergreen shrub that offers its succulent black-berry crop to those who brave the discomfort inflicted by the thorns on its long, biennial stems. In towns there is an added hazard – the risk of fruit being contaminated with lead from petrol fumes. An extremely variable plant, with over 2,000 microspecies in Europe. Bramble stems root at their tips on touching the ground, and the plant also spreads by seed. T, ex Ic.

Silver Birch

Elder

male catkins

Pussy Willow

berries

Butterfly Bush

Bramble

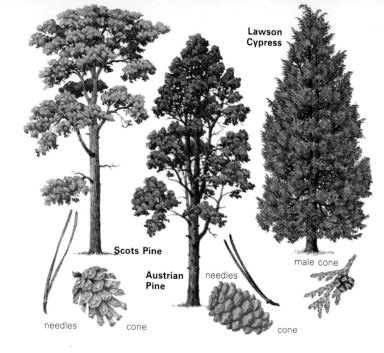

Lawson Cypress

Scots Pine

Austrian Pine

needles

needles

cone

male cone

needles   cone

Trees Conifers and *Ginkgo*

More conifers are now planted in town parks, gardens and cemeteries than was once possible. Evergreens are seriously harmed by smoke pollution, for their leaves cannot effectively perform their natural functions of transpiration and photosynthesis when covered with tarry deposits. Sulphur dioxide emission is still a problem and wind-borne industrial pollutants falling as 'acid rain' are causing ecological damage, especially in Scandinavia.

Scots Pine *Pinus sylvestris*   Pinaceae
35m or more. The commonest pine with scaly, rust-red bark on its upper parts when mature. Grey-green needles, 5–7cm, in pairs, often twisted. Cones 3–8cm, fairly symmetrical, woody and dull brown. A true native of the Scottish Highlands, N. C. and S. Europe and temperate Asia. Introduced elsewhere but planted less frequently in town than *P. nigra*. Often naturalised, and well established in the wilder urban open spaces on sandy soils.

Austrian Pine *Pinus nigra* var. *nigra*   Pinaceae
33m or more. More pyramidal in shape than the Scots pine. Fissured, dark grey bark. Needles in pairs, 10–15cm, dark, straight or twisted. Cones 5–8cm, yellowish before opening. A widely planted native of Austria, Balkans and C. Italy; wind-resistant, salt-tolerant; will grow on calcareous soils.

Cedars *Cedrus* spp.   Pinaceae
Cedars have barrel-shaped cones and, on shoots of over a year old, their

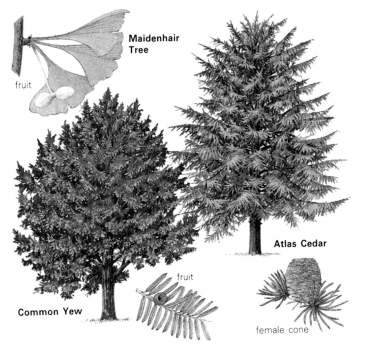

Maidenhair
Tree

fruit

Atlas Cedar

fruit

Common Yew

female cone

needles grow in whorls. The **deodar** *C. deodara*, a Himalayan species, can usually be distinguished by the *drooping* tips of its young branches. Those of the N. African **Atlas cedar** *C. atlantica* are *ascending*, and *horizontal* branches distinguish the **cedar of Lebanon** *C. libani* throughout maturity.

Lawson Cypress *Chamaecyparis lawsoniana* Cupressaceae
30–60m. A steeple-like evergreen from western USA, usually with a floppy leading shoot. Foliage resembles that of **western red cedar** *Thuja plicata*, with small scale-like leaves hiding the stems, but the tips of the leafy sprays are thinner and smell resinous when crushed. *Thuja* smells of pineapple. Widely planted, along with numerous cultivars, seeds itself freely. A fast-growing hybrid, **Leyland cypress** × *Cupressocyparis leylandii* is also popular.

Common Yew *Taxus baccata* Taxaceae
Up to 25m. A sombre, notoriously poisonous evergreen with small, narrow, flattened leaves, spirally arranged in pairs. The fleshy, cup-shaped, berry-like fruits (which distinguish yews from other conifers) are red and sticky. The flesh is not poisonous, but the seeds are. Male and female flowers on separate trees. The fruits are eaten by birds, which disperse the seeds in their droppings. T, ex Ic, but locally distributed in the W.

Maidenhair Tree *Ginkgo biloba* Ginkgoaceae
Under 30m. A primitive deciduous Chinese relative of the conifers, with leaves resembling the leaflets of the maidenhair ferns *Adiantum* spp., and, as the sole survivor of a genus which flourished in Jurassic times, a 'living fossil'. Male and female flowers on separate trees.

95

Herbaceous Plants   Grasses

Grasses (Gramineae) are often hard to identify, and, as much of the urban grassland is mown, flowers may be hard to find. The following descriptions are over-simplified, but the plates should make identification possible.

Perennial Rye-grass *Lolium perenne*
10–90cm. Flowers May–August. Flower-spikes stiff, with hairless, stalkless spikelets arranged alternately and spaced at intervals up the stem, each with one of its narrow sides adjacent to it. The typical (hard wearing) grass of recreation grounds; also grows on waste ground. T, ex Ic.

Couch Grass or Twitch *Agropyron repens*
30–120cm. A dull green perennial, often forming large clumps. Flowers June–September; stalkless spikelets alternately arranged on stiff stem, each with a broad side pressed against it. This hated garden and allotment weed spreads by means of wiry underground stems (rhizomes), severed pieces of which can produce new plants. Also grows on waste ground and roadsides. T.

Yorkshire Fog *Holcus lanatus*
20–100cm. A perennial with soft, downy, grey-green leaves, flowering May–August. Stalked spikelets form a plume-like, green, whitish or pinkish head. Grows in rough grassland, open woodland and waste places. It tolerates wet conditions. T.

Cocksfoot *Dactylis glomerata*
15–140cm. A distinctive, coarse-leaved, tussock-forming perennial, flowering from May onwards. Flower-heads suggest a chicken's foot, with green or purplish spikelets crowded together to form the 'toes'. Cocksfoot is fairly ubiquitious and does well on dry sites. T, ex Ic.

Wall Barley *Hordeum murinum*
6–60cm. A coarse annual with pale green leaves. Flowers June–July, the long bristles (awns), three to each spikelet, the most obvious feature. Mainly a plant of disturbed ground, roadsides and the neighbourhood of walls and buildings. T. ex Fi, Ic and much of Sco; introduced D, Ir, FS.

False Oat-grass *Arrhenatherum elatius*
50–150cm. A tall, coarse perennial with acutely pointed leaves, flowering June onwards. Flower-heads branched and loose, the awned spikelets shining green or purplish. A drought-resistant grass of waste ground, roadsides and railway banks. T.

Barren Brome *Bromus sterilis*
15–100cm. A downy annual, flowering May–July. Awned spikelets, sometimes solitary, in drooping tassels on long, widely spreading branches. A plant of open situations, especially waste ground and roadsides. Sometimes turns purplish red. T.

Annual Meadow-grass *Poa annua*
3–30cm. Green, slightly keeled, hairless, strap-shaped, sometimes crinkly leaves, abruptly ending in a pointed tip. Flowers and sets seed throughout the year. Flower-heads branched, triangular in outline, the branches pointing down after flowering. This is the commonest short grass of urban wasteland, flower-beds, paths and roadsides, found the world over.

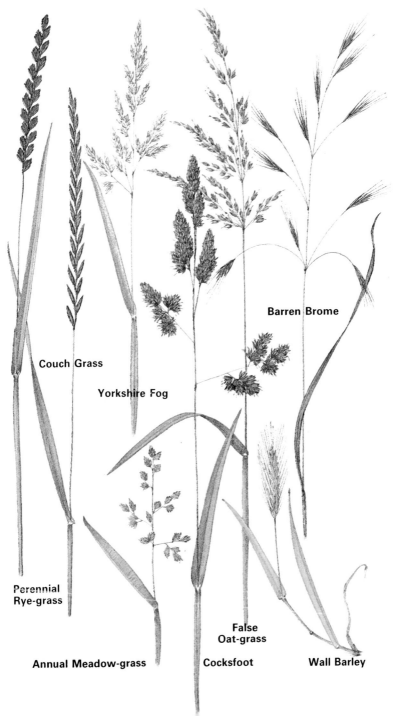

Couch Grass

Yorkshire Fog

Barren Brome

Perennial
Rye-grass

Annual Meadow-grass

Cocksfoot

False
Oat-grass

Wall Barley

Herbaceous Plants   In Tall Grass

Frequent grass-mowing is usually considered essential to park and garden management, but there are always places in towns where the herbage is left relatively undisturbed – wild commons, steep slopes, railway banks, neglected gardens churchyards and cemeteries, and the 'rough' areas of golf courses. The following wild flowers may flourish in such places.

Hogweed *Heracleum sphondylium*   Umbelliferae
A tall (50–200cm) biennial, flowering June–September and much visited by hover-flies (Syrphidae) and soldier-beetles (Cantharidae). Recognisable by its size, the umbrella-shaped inflorescence or umbel (typical of this family), and the coarse, pinnate leaves with broad-lobed leaflets. The hollow stems remain standing in autumn. T, ex Ic.

Ox-eye Daisy *Leucanthemum vulgare*   Compositae
20–70cm. A familiar perennial, also known as **dog daisy, moon daisy** and **marguerite**, with its small, dark green, toothed leaves and, like all the Compositae, a flower-head composed of tiny, close-crowded florets. Long white ray-florets surround the central mass of yellow disc-florets. T, ex Ic.

The **Shasta daisy** *L. maximum*, its larger garden relative, has escaped from cultivation in some places, e.g. around London and Birmingham.

Common Knapweed *Centaurea nigra*   Compositae
15–90cm. A tough-stemmed perennial, also known as **lesser knapweed, black knapweed** and (from the hard spherical buds) **hardheads**. Flowers from June onwards, the flower-heads thistle-like, with red-purple florets surmounting a bulbous brown or blackish, bract-covered base. Leaves hairy, the lower ones stalked and toothed. Mainly occurs in the W, ex Ic. Local in mainland Sca. Absent from most of G.

Ribwort Plantain *Plantago lanceolata*   Plantaginaceae
Up to 60cm. Perennial, flowering from April onwards. Lance-shaped leaves, prominently ribbed on underside, up to 30cm long in this habitat, but forming small rosettes on mown lawns. Flower-heads shaped like a pine cone, on an unbranched, squarish stem; blackish at first, then turning brown, with creamy anthers looking like heads of inserted pins. T.

Red Clover *Trifolium pratense*   Leguminosae
Up to 60cm. Perennial, flowering from May onwards, its stems and leaves distinguishable from those of white clover (p. 100) by their hairiness. T.

Common Sorrel *Rumex acetosa*   Polygonaceae
Up to 100cm. Perennial. Flowers May–August, but more readily known from its edible but bitter-tasting, arrow-shaped leaves, the lower ones stalked, the upper ones clasping the unbranched stem. T.

Cuckoo Flower or Lady's Smock *Cardamine pratensis*   Cruciferae
15–40cm. A hairless, damp-loving perennial, flowering April–June. Flowers with four petals, arranged crosswise (a family characteristic), pale lilac, sometimes white, with yellow anthers. Leaves pinnate; root leaves with rounded leaflets, stem-leaves with very narrow leaflets. Seeds produced in a long pod, typical of many crucifers. This attractive plant often survives in ill-drained park grassland, and may reach the flowering stage when prolonged rain makes the ground too wet to mow. T.

Ox-eye Daisy

Hogweed

Ribwort Plantain

Cuckoo Flower

Common Knapweed

Common Sorrel

Red Clover

Herbaceous Plants of Mown Grassland

Mown grassland includes playing fields, bowling greens, golf courses, road verges and (especially in Britain) the lawns of parks and gardens. Many plants tolerate regular mowing and continue flowering, to the annoyance of meticulous gardeners and the delight of naturalists. Besides those described you may also find **dandelion** (p. 104), **common knapweed** (p. 98), **lesser hawkbit** *Leontodon taraxacoides*, **autumn hawkbit** *L. autumnalis* and **common cat's-ear** *Hypochoeris radicata* (Compositae); **black medick** *Medicago lupulina* and **lesser trefoil** *Trifolium dubium* (Leguminosae); **field woodrush** *Luzula campestris* (Juncaceae); and **greater plantain** (p. 116). Heights given are of unmown plants.

Daisy *Bellis perennis*   Compositae
Up to 12cm. Perennial. Mainly flowers March–October. Flowers close at night ('daisy' = 'day's eye'). Hairy, spoon-shaped leaves forming rosette. Daisies can withstand cutting and trampling, and regenerate from severed stems if mowings are not removed. May appear to die out when grass left uncut, but plants persist in the soil and flower again once mowing is resumed. T, ex Ic.

Yarrow or Milfoil *Achillea millefolium*   Compositae
Up to 45cm. Aromatic perennial. Flowers from June onwards, but presence in lawns more likely to be noted from dense 'mossy' mats of feathery leaves. The prostrate stems of yarrow develop roots, enabling the plant to spread as much as 20cm in a year. T.

Bird's-foot Trefoil *Lotus corniculatus*   Leguminosae
Up to 15cm. Perennial. Flowers from May onwards. Red-tinged flowers are responsible for the nickname 'bacon-and-eggs'. Leaflets in fives, but two bent back, creating a trefoil appearance. Pods resemble the splayed toes of a bird. Very common plant of dry grassland; flowers when only a few mm high. T.

White Clover *Trifolium repens*   Leguminosae
A low, hairless, creeping perennial. Leaflets usually marked with a whitish chevron. Flowers from June onwards; sometimes pinkish. Usually found on lawns relies more on vegetative reproduction than on seed. T.

Selfheal *Prunella vulgaris*   Labiatae
Up to 20cm. A downy, creeping perennial with square stems and opposite leaves (both features of Labiatae). Flowers, from June onwards, in dense oblong head with a pair of leaves beneath; violet, sometimes white or pink. Selfheal will flower on a very short stem, but sometimes its presence has to be detected from its pointed oval leaves. T.

Creeping Buttercup *Ranunculus repens*   Ranunculaceae
Up to 60cm. A creeping perennial with hairy three-lobed leaves, each lobe divided into three segments. Flowers with upturned sepals and grooved stalks; from May onwards. Creeping buttercup spreads rapidly by producing a network of runners. It grows well on wet ground. T.

Slender Speedwell *Veronica filiformis*   Scrophulariaceae
A downy, prostrate perennial, forming large mauvish-blue patches. Single flowers on long thread-like stalks; April–June. Small kidney-shaped leaves. A native of W. Asia, originally introduced as a garden plant. It roots easily from severed stems and mowing only encourages its spread. T, ex Ic and Fi, but local in south Sw and No.

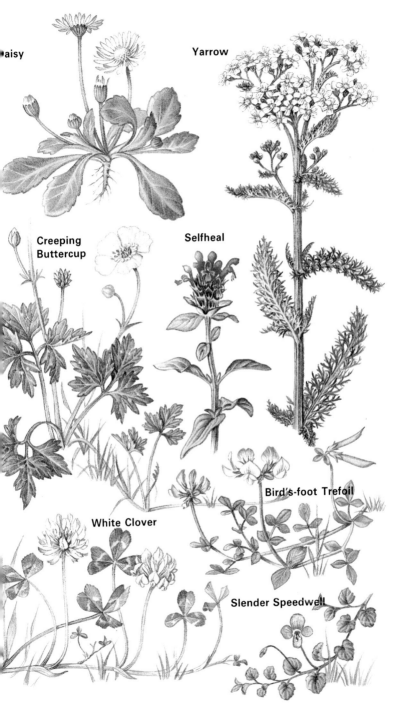

aisy

Yarrow

Creeping Buttercup

Selfheal

Bird's-foot Trefoil

White Clover

Slender Speedwell

Herbaceous Plants   Garden Weeds

When making a flower-bed the gardener also prepares the ground for the plant invaders we call 'weeds'. All the following are widely distributed.

Chickweed *Stellaria media*   Caryophyllaceae
5–40cm. A sprawling, shallow-rooted annual, flowering at all seasons and found worldwide. Since its average seed production is about 2,500 per plant and three generations are quite normal, one plant could theoretically be responsible for more than 15,000 million descendants within one year. Seeds, viable for 25 years or more, can be spread by birds or muddy boots. T.

Groundsel *Senecio vulgaris*   Compositae
8–45cm. A prolific annual, flowering January–December. Flower-heads normally consist only of disc-florets, but ray-florets are sometimes present, this variety occurs in Edinburgh gardens. Seeds are mainly wind-dispersed, each one carried on a tuft of hairs (a pappus). T.

Shepherd's Purse *Capsella bursa-pastoris*   Cruciferae
8–40cm. An annual or biennial, flowering all the year; name from shape of seed capsule. Leaves variable in appearance; basal leaves form rosette. Seeds can be transported in mud on boots, tyres or garden tools, or spread by birds, either through the gut or by adhering to their feet. T.

Scarlet Pimpernel *Anagallis arvensis*   Primulaceae
An attractive annual, flowering from June onwards, normally prostrate but sometimes reaching a height of 30cm. Nicknamed the 'poor man's weather-glass' because the flowers remain closed on cloudy days. Leaves opposite, unstalked and pointed, with faint black dots on underside. T, ex Ic.

Petty Spurge *Euphorbia peplis*   Euphorbiaceae
10–30cm. A branching annual, flowering all the year, entirely green except for the reddish main stem, and like all spurges, exuding an irritant milky juice when damaged. Flower-head a confused mass of branches, leaves and bracts, the uppermost bracts round the tiny, inconspicuous flowers. They have no petals or sepals, and close examination reveals four glandular structures, each with a pair of outcurved horns. T, ex Ic.

Red Dead-nettle *Lamium purpureum*   Labiatae
Normally under 30cm. A downy, aromatic annual, with the square stems characteristic of the family. Flowers at all seasons. Leaves heart-shaped and stalked. As in the next species, the flowers are two-lipped, with the upper lip forming a hood; are arranged in whorls in the axils of the upper leaves. Seeds, each contained in a nutlet, are carried off by ants; germinate at all seasons. Plant also spreads by producing prostrate rooting stems during the winter. Very common on allotments as well as in gardens. T.

White Dead-nettle *Lamium album*   Labiatae
Normally c. 30cm. A hairy perennial with stalked leaves resembling those of a stinging nettle (p. 110) but safe to touch. Unmistakable from March onwards when in flower. Like the previous species it spreads by means of rooting stems and its nutlets are dispersed by ants, but it only becomes common as a flower-bed weed in badly neglected gardens. T, but casual in Ic.

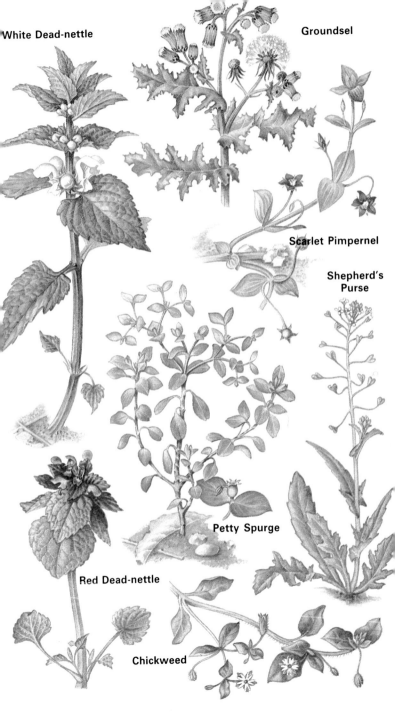

White Dead-nettle

Groundsel

Scarlet Pimpernel

Shepherd's Purse

Petty Spurge

Red Dead-nettle

Chickweed

Herbaceous Plants   More Garden Weeds

Annual Nettle or **Small Nettle** *Urtica urens*   Urticaceae
10–60cm. Armed with stinging hairs like the stinging nettle (p. 110), but has smaller leaves with unbranched veins, the lower leaves shorter than their stalks. Also differs in having male and female flowers on the same plant. Flowers June–September. T.

Black Nightshade *Solanum nigrum*   Solanaceae
Up to 60cm. A poisonous, hairless, or downy annual, flowering July–September, its white flowers resembling those of its relative, the potato. Fruit is a pea-sized, shiny black berry. T, ex Ic, but only as a casual in Sco and Ir.

Common Field Speedwell or **Buxbaum's Speedwell**
Veronica persica   Scrophulariaceae
A low-growing annual with hairy leaves and hairs on the veins on the underside of its oval, toothed leaves. Solitary blue flowers, January–December. A native of W. Asia which has been spreading across Europe since early last century, reaching Britain in 1825. T.

Ivy-leaved Speedwell *Veronica hederifolia*   Scrophulariaceae
There are two forms of this trailing, hairy, tiny-flowered weed of cultivation. *V. h. lucorum* has lilac flowers and its leaves have five to seven lobes. *V. h. hederifolia* has blue flowers and its leaves have three to five lobes. T, ex Ic.

Ground Elder, Goutweed or **Bishop's Weed**
Aegopodium podagraria   Umbelliferae
40–100cm. A hairless perennial, flowering May–August. Spreads both by seeds and rhizomes.

Once valued as a pot-herb and a possible cure for gout, this is now one of the worst of garden weeds, virtually ineradicable because of the near impossibility of removing the last fragment of rhizome from the soil. T. ex Ic.

Another umbellifer, the poisonous **fool's parsley** *Aethusa cynapium*, may also occur. It has more divided leaves and long down-pointed bracts under its umbels. T, ex Ic.

Dandelion *Taraxacum offinale* agg.   Compositae
Up to *c.* 30cm. Familiar to most people as a deep-rooted, yellow-flowered perennial with large-toothed leaves, evoking childhood memories of 'telling the time' by blowing away the plum-headed, single-seeded fruits. Appears in all parts of the garden, especially the lawn, where the leafy rosettes suppress all plant competitors. Leaves and stems contain a milky juice. Flowers all year; peak period April–May. To botanists the name 'dandelion' embraces a host of microspecies, very difficult to separate. Dandelions produce viable seeds without fertilisation, and any mutations which arise are inherited by succeeding generations, creating endless variety. T.

Smooth Sow-thistle *Sonchus oleraceus*   Compositae
20–150cm. An erect, greyish, hairless annual, exuding milky juice when damaged. Leaves distinctively lobed, edged with soft-pointed teeth and clasping the stem with pointed lobes, suggesting an arrow-head. Flowers June onwards; of 'dandelion-type' but paler yellow.

The **prickly sow-thistle** *S. asper* is similar but with greener, spiny leaves with rounded bases. Both species also occur on wasteland. T, ex Ic.

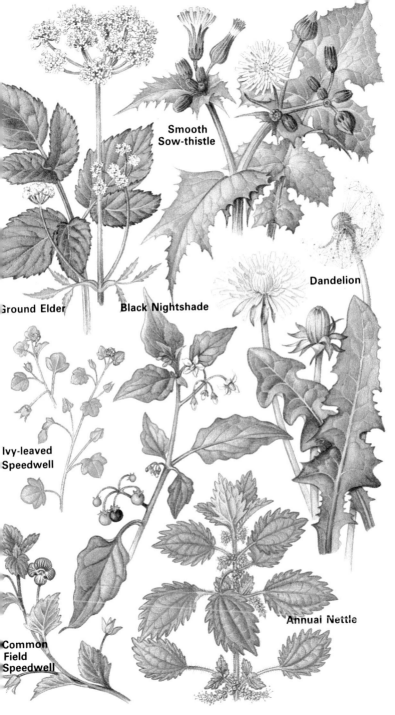

Smooth
Sow-thistle

Dandelion

Ground Elder

Black Nightshade

Ivy-leaved
Speedwell

Annual Nettle

Common
Field
Speedwell

Herbaceous Plants Shade Lovers

The following plants often grow in shady, undisturbed parts of gardens, or in parks and private grounds which are not too intensively managed.

Enchanter's Nightshade *Circaea lutetiana* Onagraceae
Usually under 60cm. A hairy-stemmed perennial, unrelated to the true nightshades and not poisonous. Flowers June–August; each has two petals which look like four. Fruits pear-shaped and covered with hooked bristles.

A woodland plant which often appears in garden shrubberies and shaded borders. Its fruits get caught in clothing and animals' fur, but it also spreads by underground shoots that become detached from the parent plant in the autumn. T, ex Ic and Fi; local in southern No and Sw.

Cow Parsley or Keck *Anthriscus sylvestris* Umbelliferae
A tall perennial (60–120cm), flowering April–June, the well known 'Queen Anne's lace' of English country lanes. In towns it may be regarded as a survivor rather than a colonist, flowering in profusion on river, canal and railway banks, and in private grounds, cemeteries, churchyards and so on T, ex Ic.

Ground Ivy *Glechoma hederacea* Labiatae
Low, softly hairy, creeping perennial with long, rooting runners and ascending, flower-bearing stems (10–30cm). Roundly toothed, long-stalked leaves, more kidney- than ivy-shaped, often purplish. Flowers March–June. T. ex Ic.

Nipplewort *Lapsana communis* Compositae
20–90cm. A stiffly erect annual, the basal leaves of which have a large, heart-shaped terminal lobe, with much smaller lobes below it. Flowers from June onwards; a branching cluster of 15–20 small dandelion-like flower-heads which remain closed in dull weather. Flower-buds nipple-shaped – hence the name. Occurs on walls and waste ground as well as in gardens, hedges and tree-shaded places. T, ex Ic.

Foxglove *Digitalis purpurea* Scrophulariaceae
50–150cm. A familiar woodland plant of acid soils, flowering June–September. Although it can be a legitimate member of the urban flora (as in Birmingham, England, where it is particularly common), its status is complicated by the popularity it and other *Digitalis* spp. enjoy as garden plants. The fact that packets of 'wild' foxglove seeds are now sold commercially has added to the confusion. Mainly found in the SW. part of the area; absent from Ic and much of Ne and G; introduced into D, south Sw and central G.

Cuckoo Pint or Lords-and-Ladies *Arum maculatum* Araceae
30–50cm. A hairless perennial with large, arrow-shaped leaves. Unmistakable in flower (April–May) with its purple flower-spike (the spadix) standing like a small Gothic statue in an outsized, pale green, hooded niche (the spathe), and in summer when its poisonous berries become conspicuous. This is another plant that survives in towns in places resembling its normal woodland or hedgerow habitat. Mainly a southern species, absent from Ic, No, Fi and most of Sw.

Small Balsam *Impatiens parviflora* Balsaminaceae
30–100 cm. A fleshy-stemmed annual with alternate leaves. Insignificant straight-spurred flowers, June–September. Fruit capsules explode when ripe. From central Asia. T, ex Ic and Ir; rare in Sco.

Small Balsam

Foxglove

Nipplewort

Cow Parsley

Ground Ivy

Cuckoo Pint

Enchanter's Nightshade

Herbaceous Plants   Waste Ground Species 1
Crucifers and Mallows

Rubble-strewn demolition sites, ruined walls and basements, old gardens acquired for building development, abandoned industrial or railway property, cleared areas serving as temporary car parks – all these provide habitats for plants and animals. Some last but a short period; others for years, and some industrial sites have lain derelict for decades. The plant colonists are a mixture of natives and aliens, arable weeds, garden escapes, and the natural vegetation of such features as landslips and glacial moraines.

Annual Wall-rocket or **Stinkweed** *Diplotaxis muralis*   Cruciferae
15–30cm. Also biennial and occasionally perennial in spite of its name. Distinguished from the next species by smaller flowers and absence of short stalk between seed-pod and former site of sepals (a slight bulge). Pods held at an angle to main stem. Flowers May–September. Leaves mostly in basal rosette; smell revolting when crushed. A native of S. Europe, now widespread but absent from Ic, much of Sco, Ne and southern No, Sw and Fi. Mainly by railways in Ir.

Perennial Wall-rocket *Diplotaxis tenuifolius*   Cruciferae
30–80cm. Bushier and more branched than last, with almost woody stems and no basal rosette. Larger flowers, May onwards. Pods with short stalk above sepal-scar (see entry above) and held almost parallel to main stem. A native of C. and S. Europe now T, ex Ic and Ir; mainly coastal in mainland Sca; casual in Sco. Particularly common in Kent and Sussex towns.

Hedge Mustard *Sisymbrium officinale*   Cruciferae
30–90cm. A wiry, branching annual. Tiny flowers, June–July; seed-pods closely pressed against the stem. T.

Eastern Rocket *Sisymbrium orientale*   Cruciferae
25–90cm. An untidy annual from S. Europe, N. Africa and W. Asia, flowering May–August. Occurs T, ex Ic, but is a casual in Sco, Ir and Fi. Often confused with London rocket. *S. irio*, a Mediterranean species now widespread in Europe, except the far N., but scarce in Ir (in Dublin) and B. Although abundant after the Great Fire of 1666 it is now a London rarity.
   London rocket has *hairless* pods with partially transparent walls. Eastern rocket has larger flowers and its opaque pods are hairy when young.
   Other yellow-flowered crucifers likely to be found are **charlock** *Sinapis arvensis* (very common), **black mustard** *Brassica nigra*, **wintercress** *Barbarea vulgaris*, **marsh yellowcress** *Rorippa palustris*, **false London rocket** *Sisymbrium loeselii*, **tall rocket** *S. altissimum*, **hoary mustard** *Hirschfeldia incana*, **warty cabbage** *Bunias orientalis* and **gold-of-pleasure** *Camelina sativa*. Leaves and seed-pods are the best characters for distinguishing members of this rather intimidating group of plants.

Common Mallow *Malva sylvestris*   Malvaceae
30–90cm. A hairy, straggly perennial with coarse, crinkly, five-lobed leaves. Flowers (June–September) 2·5–4cm across, rosy purple with darker streaks. A common plant of banks, roadsides, canal towpaths and rubbly waste. T, ex Ic, rarer in the N. The smaller, prostrate paler-flowered **dwarf mallow** *M. neglecta* occurs in similar places. T, ex Ic.

Perennial
Wall-rocket

Hedge
Mustard

Annual
Wall-rocket

Common
Mallow

Eastern
Rocket

Herbaceous Plants   Waste Ground Species 2

Japanese Knotweed *Reynoutria japonica*
(= *Polygonum cuspidatum*)   Polygonaceae
Up to 180cm. A thicket-forming perennial with stout, reddish, zigzagging stems, shield-shaped leaves, creeping roots and (June–September) loose sprays of whitish flowers. A regrettable introduction from Japan, once actually admired as a garden plant! T, ex D, Ic, Sw.

Docks (Polygonaceae) have inconspicuous (usually green) flowers, arranged in whorls on their branched stems. They are more noticeable in autumn with their dead brown leaves and clusters of reddish-brown fruits. Examination of these tiny, three-sided nuts needed for identification of some species; the two common urban docks below recognised by their leaves. Both are perennials, flowering from June onwards, and difficult to eradicate. Their 90cm tap-roots can survive mutilation, new plants arising from the broken pieces.

Broad-leaved Dock *Rumex obtusifolius*
50–100cm. Has broad, oblong leaves with a heart-shaped base. T, ex Fi.

Curled Dock *Rumex crispus*
50–100cm. Has narrower, wavy leaves with curled edges. A plant of shingle beaches well adapted to live amongst urban rubble. T.

Stinging Nettle *Urtica dioica*   Urticaceae
30–150cm. The familiar perennial with hairy, pain-inflicting leaves and bright yellow roots. Flowers from June onwards; males and females on separate plants (*cf.* annual nettle, p. 104). Leaves differ from those of annual nettle; veins are branched and lower leaves are longer than their stems.
  Stinging nettles spread by seed and creeping, rooting stems, forming large patches on loose, nitrogen-rich soils. Their occurrence ensures the presence of several attractive butterflies. T.

Fat Hen or **White Goosefoot** *Chenopodium album*   Chenopodiaceae
Up to 100cm. A branching, fleshy annual. Leaves grey-green, mealy and variable: toothed, untoothed, oval, lance-shaped or rhomboid. Stems often reddish. Hermaphrodite flowers (June onwards) in dense greenish clusters. This is the commonest member of a difficult genus. T.
  Several other *Chenopodium* spp. occur, especially on rubbish tips. Leaf-shape is an important but not infallible guide to identity, and for some spp. the investigator may need to examine the seed-coat under a microscope.

Common Orache *Atriplex patula*   Chenopodiaceae
30–90cm. A variable, branching annual. Leaves mealy, lance-shaped, triangular, or three-lobed like a goose's foot. Greenish flowers (July–October); males and females separate although on the same plant. Fruit enclosed by a pair of bracts (characteristic of *Atriplex*). This is the usual orache of inland towns, but the more erect, less mealy **spear-leaved orache** A. *prostrata* can also occur. Both species found T.

Thorn-apple *Datura stramonium*   Solanaceae
Up to 100cm. An unmistakable annual with large, coarsely toothed, evil-smelling leaves. Flowers (July–October) trumpet-shaped, usually white, sometimes purple. Seed capsules large, green and usually spiny. A highly poisonous alien of unknown provenance, once used by apothecaries. Its seeds remain viable for decades and its reappearance on disturbed ground can provide copy for the more sensational newspapers. T, ex Ic and Ir; rare in Sco.

Fat Hen

Thorn-apple

Curled Dock

Stinging Nettle

Common Orache

Japanese Knotweed

Broad-leaved Dock

Herbaceous Plants   Waste Ground Species 3
Compositae

Oxford Ragwort *Senecio squalidus*
20–30cm. Normally an annual, but can be biennial or perennial. More straggly than the agricultural (and occasionally urban) weed **common ragwort** *S. jacobaea*, in which the flower-heads form a level-topped terminal cluster. Leaves have narrow, pointed lobes; ray-florets are notched, not toothed. Flowers April–December. A Sicilian plant which escaped from the Oxford Botanic Garden in the 1790s; spread across England and Wales with the railways. Railway ballast provided a suitable habitat; rushing trains dispersed the pappus-flighted fruits. Aerial bombardment encouraged its spread in the 1940s. Did not colonise Edinburgh until 1954; reached Belfast and Dublin even later. Introduced into F and D, occurs in G.

Coltsfoot *Tussilago farfara*
Under 15cm. A creeping perennial, flowering March–April. Leaves appear later; large (10–20cm wide) with white-felted undersides. Pappus-headed fruits wind-dispersed, but underground stems provide a more effective means of spreading. Railway banks, building sites, mounds of clay and piles of loose rubble are soon covered. T, ex Ic.

Creeping Thistle *Cirsium arvense*
60cm or more. A grey-green perennial with spiny, wavy-edged leaves; upper ones clasp spineless stem. Flowers June onwards; relatively small lilac flower-heads, fragrant, but often sterile. Failure to produce seed is compensated by development of lateral roots which produce new shoots when broken. T.

Spear Thistle *Cirsium vulgare*
30–150cm. A common biennial. Cottony, spiny-winged stems, large reddish-purple flower-heads (July onwards) and yellow-tipped prickles. T, ex Ic.

Lesser Burdock *Arctium minus*
60–120cm. A downy biennial with large, heart-shaped, hollow-stalked leaves. Flowers July–September. Well-known in fruit when its burs get caught in clothing. Often banks and roadsides, and commoner in towns than the **greater burdock** A. *lappa*. T, ex Ic. Seeds of thistles and burdocks eaten by goldfinches.

Mugwort *Artemisia vulgaris*
60–120cm. A faintly aromatic perennial. Small dowdy flower-heads, July–September. Leaves dark green above, covered with whitish down below. T, ex Ic. A drab plant compared with the strongly scented, silver-leaved, yellow-flowered **wormwood** A. *absinthium*, which is less widespread. but is common in the English Midlands.

Scentless Mayweed *Tripleurospermum maritimum inodorum*
10–60cm. An annual or perennial with daisy-like flower-heads (June onwards) and finely divided leaves. A prolific agricultural weed equally able to invade disturbed ground in towns. Each plant can produce up to 210,000 seeds. T, ex Ic, where larger coastal subspecies *T. m. maritimum* is found.

Feverfew *Tanacetum parthenium*
25–60cm. An aromatic perennial once used to combat headaches and fever symptoms. Daisy-like flowers (July onwards) and yellowish-green leaves. Probably a native of S. Europe, but cultivated for centuries. Now naturalised throughout most of Europe, especially near gardens and on walls.

Mugwort

Spear
Thistle

xford Ragwort

Scentless Mayweed

Feverfew

Creeping Thistle

Coltsfoot

Lesser
Burdock

Herbaceous Plants   Waste Ground Species 4

Bristly Ox-tongue *Picris echioides*   Compositae
30–90cm. A bristly annual or biennial. Some leaf-bristles large and white, with swollen bases. Flowers June onwards, flower-heads with broad, triangular outer bracts. Most fruits small, with a large pappus for long distance travel. A few marginal florets produce larger, poorly-flighted fruits, which drop near the plant. A southern species of clay soils, absent from Sca and most of G; rare Sco and Ir.

Canadian Fleabane *Conyza canadensis*   Compositae
8–100cm. A stiff, bristly, candelabra-like annual. Flower-heads with whitish rays and yellow disc-florets, June onwards. An American bird skin, stuffed with its fluffy fruits, is reputedly responsible for its arrival in England *c.* 1686. Common from bombed sites in S. England in 1940s. T, ex Fi, Ic, Sco, Sw.

Canadian Golden-rod *Solidago canadensis*   Compositae
A tall (60–250cm), downy-stemmed perennial. Dense pyramidal plumes of tiny yellow flower-heads, August onwards. A naturalised garden escape, often forming large clumps on derelict allotments and railway banks. T, ex Ic.

Black Horehound *Ballota nigra*   Labiatae
40–100cm. A hairy, branching, malodorous perennial with stalked, nettle-like leaves. Flowers in whorls at base of upper leaves, June onwards. An unattractive roadside plant even when flowering. T, ex Ic and Fi; casual Ir; absent most of Sco.

Rosebay Willowherb or **Fireweed** *Chamerion (Epilobium, Chamaenerion) angustifolium*   Onagraceae
30–120cm. A handsome, prolific perennial now so closely associated with urban dereliction that it generates contempt. Its phenomenal increase is linked with several factors involving fire, including war damage; it benefits from the wealth of nitrates in burnt areas. Its fruits release an average of 380 wind-borne seeds; one plant may produce over 80,000 seeds. T.

Great Willowherb *Epilobium hirsutum*   Onagraceae
80–150cm. A softly hairy perennial. Flowers July–August; notched petals, white-lobed stigma held *above* anthers. Common on wet industrial sites, canal banks, etc, but not confined to wetland. T, ex Ic and Fi; rare in No.

Broad-leaved Willowherb *Epilobium montanum*   Onagraceae
Up to 60cm. An almost hairless perennial. One of several willowherbs with smaller, paler flowers than the two preceding spp. Opposite, short-stalked leaves with rounded bases. Flowers June–August; petals deeply notched, four-lobed stigma held *below* top of higher anthers. T, ex Ic.

Evening Primroses *Oenothera* spp. (Onagraceae) are identifiable as such from their broad, funnel-shaped, aromatic, short-lived flowers, which open at dusk; the urban species are yellow. They are long-naturalised garden escapes, no longer identical with their American ancestors. Seven spp. occur in London alone. Identification is difficult. The following are usually biennial, flowering June onwards.

Large-flowered Evening Primrose *Oenothera erythrosepala*
60–20cm. Red swollen-based hairs on stems. En, Wa, F, Be, D, G.

Common Evening Primrose *Oenothera biennis*
50–100cm. Smaller flowers. No red-based hairs. T, ex Ic; rare Sco and Ir.

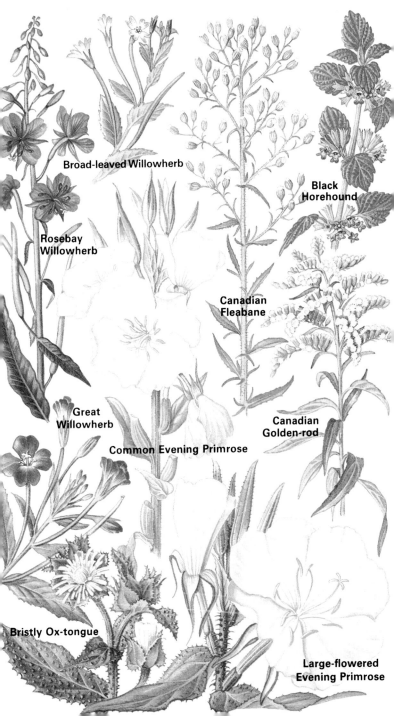

Broad-leaved Willowherb

Black Horehound

Rosebay Willowherb

Canadian Fleabane

Great Willowherb

Canadian Golden-rod

Common Evening Primrose

Bristly Ox-tongue

Large-flowered Evening Primrose

Herbaceous Plants Plants Underfoot

Unmetalled tracks, yards and pavements support vegetation that can withstand a good deal of human traffic. Some plants even benefit from it.

Procumbent Pearlwort *Sagina procumbens* Caryophyllaceae

A prostrate perennial with lateral stems proliferating from a dense, non-flowering rosette, rooting at intervals and producing more laterals. Narrow, bristle-tipped leaves. Flowers on the lateral stems, May–September, normally with minute white petals but sometimes without. Sepals larger than petals, spreading round a seed capsule which bends downwards as it ripens. Unripe capsules are usually bright yellowish-green.

Procumbent pearlwort spreads by means of its lateral shoots and its dust-like seed, which is easily blown into cracks where it can germinate. Its small size and prostrate habit enable it to grow between paving stones, and it occurs in a variety of other well-trodden places, including lawns. T.

Annual Pearlwort *Sagina apetala* Caryophyllaceae

A prostrate annual. Does not produce a lasting rosette or rooting lateral shoots. Flowers (May–August) on the main stem; petals, if present, minute and greenish. Unripe capsules dull green or purplish, remaining erect while ripening. Annual pearlwort is less often found in damp places than procumbent pearlwort. T, ex Ic, FS.

Pineapple Weed *Matricaria matricarioides* Compositae

Almost prostrate in trampled places, but can reach 40cm. A branching annual, smelling of pineapple when crushed. Rayless flower-heads with greenish-yellow disc-florets on a hollow, conical receptacle; flowers May onwards. Finely divided leaves with thread-like segments.

Pineapple weed is probably a native of NE. Asia, but reached Europe from N. America. Its spread during the early 1900s is associated with motor transport. The fruits were carried in mud adhering to car tyres (and human footwear) – muddy roads were commonplace in the early days of motoring. Farm tracks are now the main rural habitat, but the plant is equally characteristic of unmetalled thoroughfares in town. T.

Greater Plantain *Plantago major* Plantaginaceae

A perennial, varying in size according to habitat; on good soil flower-spikes may reach 60cm. Broad, long-stalked leaves with prominent, unbranched veins below. Tiny flowers, May onwards, in a greenish cylindrical spike. The name **ratstail plantain** aptly describes the plant in fruit.

Greater plantains flourish in all open places lacking in tall vegetation, including lawns. Their seeds become sticky when wet and human feet have carried them everywhere – hence the alternative name 'white man's foot'. The fruiting spikes are attractive to birds and are often collected for caged songsters. T.

Knotgrass *Polygonum aviculare* agg. Polygonaceae

The scientific name embraces several forms sometimes regarded as distinct spp. Some reach heights of 100cm when growing amongst tall vegetation, but on sparsely covered ground they are often prostrate. They are wiry, branching annuals with ragged, silvery, tubular sheaths (ochreae) at the base of the leaves. Tiny pink or white flowers in the axils of the upper leaves, June onwards. A tough tap-root, sometimes 90cm long, enables the plant to survive surface damage. T.

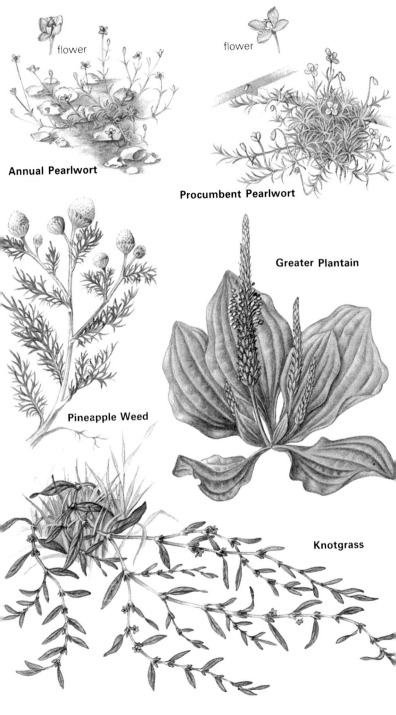

flower

Annual Pearlwort

flower

Procumbent Pearlwort

Greater Plantain

Pineapple Weed

Knotgrass

Herbaceous and Woody Climbers

The following plants are found festooning other vegetation and such unattractive urban features as the chain-link fence.

Black Bindweed *Bilderdykia convolvulus* Polygonaceae
A rather mealy annual which is both a scrambler and a clockwise-twining climber. Leaves shaped rather like those of true bindweeds (Convolvulaceae) but mealy below. Flowers (July onwards) are quite different; greenish-pink and insignificant. A prolific plant; one specimen can produce *c.* 200 dull black nuts. Prefers nutrient-rich soil and rubbish tips; will grow on railway banks. T.

Russian Vine *Bilderdykia baldschuanicum* and
B. aubertii Polygonaceae
Fast-growing, deciduous, woody climbers capable of reaching a height of 12m. Large, pale green leaves. A profusion of flowers July/August–September. Plants with pinkish flowers are regarded by some authorities as *B. baldschuanicum* and those with white flowers as *aubertii*, but the former name is often used to cover both forms. They are of Asian origin. Usually planted in gardens to hide unsightly objects,

Field Bindweed *Convolvulus arvensis* Convolvulaceae
Smallest of the urban bindweeds, all of which are perennial and twine anti-clockwise. More of a prostrate scrambler and less of a climber than the others. Flowers June–September; pink, white or both together; pleasantly scented and attractive to insects. Field bindweed spreads partly by seed but mainly by its underground stems. If the stems are severed they heal themselves by exuding a sealant latex. The roots can penetrate to depths of nearly 7m – hence the uncomplimentary name of 'devil's guts'. T, ex Ic.

Hedge Bindweed *Calystegia sepium* Convolvulaceae
Much larger than field bindweed, with white, sometimes pink-veined flowers, July–September. Broad, sepal-like bracts enfold the true sepals. A true climber, swarming over fences, hedges and trees. The problems of eradicating its deeply penetrating roots and underground stems have given rise to names like 'hellweed'. T, ex Ic.

Hybridises with **large bindweed** *C. silvatica*, an introduction of SE. Europe, which is larger in all its parts, with the bracts inflated and overlapping. The hybrid is fertile and will backcross with parent spp.

Bittersweet or **Woody Nightshade**
Solanum dulcamara Solanaceae
A poisonous, woody-based, downy perennial, twining in both directions. A sprawler rather than an efficient climber, often found in wettish places. Flowers June–September, like tomato flowers in form. Egg-shaped berries, green, yellow and finally scarlet. Bittersweet is often wrongly thought to be deadly nightshade. T, ex Ic.

Broad-leaved Everlasting Pea *Lathyrus latifolius* Leguminosae
A gaudy, deep-rooted perennial with winged stems, climbing to 3m and scrambling along the ground. Leaves consist of two broadly elliptical leaflets and a branched tendril. Flowers July–September. A native of S. Europe including southern F; introduced (Be, B, northern F, G) and growing as a garden escape. Frequent on English railway banks.

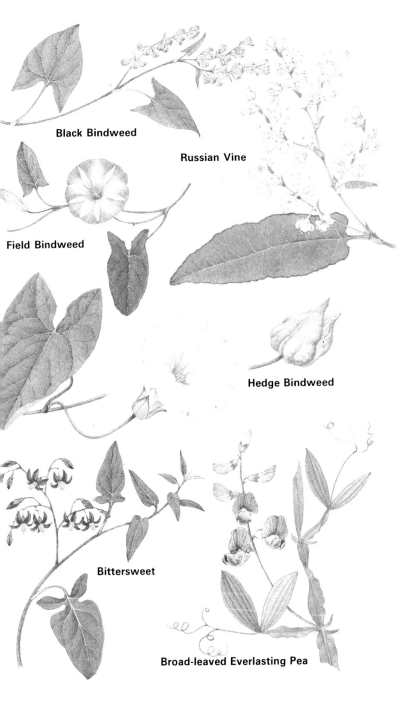

Black Bindweed

Russian Vine

Field Bindweed

Hedge Bindweed

Bittersweet

Broad-leaved Everlasting Pea

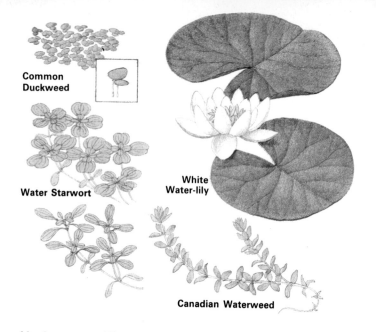

Common Duckweed

Water Starwort

White Water-lily

Canadian Waterweed

Herbaceous Plants Aquatic Species

Although many urban streams and rivers have been cleared of vegetation or have become too polluted for higher plants, there are still canals, canal reservoirs and other botanically interesting wetland sites. They include pools on urban commons and industrial wasteland and some park lakes. Some aquatic species may be introduced by aquarists disposing of unwanted plants. Some grow from seeds or regenerate from broken pieces transported in anglers' tackle or by waterfowl. Birds may deposit undigested seeds in droppings.

White Water-lily *Nymphaea alba* Nymphaeaceae
A well-known perennial with almost circular floating leaves and large fragrant flowers, June–August. A European native but those seen in towns most likely to be of nursery origin.T, ex Ic.

Common Duckweed *Lemna minor* Lemnaceae
A tiny, floating, unobtrusively flowering plant. Spreads rapidly by vegetative means, covering still waters like green confetti. Flat on both sides and with a single root. Other spp. occur in towns but this is the commonest; found on small ponds and little-used canals. T.

Pondweeds (Potamogetonaceae) are perennial plants of still or slow-flowing waters; canals have played an important part in their distribution. Wholly submerged or with some floating leaves. Greenish, inconspicuous flowers at leaf-base; four sepals but no petals. Seeds are eaten by waterfowl and germination is dependent on passage through a bird's digestive tract. Narrow-leaved pondweeds are particularly difficult to identify and hybridisation adds to the problem.

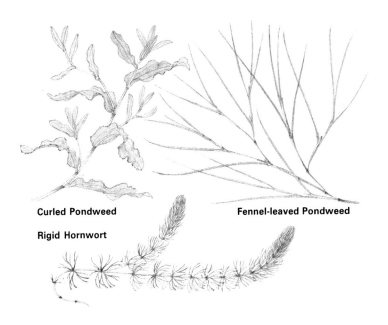

Curled Pondweed

Rigid Hornwort

Fennel-leaved Pondweed

Fennel-leaved Pondweed *Potamogeton pectinatus*
Commonest of narrow-leaved spp. found in urban canals and ditches; some-times in park lakes. Submerged leaves, dark and thin, rather like bootlaces. The plant is tolerant of lime and moderate pollution and can live in brackish water. T.

Curled Pondweed *Potamogeton crispus*
Submerged leaves, oblong, wavy-edged, translucent and stalkless; on a four-angled stem. T, ex Ic and Fi; rare in No.

Rigid Hornwort *Ceratophyllum demersum* Ceratophyllaceae
A submerged, dark green perennial of nutrient-rich ponds and ditches. Finely divided, stiff, once- or twice-forked leaves which, at the top of the stem, are crowded into a 'bushy tail'. Brittle; able to regenerate from small fragments. T, ex Ic; rare in No, Sco, Ir and Wa.

Canadian Waterweed *Elodea canadensis* Hydrocharitaceae
A submerged, dark green, brittle-stemmed perennial. Leaves in overlapping whorls of three. Tiny, purple-tinged white flowers on long thread-like stalks, May–September.
  Canals and rivers were choked with this plant soon after its introduction into Europe in the 19th century, but it is now only moderately common. Spreads vegetatively. T, ex Ic; rare in No.

Water Starwort *Callitriche* spp. Callitrichaceae
A difficult group of annuals and perennials for which fruit is needed for specific identification. Variable leaves, submerged or partially so, or growing on mud at the water's edge, a habit of **common water starwort** *Callitriche stagnalis*, the most likely urban sp. T.

Herbaceous Plants   Marsh and Waterside

Flood control measures and an obsession with tidiness have often robbed town-dwellers of the pleasure of seeing the colourful plants that naturally adorn the banks of pools and watercourses, but there are some town parks, particularly in The Netherlands, where such vegetation is now cherished and carefully managed. The canals, canal reservoirs and the pools on industrial wasteland already mentioned (p. 120) are sometimes the richest urban localities for marsh plants. This is certainly so in Britain. **Reed-mace** *Typha latifolia* and **reed sweetgrass** *Glyceria maxima* are often abundant. **Soft rush** *Juncus effusus* and **common rush** *J. conglomeratus* occur, especially on acid ground; **hard rush** *J. inflexus* prefers calcareous soils. **Meadowseet** *Filipendula ulmaria* and **marsh ragwort** *Senecio aquaticus* are two of the more colourful plants. The following spp. are found in a variety of wetland sites.

Indian Balsam or Policeman's Helmet
Impatiens glandulifera   Balsaminaceae
1–2m. A handsome annual with reddish, fleshy stems. Flowers, sometimes white, July–October. Fruits burst explosively when touched, expelling the seeds. A garden escape of Himalayan origin, forming dense masses along many urban river banks; the seeds are carried downstream to found new colonies. The plant also occurs on waste sites. T, ex Ic.

Giant Hogweed *Heracleum mantegazzianum*   Umbelliferae
Up to 5m, a giant indeed, with umbels *c.* 50cm across and leaves up to 1m long. Flowers June–July. A Caucasian plant of parks and gardens, often naturalised on river banks. Children tempted to use its hollow stems as blowpipes may find the plant contains a chemical which blisters the skin under strong sunlight. B, Ir, F, Ne, G and Sca, ex Ic.

Water Dock *Rumex hydrolapathum*   Polygonaceae
Up to 2m. An impressive perennial with lance-shaped leaves reaching to 110cm, brick-red in autumn. Flowers July–September. The largest of the urban docks, especially frequent on canal banks. T, ex Ic; rare in No; probably absent from Scottish towns.

Yellow Flag *Iris pseudacorus*   Iridaceae
40–150cm. A robust perennial, unmistakable in flower, May–July. Sword-shaped leaves in a flattened fan. One of the attractive flowers which are lost when urban streams are artificially channelled but surviving on canal banks and any wetland that escapes drainage and infilling. It may even be deliberately planted round oramental lakes in the more formal parks. T, ex Ic.

Gipsywort *Lycopus europaeus*   Labiatae
30–100cm. A rather hairy perennial. White, purple-dotted flowers in tight whorls at base of upper leaves, June–September. A plant of all urban wetland sites, most plentiful around pools on industrial wasteland, but also found on canal banks and, if tolerated, even on the shores of the conventional park lake. T, ex Ic.

Skullcap *Scutellaria galericulata*   Labiatae
15–30cm. A creeping perennial, often downy, with opposite pairs of bluntly toothed, short-stalked leaves. Blue-violet flowers in pairs on the leafy stems, June–September. Canal walls are its usual habitat but, like gipsywort, it can also enliven the artificial banks of a park lake. T, ex Ic.

Indian Balsam

Water Dock

Giant Hogweed

Skullcap

Yellow Flag

Gipsywort

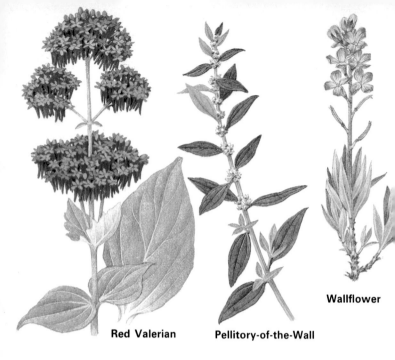

Red Valerian   **Pellitory-of-the-Wall**   **Wallflower**

Herbaceous Plants (and Ivy)   Wall Plants

A wall may be regarded as a man-made rock face, and walls present an open
invitation to plants which normally occupy this kind of habitat in a natural
situation. The greatest botanical variety is found on old, irregularly surfaced
walls in which lime mortar has been used. Some of the plants are aliens from
warmer lands and need a well-drained position to survive the wet winters of
NW. Europe; walls provide ideal conditions.

Wallflower *Cheiranthus cheiri*   Cruciferae
20–60cm. The familiar garden perennial with flowers of various shades of red
or yellow, March–June. An eastern Mediterranean plant well established on
walls and cliffs, and in railway cuttings. Usually self-sown, the seeds carried
by the wind, but sometimes sown deliberately. Absent from Sca and most of
G; elsewhere T.

Red Valerian *Centranthus ruber*   Valerianaceae
30–80cm. A showy perennial, sometimes with bluish-green leaves. Terminal
clusters of tiny asymmetrical flowers, pink, red and sometimes white; May
onwards. Feathery-flighted, single-seeded fruits dispersed by wind. Another
long-naturalised Mediterranean garden plant of walls and cliffs, particularly
common in coastal towns of S. England. T, ex Sca, Ne and much of G.

Yellow Corydalis *Corydalis lutea*   Fumariaceae
15–30cm. A slender, branching perennial with pinnate, long-stalked leaves.
Canary yellow flowers, May onwards. The large seeds provide food for and

124

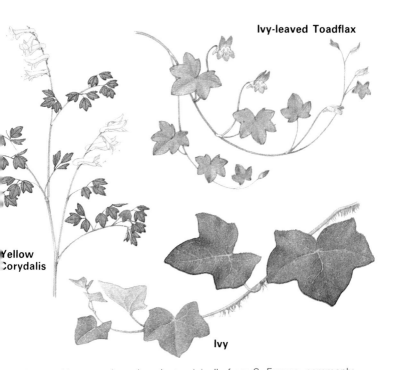

Ivy-leaved Toadflax

Yellow Corydalis

Ivy

are dispersed by ants. A garden plant, originally from S. Europe, commonly naturalised on old walls except in the N.; uncommon in W. Sco and Ir.

Ivy-leaved Toadflax *Cymbalaria muralis* Scrophulariaceae
A prolific perennial that clings to the wall surface and roots itself between the stones. Long-stalked ivy-like leaves, some tinged with purple on underside. Flowers (April onwards) normally lilac with a yellow spot at corolla mouth, but sometimes white. Their supporting stalks bend away from the light when fruits ripen and seeds are shed into mortar. A naturalised Mediterranean sp. introduced as a garden plant. Reached England around 1618. Cultivated varieties are still grown, but original form now considered a garden weed. T, ex Ic and Fi.

Pellitory-of-the-Wall *Parietaria judaica* Urticaceae
30–100cm. A hairy, branching, reddish-stemmed perennial. Slightly glossy, alternate leaves. Tiny greenish flowers in clusters, the sexes separate; June onwards. A native plant, often growing below the wall as well as on the wall itself. B (uncommon in Sco), Ir, Fr, Be, Ne; local in G.

Ivy *Hedera helix* Araliaceae
The familiar woody, evergreen climber with variously shaped leaves, draping itself over trees and ground as well as walls. The plant is not wholly undesirable. It is not a tree-parasite; its flower-buds are food for larvae of holly blue butterflies (p. 132); its flowers (September onwards) attract wasps, drone-flies, moths and late butterflies, and its ripe berries (March–April) are eaten by birds. T, ex Ic and Fi.

125

Flowerless Plants   Ferns and Horsetails

Many of the spores of ferns and horsetails present in the urban atmosphere can find the damp conditions they need for the early stages of their develop ment. Tunnel entrances, basement areas and walls often meet the ferns requirements. In the following fern species the spores are produced on the underside of the fronds.

Hart's-tongue Fern *Phyllitis scolopendrium*   Aspleniaceae
Usually less than 60cm. Immediately known by its strap-shaped, undivided leaves. Spores are produced in parallel brown lines on either side of the midrib A moisture-loving fern of damp, shady banks and walls. T, ex Ic and Fi, commonest in Ir and western B, scarce on the Continent.

Wall Rue *Asplenium ruta-muralis*   Aspleniaceae
A dark, dull-green, mural fern with long-stalked, leathery leaves, usually 2–12cm, with wedge-shaped leaflets. Often found in mortar joints. T, ex Ic; another fern of canal walls in Ne.

Male Fern *Dryopteris filix-mas*   Aspidiaceae
'Male' because it is less graceful than the **lady fern** *Athyrium filix-femina*, which is rare in towns. Pinnate fronds 60–120cm or more, arranged in tall leafy crowns, usually one crown. The leaf segments (pinnae) are further divided into toothed pinnules, on which the spore capsules are arranged on either side of the midrib, each protected by a kidney-shaped membrane. Leaf-stalks are clothed with chaffy brown scales. Male ferns are frequently grown in wooded parks and shady gardens, and are widely naturalised elsewhere, often growing on walls and railway banks. T.

Bracken *Pteridium aquilinum*   Pteridiaceae
The best-known fern, up to 180cm but usually less in towns. An aggressive plant, spreading by extensive rhizomes, and shading out its plant competitors both in summer and on dying down in autumn. Bracken occurs on sandy urban commons (often abundantly), railway banks and industrial wasteland. It colonises brick scree on derelict city centre sites and its sporelings can appear on damp brickwork anywhere. T, ex Ic.

Horsetails (Equisetaceae) are perennials with creeping rhizomes and jointed, tubular, aerial stems. Each joint is marked by a whorl of small dark leaves, joined together to form a toothed collar. The following species produce stems of two kinds – infertile stems with whorls of green branches growing from the joints, and unbranched fertile stems, pale non-green and terminating in a spore-producing cone.

Common Horsetail *Equisetum arvensis*
Barren stems 20–30cm, green, deeply grooved and rough. Fertile stems pale brown, with brown cones. A common plant of dry places, often troublesome in gardens because of its underground stems, roots and tubers. T.

Great Horsetail *Equisetum telmateia*
Both kinds of stems are ivory-white between the joints. Barren stems 100cm or more, with long, drooping branches. A plant of damp places, especially on clay; common on canal and railway banks, and sometimes in cemeteries, where grave-digging helps it to colonise new ground. T, ex Ic, No and Fi.

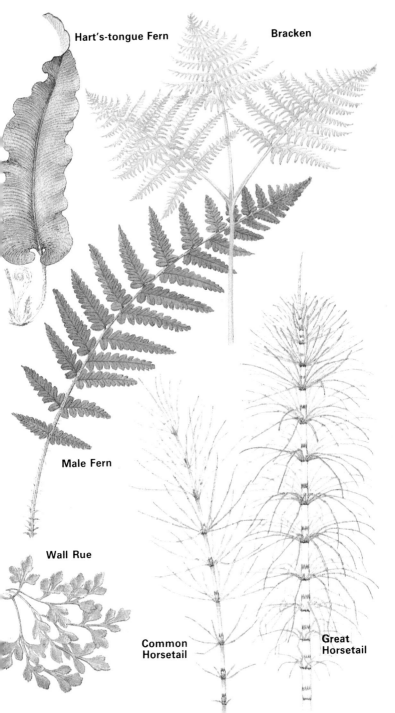

Hart's-tongue Fern

Bracken

Male Fern

Wall Rue

Common
Horsetail

Great
Horsetail

Cypress-leaved Feather Moss

spore capsule

Greater Matted Thread Moss

spore capsule

Silvery Thread Moss

spore capsule

spore capsule

Grey Cushion Moss

Wall Screw Moss

Flowerless Plants   Mosses and Lichens

Mosses are usually associated with moisture and shade, but several of the urban species can tolerate very dry conditions. The cushion shape of mosses that grow on walls, roofs and pavements is an adaptation which enables them to conserve water. Lichens, which represent a symbiotic partnership of algae and fungi, can find the town environment even more exacting, for most of them are sensitive to atmospheric pollution, especially high levels of sulphur dioxide. Those mentioned below are among the more tolerant species.

Cypress-leaved Feather Moss *Hypnum cupressiforme*   Hypnaceae
A very variable moss with curved, overlapping branches suggestive of cypress foliage. Leaves nerveless, tapering to a fine point. Typical forms grow on masonry, trees, stumps, railway tracks, paths and soil. T.

Greater Matted Thread Moss *Bryum capillare*   Bryaceae
A cushion-forming moss with oblong leaves that become spirally twisted, corkscrew fashion, when dry. Large, drooping, pear-shaped spore-capsules on 3cm stalks, changing from green to brown on ripening. This moss grows on masonry, roofs, railway tracks, trees and stumps, and flourishes on wall-tops capped with soil. T.

Silvery Thread Moss *Bryum argenteum*   Bryaceae
A silvery, cushion-forming moss growing in cracks in city pavements, on paths, railway tracks, roofs and wall-tops. Very tolerant of atmospheric pollution. T.

Grey Cushion Moss *Grimmia pulvinata*   Grimmiaceae
A moss which forms compact domed cushions which appear grey because

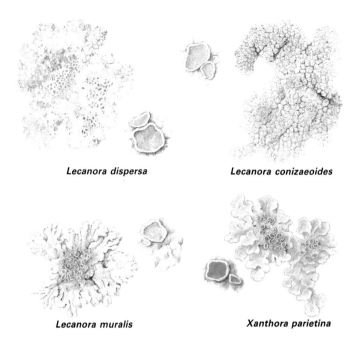

Lecanora dispersa

Lecanora conizaeoides

Lecanora muralis

Xanthoria parietina

the green leaves are tipped with long whitish hairs. Capsules oval, on curved stalks, and buried in the leaves. This moss occurs on all kinds of masonry a common feature of wall-tops. T. ex lc.

Wall Screw Moss *Tortula muralis* Tortulaceae
Another cushion moss with green leaves ending in long whitish hairs, but with erect, cylindrical, short-stalked capsules which have a pointed cap when young. It grows on masonry and dumped building materials. T, rare in lc.

Lecanora dispersa Lecanoraceae
An inconspicuous lichen, varying in appearance from a black stain in soot-polluted areas to a greyish-white crust in cleaner places. A lens reveals the densely crowded fruiting-bodies, which resemble brown jam tarts. Found on stonework, cement and mortar, this pollution-tolerant lichen is usually the only one found in city centres. T.

Lecanora conizaeoides Lecanoraceae
A grey-green lichen, forming a cracked, powdery crust over trees, woodwork, bricks and siliceous stonework. Unknown anywhere before the mid-19th century, it has actually benefited from sulphur dioxide pollution and is increasing. T.

Lecanora muralis Lecanoraceae
A rosette-forming, buff-grey lichen with brown fruiting-bodies in the centre and a pale lobed margin. It is increasingly found on pavements and asbestos-cement roofing. T.

Xanthoria parietina Physciaceae
A leafy-lobed lichen, usually bright orange. On walls trees, concrete posts and asbestos roofs; especially common in coastal districts. T.

Insects Butterflies: Nymphalids and Wall Brown

There is no sound scientific reason for dividing the order Lepidoptera into butterflies and moths, but the European butterflies can be distinguished as such by their clubbed or knobbed antennae. With a few exceptions, butterflies are welcomed in town gardens, and buddleia is often planted for their benefit. The food plants of the caterpillars, however, usually grow elsewhere, mainly on wasteland.

Wing-span measurements are given for all the butterflies and moths mentioned.

Small Tortoiseshell *Aglais urticae* Nymphalidae
44–50mm. A common and unmistakable visitor to garden flowers. Adults hibernate, often in buildings. Flies from March onwards, sometimes even earlier. Eggs laid in clusters on stinging nettles. Spiny caterpillars (May–August), living communally in silken webs amongst the leaves; black at first, becoming yellowish with black speckling and a black dorsal stripe when larger. Single-brooded in the N., double-brooded elsewhere. T.

Peacock *Inachis io* Nymphalidae
54–58 mm. Recognisable from the 'eye' markings and black underside. Very common in gardens, especially on buddleia, July onwards. Single-brooded. Hibernating insects reappear in March. Spiny, velvety-black caterpillars; feed communally on nettles, June–July. T.

Red Admiral *Vanessa atalanta* Nymphalidae
55–62mm. Another buddleia-lover, also attracted by rotting fruit. A migrant species, seen from May onwards. The immigrants' offspring may attempt to return to S. in autumn, but many die. Successful hibernation takes place in S. Europe, but is considered rare further N. Eggs laid singly, usually in nettles, sometimes thistles. Spiny caterpillars, blackish, brownish or greyish; individually construct a tent of leaves bound with silk, June–July. Chrysalis adorned with shining gold markings. T, but a vagrant to Ic.

Painted Lady *Cynthia cardui* Nymphalidae
54–58mm. A spring migrant, arriving from Africa in varying numbers, sometimes by March; has even reached Iceland. Immigrants' progeny migrate S. in autumn. Caterpillars spiny, greenish-grey to blackish with black and yellowish markings; tent-makers (see red admiral); food plants are usually thistles. Adults visit garden flowers, including buddleia. T, but only as summer visitor.

Comma *Polygonia c-album* Nymphalidae
44–48mm. Distinctive with its ragged wings and white 'comma' on the underside of each hindwing. Two generations between July and October, some insects hibernating amongst tree branches until March–April. A garden visitor; another buddleia feeder. Eggs laid singly, usually on nettles or **hops** *Humulus lupulus*. Full-grown caterpillars spiny and black, with broad white area on rear half, creating resemblance to a bird dropping. T, ex Ic, Sco, Ir and northern En; not breeding south-west No, D, Ne and Be.

Wall Brown *Lasiommata megera* Satyridae
38–50mm. Usually seen basking, wings open, on sunlit walls, paths or other bare surfaces. Normally double-brooded, first generation flying May–June, sometimes earlier; second July–August. Caterpillars green, dotted with white; second brood overwintering. Main food-plants are meadow-grasses and cocksfoot. T, ex Ic and Fi.

Small Tortoiseshell

Wall Brown

Wall Brown
caterpillar

Comma

Red Admiral

Comma
caterpillar

Painted Lady

Red Admiral
caterpillar

**Small
Tortoiseshell**
caterpillar

Peacock
caterpillar

Painted Lady
caterpillar

Peacock

Insects   Butterflies: Blues and Whites

Common Blue *Polyommatus icarus*   Lycaenidae
28–36mm. Males violet-blue; females brown, often tinged blue at the wing-bases, with orange spots near the outer margins. Both sexes have orange spots in this position on the underside. Flies April–September; double- or treble-brooded in S.; single-brooded in N. Caterpillars green and slug-like. The butterfly can complete its life cycle only in places where its food-plants (e.g. bird's-foot trefoil) can escape being mown. T, ex Ic.

Holly Blue *Celastrina argiolus*   Lycaenidae
30mm. The only blue butterfly of town parks and gardens which has a bluish-white underside marked with black specks, and with no orange spots anywhere. Usually two broods (April–May and July–August), but only one in the N. and in N. Ireland. Male lilac-blue with narrow black edge to forewings. Female has wide black margin at outer edge of forewings, even more extensive in second generation. Caterpillars of first brood (June) usually feed on flower-buds and green berries of holly; second-brood larvae (August–October) usually on flower buds of ivy. T, ex Ic and Sco.

Large White *Pieris brassicae*   Pieridae
55–66mm. Popularly known as the 'cabbage white', although the name also suits the small white. Flies April–October; two or three broods. Male has black-tipped forewings but lacks additional black markings which distinguish female. Black is usually more intense in second-brood insects. Caterpillars probably the best known of all butterfly larvae; as easily seen as the havoc they create in the cabbage patch. Chrysalis found on fences, walls and tree-trunks, and in sheds, held in a vertical position by a silken girdle.
    Many caterpillars are attacked by *Apanteles glomeratus*, a hymenopteran parasite of the family Braconidae. Over 100 *Apanteles* larvae may feed inside the living caterpillar, eventually emerging to spin yellow cocoons and pupate. So many caterpillars are parasitised in Britain that the butterfly might not survive here but for the arrival of immigrants. The biggest migration takes place in July/early August, moving S. from Sweden into C. Europe, with swarms of insects turning W. to reach the Low Countries and Britain. T, but rarer in the N.

Small White *Pieris rapae*   Pieridae
46–54mm. Similar to the large white but smaller. Black border of the forewings is less extensive and the male has a black spot on each forewing. Two to three broods, April–October. Food-plants are crucifers (including *Brassica* spp.) and garden nasturtiums *Tropaeolum majus*. Caterpillars green: rather inconspicuous on cabbage leaves due to their habit of lying along the midrib. This is the commonest town butterfly, with numbers regularly augmented by migrating insects. T, rare in Ic.

Green-veined White *Pieris napi*   Pieridae
36–44mm. Recognisable from the dark pigmentation along the veins of the yellow hindwing, blackish rather than green. Two to three broods, March–September, with little migration taking place. Caterpillars green, feeding on wild and garden crucifers, but not on *Brassica*. T, ex Ic.

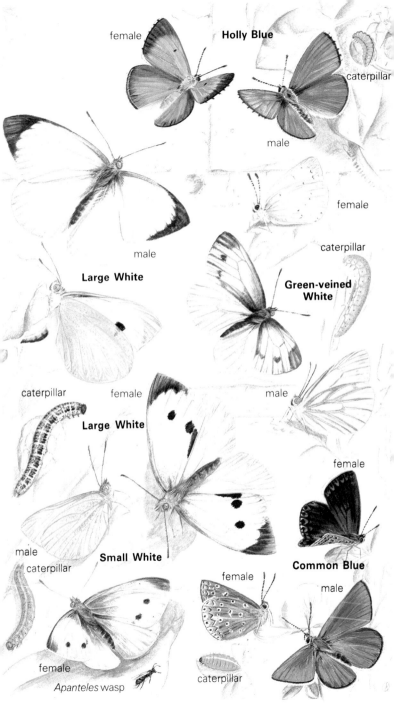

female

Holly Blue

caterpillar

male

male

Large White

female

caterpillar

Green-veined White

caterpillar

female

Large White

male

female

male

female

Small White

male
caterpillar

female

Common Blue

male

female

caterpillar

Apanteles wasp

caterpillar

Insects   Moths 1: Hawk-Moths and Others

Most moths are nocturnal and many are cryptically coloured, resting undetected during the day on tree-trunks, walls and fences. After dark a wide
range of species may be attracted to a lighted window, especially on warm,
overcast nights.

Poplar Hawk-moth *Laothoë populi*   Sphingidae
72–92mm, males smaller than females. Ash-coloured wings, rather like dead
leaves, render it inconspicuous when resting on a tree-trunk. Flies at dusk,
May-June; sometimes a second brood in autumn. Caterpillar, *c.* 60mm,
yellow-green or blue-green, with yellow diagonal stripes on sides and sometimes a row of red spots in that area. As in most hawk-moth larvae the eighth
abdominal segment has a projecting horn. Feeds on willows and poplars,
July–September; pupates in the soil. This, the commonest of hawk-moths,
can occur in city centres. T, ex Ic.

Elephant Hawk-moth *Deilephila elpenor*   Sphingidae
62–72mm. Flies in June, but less often noticed than the 85mm, green or
brown caterpillars; July–September. These attract attention because of the
large, intimidating 'eye-spots', which become dilated when the animal draws
in its slender, trunk-like head and thorax on being disturbed. Feed on willowherbs and often on garden fuchsias; pupate in the soil. They can become
abundant on waste sites where willowherbs are plentiful. T, ex Ic; local in
Sco and Ir.

Buff-tip *Phalera bucephala*   Notodontidae
55–68mm, female larger than male. Flies June–July. Strongly resembles a
newly broken twig when at rest. Caterpillars 60–70mm long, yellow with black
markings. Feed July–October on leaves of various trees, including goat willows
on waste sites and limes in streets and gardens; gregarious until nearly full-
grown, often stripping branches bare. Pupates in the soil. T, ex Ic; local in
Sco and Ir.

Puss Moth *Cerura vinula*   Notodontidae
62–80mm. Flies May–July. Disruptively camouflaged caterpillars on poplars
and willows, May–September; *c.* 70mm when full grown. Adopt a defensive
attitude if disturbed, waving whip-like 'tails' and, if still provoked, squirting
formic acid. Chrysalis overwinters in cocoon of silk and chewed wood, on
tree-trunk or fence-post. T, ex Ic.

Vapourer *Orgyia antiqua*   Lymantriidae
Males 35–38mm, day-flying, seeking the almost wingless females which
remain on their cocoons after emergence and lay eggs there. Normally two
broods, sometimes three, June–August and October; one brood in the N.
Caterpillars feed on a wide range of trees and bushes, even including London
plane; sometimes occur in vast numbers in city centres. Their hairs are easily
detached if they are handled, causing severe skin irritation. T.

Lackey *Malacosoma neustria*   Lasiocampidae
Average male 29mm; average female 40mm. Flies July–August. The colourful,
gregarious caterpillars are more often noticed than the moths, especially
when sun-bathing on the webs they spin over the leaves of orchard trees,
hawthorns, roses and other food plants. T, ex Ic, Sco; rare Ir.

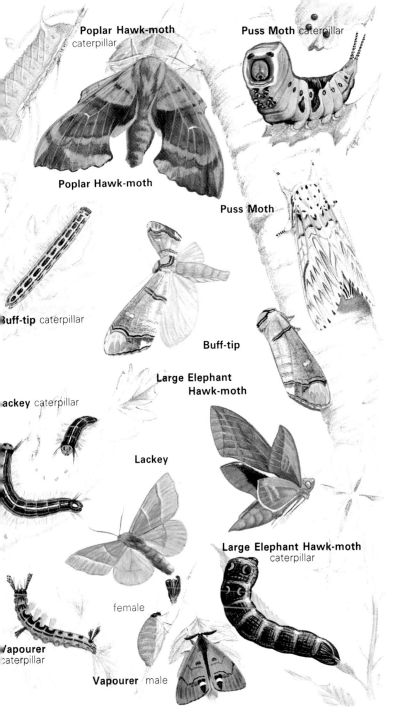

Poplar Hawk-moth caterpillar

Puss Moth caterpillar

Poplar Hawk-moth

Puss Moth

Buff-tip caterpillar

Buff-tip

Large Elephant Hawk-moth

Lackey caterpillar

Lackey

Large Elephant Hawk-moth caterpillar

female

Vapourer caterpillar

Vapourer male

Insects Moths 2: Arctiids and Noctuids

Garden Tiger *Arctia caja* Arctiidae
50–78mm. Flies late July–August. The brilliant hindwings warn predators of the moth's unpalatability. The hairy 'woolly bear' caterpillars are also distasteful; hibernate when still small, reaching c. 60mm when full-fed in June. They are not restricted to particular food-plants, and on waste sites are often found on Oxford ragwort. T, ex Ic.

Cinnabar *Tyria jacobaeae* Arctiidae
35–45mm. Nocturnal, but often disturbed by day; late May–mid-July. Its bright colours and those of the gregarious caterpillars advertise the fact that this species makes an unpleasant meal. Caterpillars found June–August, completely stripping their food-plants – groundsel and ragwort spp., mainly on Oxford ragwort in towns. The species was used in attempts to control common ragwort on Christ Church Meadow, Oxford. T, ex Ic.

Sycamore Moth *Acronicta aceris* Noctuidae
41–49mm. A variable moth; flies June–August, resting on fences and trees in daytime. Caterpillars, c. 55mm when full-grown in August; often found on paths and pavements. Urban food-plants include sycamore, birch and laburnum, but horse-chestnut the main species in Britain. A common moth in London streets and squares. T, ex Ic, Sco, Ir and northern En; rare Wa, Fi, No.

Grey Dagger *Acronicta psi* Noctuidae
33–44mm. Almost indistinguishable from the dark dagger *Acronicta tridens*. Flies late May–September; two broods in the S. A melanic form occurs in industrial areas. Caterpillar (c. 40mm) has a pointed horn on the first abdominal segment; that of *tridens* has a tuft of brown hair on its horn and is less brightly coloured. Grey dagger larvae feed on willows, limes, hawthorns and other trees and bushes, and on bracken, July–October. T, ex Ic.

Heart-and-Dart *Agrotis exclamationis* Noctuidae
35–44mm. A very common moth; flies May–June, sometimes later. Ground colour of forewings variable and markings sometimes merging; a dark mark behind the head. Caterpillars feed on most herbaceous plants, with an unfortunate partiality for lettuces. T, ex Ic.

Dot Moth *Melanchra persicariae* Noctuidae
38–50mm. Appropriately-named; flies June–August. Caterpillar varies from pale green to purplish-brown, marked with chevrons, heavily so on first two abdominal segments. Feeds July–October, accepting most plants, cultivated and wild, but especially nettles and elder. It is now commoner in and around towns than in the open countryside. T, ex Ic and No; only known from southern Sco.

Silver Y *Autographa gamma* Noctuidae
40–48mm. Variable but with 'Y' (or *gamma*) mark on forewings normally recognisable. A migrant species, active day and night; often on buddleia at dusk. Occurs May onwards, sometimes appearing earlier. Spring immigrants produce one or two generations, with caterpillars on a wide range of wild and garden plants. More migrants in late summer, sometimes vast numbers, and a return passage takes place in autumn. T as a migrant.

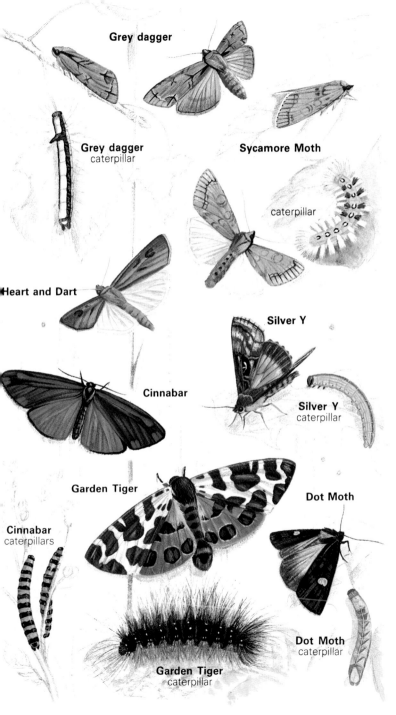

Grey dagger

Grey dagger caterpillar

Sycamore Moth

caterpillar

Heart and Dart

Silver Y

Cinnabar

Silver Y caterpillar

Garden Tiger

Dot Moth

Cinnabar caterpillars

Dot Moth caterpillar

Garden Tiger caterpillar

Insects   Moths 3: Noctuids and Geometers

Angle Shades *Phlogophora meticulosa*   Noctuidae
50–60mm. With its curiously folded wings the resting insect resembles a withered leaf. Ground colour varies from olive-green to brown or pinkish, with the angled pattern usually constant. Recorded in every month but mainly late May–early July and, with the arrival of migrants, late August–late October. Caterpillars green or brown, found throughout the year on a wide range of low-growing plants, including bracken, docks, groundsel and cultivated spinach. Sometimes a greenhouse pest, attacking *Chrysanthemum* and *Pelargonium* plants. T, but in Ic, No and Sw only as a migrant; uncommon in Ir.

Large Yellow Underwing *Noctua pronuba*   Noctuidae
50–60mm. Males with darker forewings than females, but both sexes inconspicuous when resting. Predators are confused by unexpected flashes of yellow which are glimpsed when moth is provoked into flight, and by its equally sudden disappearance upon settling. Very common; recorded April–October, but normally June–August; often visits buddleia. Caterpillars August–May, spending much time underground but feed throughout winter on grasses and low-growing herbs (including Oxford ragwort on waste sites); damages flower borders. T.

Red Underwing *Catocala nupta*   Noctuidae
75–94mm. Like the last sp. this moth evades capture by a combination of cryptic and 'flash' coloration. Flies August–October; often attracted by rotting fruit. Caterpillar feeds nocturnally on willows and poplars, and rests during the day on twigs or in a bark fissure (almost invisibly); also hides under loose bark. Red underwings are common in parks and gardens where their food-plants occur. T, ex Ic, Ir, Sco and northern En.

Peppered Moth *Biston betularia*   Geometridae
42–52mm, females larger than males. Rests on tree-trunks during the day, May–July. Provides the classic example of industrial melanism (see p. 52). The 'normal' form is white, speckled with black, well camouflaged on light, lichen-covered bark, but an obvious target for insectivorous birds when settled on a dark surface. The black variety *carbonaria*, is more likely to go undetected when resting on soot-blackened trunks. An intermediate form, *insularia*, which is black with white speckling, is found in less polluted districts where the ultra-sensitive lichens still cannot grow but the bark remains green with the alga *Pleurococcus*.
   Stick-like 'looper' caterpillars in various shades of green and brown; fall to the ground if disturbed and remain motionless for some time. Feed at night, July–September, on a variety of trees and bushes, including elm, willow, beech, birch, plum, rose and bramble. T, ex Ic.

Waved Umber *Menophra abruptaria*   Geometridae
29–48mm, females larger than males. Flies April–May; well camouflaged at rest. Melanism recorded in London, where it is particularly common, even in the centre. Caterpillars stick-like 'loopers', grey-brown to almost black, feeding on lilac *Syringa vulgaris* and privet. T, ex Ic, Fi, Sw; almost unknown Sco, Ir.

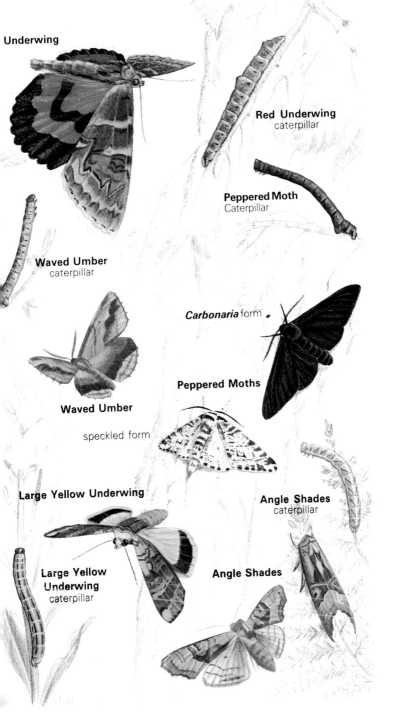

Underwing

Red Underwing
caterpillar

Peppered Moth
Caterpillar

Waved Umber
caterpillar

Carbonaria form

Peppered Moths

Waved Umber

speckled form

Large Yellow Underwing

Angle Shades
caterpillar

**Large Yellow
Underwing**
caterpillar

Angle Shades

Insects Moths 4: Geometers

All the following belong to the family Geometridae; two examples are shown on p. 138. Typical geometrid larvae have the normal three pairs of legs but only two pairs of clasping prolegs at the rear end. When walk they stretch forward, position the true legs, then draw the body up in a l as the prolegs are moved forward; hence the name 'looper caterpillars'.

Brimstone Opisthograptis luteolata
29–39mm. An unmistakable common moth, flying April–September, mainly May–June. Caterpillars twig-like, brown, tinged purplish or green with a double hump on third abdominal segment. Feed nocturnally, mainly hawthorn, but also on cultivated Prunus, including the ornamental cher of suburbia. Double-brooded; some second-brood larvae overwinter, oth pupate. T, ex Ic.

Magpie Moth Abraxas grossulariata
36–43 mm. A very common moth, usually flying July–August; remark. subject to variation. Colours are a warning to predators that it is unpalata as are those of the caterpillar and the yellow-banded black chrysalis. Ca pillars feed on hawthorn, apple, plum and, sometimes in thousands, Japanese spindle. They are notorious pests of cultivated gooseberries currants. Usually found August–May/June, but some larvae pupate early the moths emerge in autumn. T, ex Ic.

Swallow-tailed Moth Ourapteryx sambucaria
42–56mm. A common town moth, its large size and pale colour attrac attention when flying at dusk, July–early August. Caterpillar found betw August and June, feeding intermittently during winter, especially on Leaves of hawthorn, elder, holly and privet also eaten. Feeds at night, spend day on food-plant stretched at an angle, suspended by a silken line at head end and looking very like a twig. T, ex Ic, Fi, No.

Brindled Beauty Lycia hirtaria
38–50mm. Flies March–April. Caterpillars found May–July, varying from g to reddish-brown when fully grown and resembling twigs. Feed at night foliage of most broad-leaved trees, but particularly on elm, lime, plum, p and willow; remain on twigs during the day or stretched out on the bark. moth is especially common in London, sometimes found resting on t trunks in the parks in hundreds. T, ex Ic.

Winter Moth Operophtera brumata
A notorious orchard and garden pest. Average male 28mm, seen flying dusk, October–February. Females rather spider-like, with rudimentary win fruit trees are grease-banded to catch them as they crawl up the trunk lay their eggs. Caterpillars feed April–May, on buds and leaves of most bro leaved trees and shrubs, even on rhododendron. They pupate undergrou the full-fed larvae descending to earth on silken threads. T.

Garden Carpet Xanthorhoë fluctuata
22–24mm. A common moth with rather variable markings mid-forewing. F April–October; at least two generations. Caterpillars feed at nig June–October, on cabbage, wallflower and other crucifers. A common m of town gardens and wasteland, often found indoors. T, ex Ic.

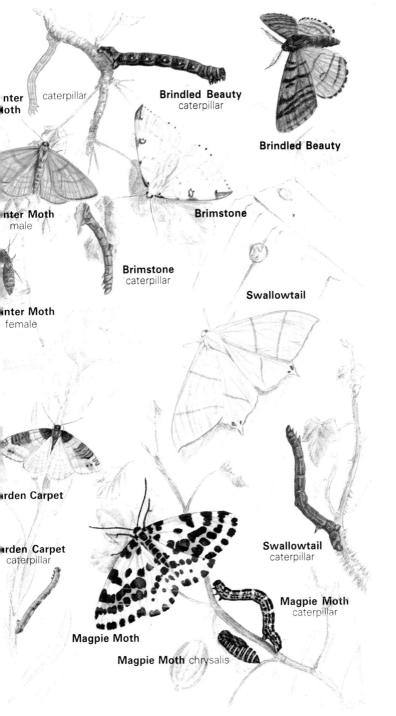

caterpillar

Brindled Beauty
caterpillar

Brindled Beauty

nter
loth

nter Moth
male

Brimstone

Brimstone
caterpillar

nter Moth
female

Swallowtail

rden Carpet

rden Carpet
caterpillar

Swallowtail
caterpillar

Magpie Moth
caterpillar

Magpie Moth

Magpie Moth chrysalis

Insects   Moths 5: 'Micros'

The following small moths belong to families which are conveniently group together as the 'Microlepidoptera', familiarly known as 'micros'. The gro includes many household pests.

Small Magpie *Eurrhypara hortulata*
30mm. Markings somewhat like those of the magpie moth (p.140). Fli June–July, often coming to lighted windows. Common in gardens and usua wherever its main food-plant (stinging nettle) occurs. T, ex Ic; most of Sco

Meal Moth *Pyralis farinalis*   Pyralidae
24mm. Found in corn mills, grain stores and outbuildings. Flies June–Augu resting on walls by day with wings flattened and abdomen curved upward scuttles away when disturbed, instead of flying. Caterpillars feed on stor grain and cereal refuse, September–May, but sometimes taking nearly tw years to reach full size. T.

Common Clothes Moth *Tineola bisselliella*   Tineidae
11–15mm. A familiar pale-coloured household pest, mainly flyi May–September, but with a longer season in heated buildings; it cannot li outdoors in temperate regions. Central heating has enabled it to extend range and produce up to four generations annually. Caterpillars feed o woollen textiles, fur and hair, as well as vegetable matter. The larva makes protective tube of silk and fibres of its food material which gets covered debris and droppings. Fabrics which have been 'enriched' with spilt food soiled with other organic matter are especially liable to be attacked. D cleaning and the increased use of synthetic fibres and chemically-treat materials have caused a reduction in the damage caused by this species recent years. T.

Tapestry Moth *Trichophaga tapetzella*   Tineidae
16–25mm. Distinguished from other 'clothes moths' by its larger size a white-and-blackish forewings; can resemble a bird dropping when restir Flies May–October. Caterpillars can feed on coarser material than oth species, including horse hair. Tapestry moths require damp conditions and a more likely to be found in outbuildings than in occupied houses. T, ex Ic.

Brown House Moth
Hofmannophila pseudospretella   Oecophoridae
19–23mm. Runs away when disturbed, with its wings overlapped across back. Each forewing is marked by three conspicuous dark spots. Brown hou moths are found between May and October, living outdoors as well as buildings; may enter houses from birds' nests in the eaves or in neighbouri trees. Caterpillars feed on both animal and vegetable matter – seeds, stor products, débris between floor boards, birds' nest materials, woollens, wir bottle corks, tennis ball coverings and even polythene and polystyrene. The need fairly damp conditions, but are able to go into a quiescent state whenev the surrounding atmosphere is temporarily unfavourable. T.

White-shouldered House Moth *Endrosis sarcitrella*   Oecophorida
14–20mm. Recognisable by white head and thorax. Occurs May–Octob Less common than last species but found in similar habitats, including bird nests. Shows the same reluctance to fly when disturbed. Caterpillars a vegetarian scavengers. T.

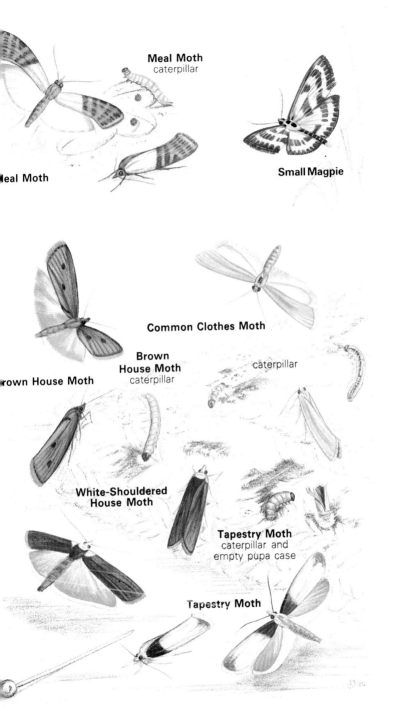

Meal Moth
caterpillar

Meal Moth

Small Magpie

Common Clothes Moth

Brown House Moth
caterpillar

caterpillar

Brown House Moth

White-Shouldered House Moth

Tapestry Moth
caterpillar and empty pupa case

Tapestry Moth

Insects More Unwelcome Guests

Buildings provide the ideal environment for harmful insects by offering them protection from the weather, freedom from natural predators, and sometimes unlimited food supplies. Following species are widely distributed.

Pharaoh's Ant *Monomorium pharaonis* Hymenoptera: Formicidae
Workers 2–2·4mm, yellow with brown-tipped abdomen; queens 4–4·8mm, similar but darker; males 3mm, black. Probably an African species but now ubiquitous. Pharaoh's ant infests bakeries, restaurants, hospitals and other heated premises, feeding on sweet substances and meat, and nesting in crevices at temperatures of around 30°C. Eradicated using baits containing a synthetic hormone which arrests development and sterilises the queens.

Cockroaches (Dictyoptera) are fast-scuttling, flat-bodied, beetle-like insects with long antennae and spiked legs. Spp. scavenging in kitchens, bakeries and other heated places are probably all of African origin despite such names as German cockroach *Blatella germanica*, American cockroach *Periplaneta americana*, etc. **Common cockroach** *Blatta orientalis* (**Blattidae**) is a nocturnal, cosmopolitan insect, probably present in B since 16th century. 17·5–28·7mm. Males dark reddish-brown. Females ('black-beetles') very dark brown, with vestigial wings. Neither sex can fly.

Bristle-Tails (Thysanura) are primitive wingless insects with long antennae and three long, thin, tail-like processes.

Silverfish *Lepisma saccharina* Lepismatidae
10mm, covered with silvery scales. Best known of bristle-tails (Thysanura), primitive wingless insects with long antennae and three long, thin long, thin, tail-like processes. Feeds on starchy matter in kitchens; also damage books and papers – can digest cellulose.

Cat Flea *Ctenocephalides felis* Pulicidae
Fleas (Siphonaptera) are small. wingless, laterally flattened, blood-sucking insects renowned for their jumping. Fleas found in buildings are dependent on the warm-blooded occupants – rodents, bats, nesting birds, human beings and their pets. The larvae do not suck blood. Cat flea (*c.* 2mm.) probably the commonest indoor flea since improved hygiene reduced numbers of *Pulex irritans*, our ancestors' constant associate. Cat fleas also attack humans.

Beetles (Coleoptera) generally have two pairs of wings, with the tough and often colourful forewings (elytra) concealing the transparent hindwings when these are present. Three serious pests are considered here.

Varied Carpet Beetle *Anthrenus verbasci* Dermestidae
1·7–3·3mm. Black and scaly, with three whitish bands.

Fur Beetle *Attagenus pellio* Dermestidae
4–6mm. Black and downy, with a white spot on each elytron. Dermestid beetles are downy or scaly, have clubbed antennae, and usually have two compound eyes and a large simple eye. They feign death when disturbed. Their hairy larvae are the notorious 'woolly bears', and those of the above species can destroy woollen fabrics, skins, furs and museum specimens.

Furniture Beetle *Anobium punctatum* Anobiidae
3–4·5mm. Reddish or dark brown, with yellowish down. The head is 'hooded' by forward-projecting thorax. Signs of presence are 'woodworm' holes in furniture, etc, made by emerging adults, and tell-tale heaps of wood-dust. Worst damage caused internally by larvae burrowing beneath the surface.

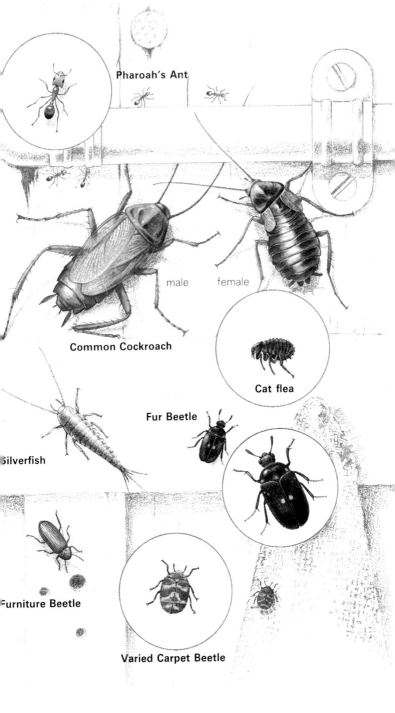

Pharoah's Ant

male   female

Common Cockroach

Cat flea

Silverfish

Fur Beetle

Furniture Beetle

Varied Carpet Beetle

Insects   Garden Species

Gardening books usually regard insects merely as 'friends' or 'foes', ignoring the possibility that anyone might find them interesting or beautiful and actually enjoy having them around. All the following are common in gardens and usually occur on wasteland. Measurements quoted are for body length.

Violet Ground Beetle *Carabus violaceus*   Coleoptera: Carabidae
22–28mm. A fast-running carnivore; black and shiny, margins of thorax and elytra tinged purple. Mainly seen June–August. T, ex Ic.

Devil's Coach-horse *Staphylinus olens*   Coleoptera: Staphylinidae
20–28mm. Entirely black. Has the short elytra and exposed abdominal segments characteristic of the rove beetle family. It curls its abdomen over the thorax when alarmed, hence the alternative name of **cocktail beetle**. A nocturnal predator and carnivorous scavenger, hiding under stones and logs by day; sometimes enters houses. T, except the N.

Cockchafer *Melolontha melolontha*   Coleoptera: Scarabaeidae
20–25mm. A bulky, unmistakable, nocturnal beetle which often thuds against lighted windows; May–June. Males have fan-like antennae. Larvae are root feeders, damaging grassland. T, ex Ic, Fi, No.

Seven-spot Ladybird *Coccinella septempunctata*
Coleoptera: Coccinellidae
5·5–7·5mm, the largest of common ladybirds. Usually has seven spots, one spot shared by both the red elytra. The smaller, extremely variable **two-spot ladybird** *Adalia bipunctata* is equally at home in towns, often hibernating in buildings. Ladybirds and their larvae prey on aphids. Both spp. T.

Blackfly or **Bean Aphid** *Aphis fabae*
Hemiptera: Homoptera: Aphididae
2–3mm. A black member of a vast group of minute, sap-sucking, honeydew-exuding bugs, many of which are known as 'greenfly'; the despair of gardeners but of great importance to ants, predatory insects and small birds. Blackfly eggs laid in late summer on primary host plants, spindle *Euonymus europaeus*, *Philadelphus* and *Viburnum*, hatch into wingless, parthenogenetic females, which produce a wingless second generation. The third generation includes winged individuals which can fly to the secondary hosts – bean plants and others – where they continue to proliferate parthenogentically. Males appear in late summer when both sexes return to primary host. T. **Rose aphids** *Macrosiphum rosae* are equally unwelcome. T, ex Ic.

Common Earwig *Forficula auricularia*   Dermaptera: Forficulidae
11–15mm; pincers strongly curved in males, almost straight in females. Hides during the day under bark, rubble or rubbish, or in garden canes, hollow plant stems and cracks in woodwork. T.

Common Field Grasshopper *Chorthippus brunneus*
Orthoptera (Saltatoria): Acrididae
15–25mm, females larger than males. Vary in colour (or colours); buff, brown, purple, green, blackish. Distinctive sharply-angled 'hour-glass' mark on thorax; underside of thorax hairy, wings well developed. Adults found late June–early November, in gardens that are not too 'neat'. They prefer dry places, often where there is concrete or asphalt; commonest on well-vegetated, rubbly waste sites, even in city centres. T, ex Ic.

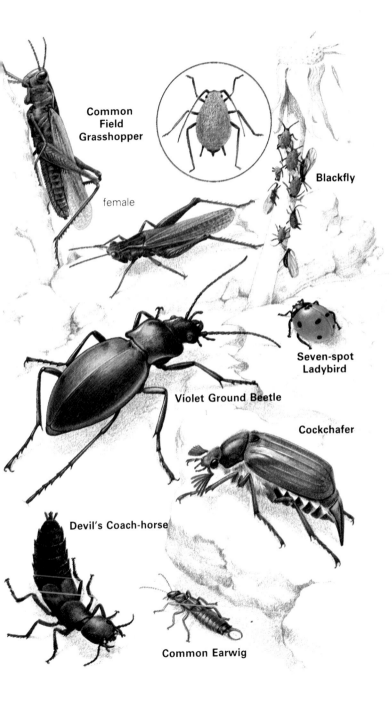

Common
Field
Grasshopper

female

Blackfly

Seven-spot
Ladybird

Violet Ground Beetle

Cockchafer

Devil's Coach-horse

Common Earwig

Insects   More Garden Species (Hymenoptera)

Flying hymenopteran insects have two pairs of membraneous wings, and all hymenopterans, except sawflies and wood-wasps, have a constricted 'waist' between abdomen and thorax. The group includes many parasites, like *Apanteles* (p.132), and insects with complex communal societies based on one or more fertile females (queens) served by sterile females (workers) and males.

Honey Bee *Apis mellifera*   Apidae
13–18mm. An introduced insect, probably from Asia, valued as a pollinator and exploited for its honey. Numbers of urban apiarists have increased since modern agricultural practices, especially crop-spraying, made the countryside a relatively hostile environment for bees. London hives, can yield over twice as much honey as country hives. Besides visiting park and garden flowers, town bees collect honeydew from limes. Introduced T.

Bumblebees
Bumblebees (Apidae), unlike honey bees, do not provide for winter. Mated females hibernate, each starting a new colony in spring. As with the honey bees, workers and queens are armed with stings. Urban spp. include: **Buff-tailed Bumblebee** *Bombus terrestris*. 18mm (workers) – 25mm (queens). The female has orange-buff tail in B and Ir, but is white-tailed elsewhere. Tail is off-white in males and workers. Nests underground, often in rodent burrows. T, ex Ic, Fi. **Common Garden Bumblebee** *Bombus pascuorum*. 14mm (workers) – 18mm (queens). Brown, with black hairs present in variable amounts, but never forming a band across thorax. Nests on the surface, carding grass blades into shreds for nest material – hence the name 'carder-bee'. T, ex Ic.

Leaf-Cutter Bees
Leaf-Cutter Bees (Megachilidae) annoy gardeners by cutting semi-circular pieces from the leaves of roses and other plants. The rolled pieces are used to form nests of cylindrical cells in decaying wood, plant stems or flower pots, each cell provisioned for a larva's benefit. *Megachile centuncularis* (10–12mm) is one of the commoner spp.; June–July. T, ex Ic.

Common Wasp *Vespula vulgaris*   Vespidae
14–18mm. Yellow band across front of thorax parallel-sided. In the very similar **German wasp** *V. germanica* thoracic band has a prominent bulge. Social insects; both spp. construct football-size paper nests from wood-pulp, in ground or buildings. Wasps are a nuisance at meal-times and sting if provoked, but they destroy many insect pests. Common wasp T, ex Ic. German wasp T.

Black Garden Ant *Lasius niger*   Formicidae
3·5–9mm, queens larger than males and workers. Social insects with wingless workers, like all ants; make galleried nests under rockery stones, paving slabs, etc; tend and protect aphids for their honeydew; sometimes invade houses for food. In summer the synchronised emergence and nuptial flight of winged males and females from different nests provide a feast for birds, and sometimes cause traffic chaos in the streets. T, ex Ic.

Horntail *Urocerus gigas*   Siricidae
18–35mm, female with long ovipositor, much larger than the male. A perfectly harmless wood-wasp which sometimes emerges from new woodwork. T.

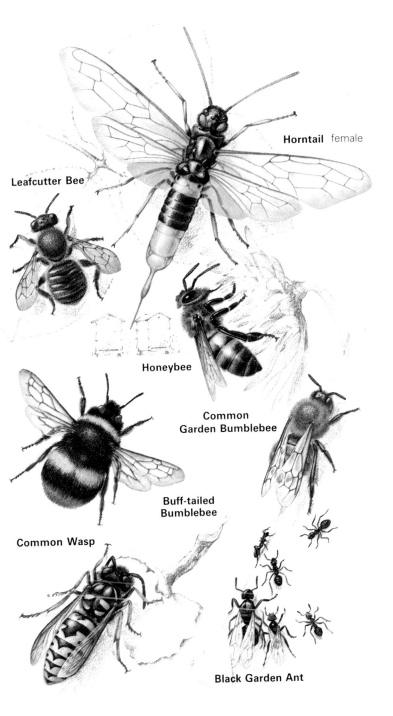

Horntail female

Leafcutter Bee

Honeybee

Common
Garden Bumblebee

Buff-tailed
Bumblebee

Common Wasp

Black Garden Ant

Insects   Flies (Diptera) and Lacewings (Neuroptera)

Flies have one pair of wings, the hind wings having been replaced by two balancing organs (halateres). Sizes given are body lengths.

Crane-flies ('Daddy-long-legs')   Tipulidae
Slim-bodied, narrow-winged, long-legged flies of many genera. *Tipula paludosa* (c. 25mm) is common in August and September. Larvae ('leather-jackets') infest the soil, damaging grassland by attacking the roots. T, ex Ic, Ir.

House-fly *Musca domestica*   Muscidae
8–9mm. Grey thorax, buffish abdomen. Follows man everywhere, breeding in organic waste, contaminating food and spreading disease. T.

Lesser House-fly *Fannia canicularis*   Fanniidae
6–8mm. Females similarly coloured to *domestca*; males with pale patches at base of abdomen. Males circle centre of room under a hanging lamp or other focal point. Eggs laid in wet decaying matter, including excrement. T.

Bluebottles (Blow-flies) *Calliphora* spp.   Calliphoridae
8·5–11mm. Hairy and blue-bodied; buzz noisily. Two commonest species are *C. vicina* and *C. vomitoria*. Males are nectar-feeders. Females lay eggs in animal flesh. Larvae are the 'gentles' fishermen use for bait.

Greenbottles *lucilia* spp.   Calliphoridae
Metallic-green sun-lovers, seldom coming indoors. *L. caesar* (9–10mm) is one of commonest species, often numerous around dustbins. T, ex Ic.

Flesh-flies *Sarcophaga* spp.   Sarcoghagidae
Grey, with striped thorax and speckled abdomen. *S. carnaria* (14·5–15·5mm) is one of commonest. Eggs hatch within female. Larvae, when deposited on meat or carrion, prepare it for consumption with a liquefying enzyme. T, ex Ic.

Episyrphus balteatus   Syrphidae
10mm. One of the more easily recognisable hover-flies, so-called from their ability to hang, apparently motionless, on rapidly vibrating wings. Seen with related species on flower beds, especially umbels. Numbers sometimes greatly increased by influx of migrants. Larvae prey on aphids. T, ex Ic.

Syrphus ribesii   Syrphidae
11–14mm. One of several hover-flies superficially resembling a black-and-yellow wasp. Harmless and worth encouraging; slug-like larvae eat aphids. T.

Drone-fly *Eristalis tenax*   Syrphidae
12–14mm. A common hover-fly resembling a male hive bee. Feeds on nectar and pollen; often seen on ivy flowers in autumn. Larvae ('rat-tailed maggots') live on and in putrefying matter in ponds, water-butts, gutters and wet vegetable refuse, and breathe when submerged through a long extensible tube like a snorkel. T, ex Ic, D, FS.

Lacewings have four gauzy, netted wings and long antennae. Wings are held tent-wise when at rest. ***Chrysopa carnea*** (Chrysopedae) 7–10mm, is one of the green lacewings attracted to lighted windows at night. Hibernates in buildings. Lays each egg at the end of a stalk formed of hardened mucus. Both larvae and adults feed on aphids. T, ex Ic.

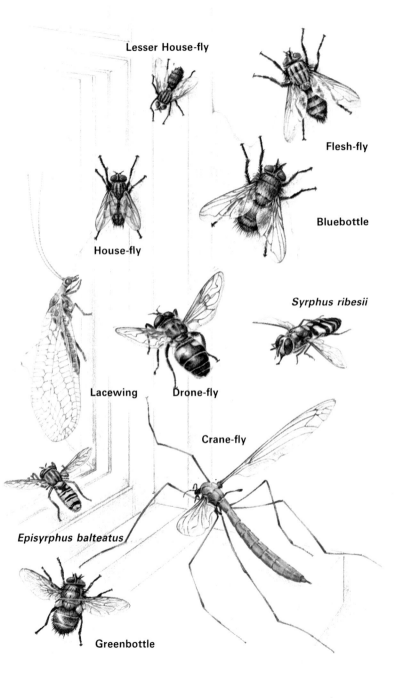

Lesser House-fly

Flesh-fly

House-fly

Bluebottle

Lacewing

Drone-fly

Syrphus ribesii

Crane-fly

Episyrphus balteatus

Greenbottle

Insects   Aquatic Species

Urban development often means the loss of wetland habitats, and garden ponds can help to conserve aquatic life. All the following insects can fly and are therefore able to take advantage of these additional habitats.

Great Diving Beetle *Dytiscus marginalis*   Coleoptera: Dytiscidae
26–35mm. A typical carnivorous water beetle – stream-lined, with hind legs specially adapted for swimming; both adults and larvae dependent on air taken from the surface. Adults' prey includes tadpoles, young fish and others of its own kind. The larvae are equally voracious. T, ex Ic.

Whirligig Beetle *Gyrinus natator*   Coleoptera: Gyrinidae
5–7mm. Commonest member of a difficult group of gregarious beetles which attract attention by their habit of rapidly swimming in circles on the surface of still or slow-flowing water. Black and oval, with front legs longer than the others. Each eye is divided into two, for vision above and below water. Both adults and larvae are predatory. T, ex Ic.

Bugs (Hemiptera) of several spp., all belonging to the Sub-Order Heteroptera, are adapted for life in water or on its surface.

Common Pondskater *Gerris lacustris*   Gerridae
8–10mm. The sp. of *Gerris* most likely to appear on garden ponds; common on most still waters, rapidly covering the surface with sweeping movements of its long middle legs, which are placed well behind the front pair. Preys on anything touching the water, sometimes egg-laying damselflies. T, ex Ic.

Backswimmer *Notonecta glauca*   Notonectidae
14mm. The sp. of *Notonecta* usually found in towns. Swims upside-down, propelling itself with its long, hair-fringed back legs. A predator with piercing mouth-parts, Often called 'water boatman', a name now usually reserved for the corixid bugs, which are smaller. T, ex Ic.

Dragonflies and **Damselflies** (Odonata) have two pairs of wings. Dragonflies (Anisoptera) rest with them outspread and, in most cases, their eyes touch each other. Damselflies (Zygoptera) rest with wings held vertically or pointing backwards; their eyes are widely separated. Damselfly nymphs have three leaf-like external gills at the hind end; dragonfly nymphs have gills concealed in the rectum. Both adults and nymphs are predatory, the nymphs seizing prey with an extending lower lip, the 'mask'.

Brown Hawker *Aeshna grandis*   Aeshnidae
c. 73mm. A brown dragonfly with amber wings; wingspan 102mm male has blue markings at base of abdomen. Frequents most urban wetland sites, but often seen away from water, even over city traffic; July–October. T, ex Ic, Sco; rare north and west En.

Common Darter *Sympetrum striolatum*   Libellulidae
c. 37mm. The commonest small dragonfly; wingspan *c.* 58mm; June–November, numbers swelled by migrants. Frequents park and garden ponds; often basks on sun-warmed surfaces. Bred in emergency water tanks on London bomb sites. T, ex Ic, Fi.

Blue-tailed Damselfly *Ischnura elegans*   Coenagriidae
c. 31mm. The commonest urban damselfly, frequenting pools and canals, even moderately polluted waters; mainly May–August. T, ex Ic.

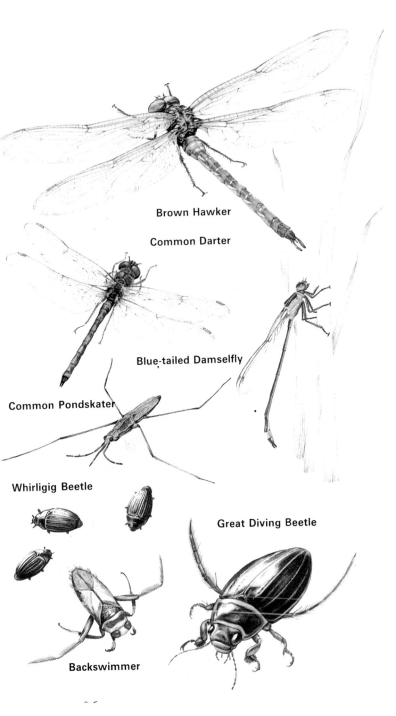

Brown Hawker

Common Darter

Blue-tailed Damselfly

Common Pondskater

Whirligig Beetle

Great Diving Beetle

Backswimmer

Arachnids   Scorpions, Harvestmen and Spiders

Like the insects, the invertebrates covered by the next three plates have segmented bodies and jointed legs, and are therefore classed with them as arthropods. Insects are arthropods with three pairs of legs; arachnids, (spiders, harvestmen, scorpions, pseudoscorpions, mites and ticks) are wingless arthropods which usually have four pairs of walking legs. Unlike insects, they have no antennae. Measurements given are of body length. More detailed descriptions can be found in *The Country Life Guide to Spiders*.

Euscorpius flavicaudis   Scorpiones: Chactidae
Up to 40mm. A harmless scorpion of the Mediterranean region recorded from town buildings in C. and N. France, and several places in England. Early occurrences attributable to movement of goods by rail and water; now spread by motor vehicles, especially holiday traffic. Able to establish itself in places beyond its normal range. Present at Sheerness, Kent for over a century; also known from a railway station NE. of London.

Harvestmen (Opiliones) bear a superficial resemblance to spiders, but their bodies are not divided into two parts. Are not venomous and do not produce silk. **Phalangium opilio** (Phalangiidae) is common in gardens and waste places. 4–9mm. Long legs, dark brown 'saddle' on dorsal surface; white, unspotted underside. Eyes on a turret-like protruberance. The male recognisable from 'horns' on its jaws (*chelicerae*)..

Spiders (Araneae) have the body divided into two sections; carapace (head and thorax) and abdomen. Chelicerae armed with poison fangs. Produce silk from spinners at end of abdomen, but do not all make webs.

Cross Spider or Garden Spider *Araneus diadematus*   Araneidae
Female *c*. 12mm, male *c*. 8mm. Recognisable by cross-shaped pattern of white spots on abdomen. Full-grown in summer, when large orb webs adorn trees and shrubs everywhere. T.

Araniella cucurbitina   Araneidae
Female *c*. 6mm, male *c*. 4mm. Green abdomen with red blotch above spinners. Usually on bushes. Web small, shape varies according to space occupied; often placed horizontally between leaves. T, ex Ic.

Zygiella x-notata   Araneidae
Female *c*. 6mm, male *c*. 4mm. A silver-grey, brown-edged leaf-pattern (folium) on abdomen. Web with one segment missing; often across window frames, T? (an unconfirmed 1983 record from Ic).

Linyphia triangularis   Linyphiidae
Both sexes 5–6mm. A brown pattern with toothed edges down middle of abdomen. Webs hammock-like, with silken scaffolding above and below; obvious in garden hedges when covered with dew. T, ex Ic.

Dysdera crocata   Dysderidae
Female *c*. 11–15mm, male 9–10mm. Abdomen pale grey to nearly white; carapace dark red, legs a brighter red. Large chelicerae, with which it captures woodlice. Has six eyes – most spiders have eight. Lives under stones in waste places, rubbish tips and gardens. T, ex Fi, Ic, Sw.

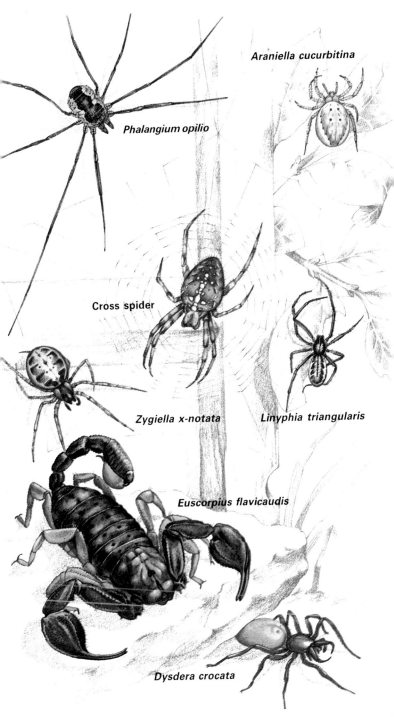

Phalangium opilio

Araniella cucurbitina

Cross spider

Zygiella x-notata

Linyphia triangularis

Euscorpius flavicaudis

Dysdera crocata

Arachnids More Spiders

The spiders illustrated here are associated with buildings, some living inside, others outside.

Amaurobius similis Amaurobiidae
Female 9–12mm, male 6–8mm. Carapace reddish-brown, head darker than thorax. Abdomen has dark central stripe divided longitudinally by a lighter streak and flanked by a yellowish area. Legs marked with dark rings (annulations). Frequents outhouses, old weather-boarding and crumbling walls. Constructs silken retreat in a crevice and builds ragged, matted web of sticky, bluish-white, finely-combed silk round entrance. T, ex Fi, Ic, Sw.

Segestria senoculata Segestriidae
Both sexes 7–10mm. Six-eyed. Elongated abdomen usually light brown with chestnut markings suggesting dorsal pattern of an adder *Vipera berus*. Another inhabitant of old walls; also found under stones and bark. Makes silken tube in wall crevice with 'trip wires' radiating from entrance. T, ex Ic.

Zebra Spider *Salticus scenicus* Salticidae
Female 5–7mm, male 5–6mm. Black abdomen with white band near 'waist' and two pairs of white stripes at sides. A sun-loving jumping spider of walls, parapets, fences, rockeries and pavings. Stalks prey and pounces on it. T, but of only casual occurrence in Ic.

Spitting Spider *Scytodes thoracica* Scytodidae
Both sexes 5–6mm. Six-eyed. Carapace and abdomen of similar size and coloration; hind part of carapace raised above fore part; abdomen rather globular. Slender, annulated legs. Slow-moving immobilises prey with gum from chelicerae; falls on victim as two sets of sticky threads. Frequents houses but not common. T, ex D, FS, Ic, Ir, Sco.

Daddy-long-legs Spider *Pholcus phalangioides* Pholcidae
Both sexes 8–10mm. Cylindrical pale grey abdomen with darker markings. Very long legs; first pair over five times length of head and body. Frequents outhouses, lofts, outside lavatories, and room corners. Usually seen on ceiling, or in irregular scaffolding of its web, between wall and ceiling. T, ex FS, Ic; in S. only in Ir, mainly in S. in En; has been found in Sco (Morayshire).

Steatoda bipunctata Theridiidae
Female 4·5–7mm, male 4–5mm. Abdomen glossy, light brown to almost black; thin white line curving round foremost end; white marks sometimes form a broken, median dorsal stripe. Found in lofts, outbuildings, cellars, and sometimes outdoors. Web a collection of short strands stretching in all directions; a denser tangle near centre and gum-studded threads anchoring structure to the floor. Snares crawling insects. Probably in Ic; T elsewhere.

House spiders *Tegenaria* spp. Agelenidae
Large yellow-brown spiders with black markings that build sheet webs and cause alarm by scuttling across the carpet and appearing in the bath. At least five urban spp., but no adequate guide to their specific identification can be attempted here; their classification has been repeatedly revised. One large sp. (up to 18mm) is *T. duellica*, formerly *gigantea* and before that *propinqua*! Information on distribution is incomplete.

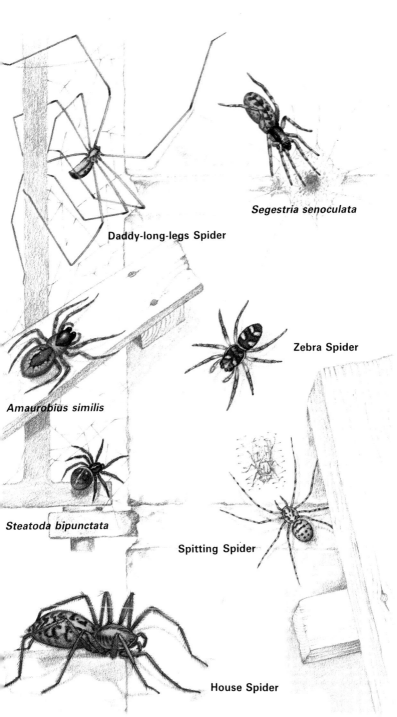

Segestria senoculata

Daddy-long-legs Spider

Zebra Spider

Amaurobius similis

Steatoda bipunctata

Spitting Spider

House Spider

Other Arthropods   Woodlice and Myriapods

Other urban arthropods include woodlice (land-living crustaceans belonging to the order Isopoda) and the unrelated animals sometimes classed together as 'myriapods', the centipedes (Chilopoda) and millipedes (Diplopoda). Measurements given are of body length.

Woodlice have seven pairs of walking legs. They have two pairs of antennae, but only one pair is obvious. Each of these larger antennae ends in a section called the flagellum – worth examining when identifying these animals. Woodlice damage seedlings but they also help break down vegetable matter to form humus. They frequent damp, dark places; those that invade houses usually die of desiccation. Only a few spp. can roll into a ball. *Oniscus asellus* (Oniscidae) is commonest sp. in gardens and waste places, especially in compost heaps and rotten wood. *c.* 16mm. Grey, with paler patches; rather shiny. Flagellum has three segments. T, ex Ic. *Porcellio scaber* (Porcellionidae) is common; often found under loose bark and in crumbling walls; can live in drier places than *Oniscus*. *c.* 17mm. Has rough 'pimply' (tuberculate) surface. Colour variable; usually slate grey, often reddish or purplish. T. *Armadilliduim vulgare* (Armadillidiidae) is commonest of spp. which roll up (pill bugs). *c.* 18mm. More 'domed' than preceding spp. Variable; usually dark slate but often yellowish with black markings. Flagellum has two segments. Common under stones, especially in calcareous districts. T, but rare in Sco. *Androniscus dentiger* (Trichoniscidae) is locally common in gardens (sometimes in greenhouses) and waste places, also in cellars and tunnels. *c.* 6mm. Usually rose-pink with dark dorsal streak. Body surface tuberculate; rear end noticably narrower than rest of body. Flagellum ends in narrow tuft of bristles. T, ex Ic, but rare in Sco and as a greenhouse animal in G and mainland Sca. Has apparently been spread by man.

Centipedes have one pair of legs per body segment, the total number rarely reaching a hundred! The animals are predators, equipped with poison claws which curve round either side of the head. *Lithobius forficatus* (Lithobiidae) is the commonest garden and wastland sp. 18–30mm. Has fifteen pairs of legs, hides under stones, etc. by day. T. *Necropholeophagus longicornis* (Geophilidae) is a common soil-dweller. 30–45mm. Bright yellow with a darker head; 49–51 pairs of legs. T, ex Ic. **House Centipede** *Scutigera coleoptrata* (Scutigeridae) measures up to 30mm. A fast-running centipede with long antennae and fifteen pairs of legs. The latter are also long, especially the last pair. Found in and around buildings. An occasional introduction into B (recorded Edinburgh, Aberdeen and Colchester) and found in Channel Islands. Otherwise T, ex FS and Ic.

Millipedes have two pairs of legs on most segments and are mainly vegetarian. *Polydesmus angustus* (Polydesmidae) 17–25mm. Largest and probably commonest of the flat-backed millipedes, in all of which the segments are heavily embossed on the dorsal surface. Found under logs, stones, etc. Has a liking for lupin roots. T, ex east G and the north.

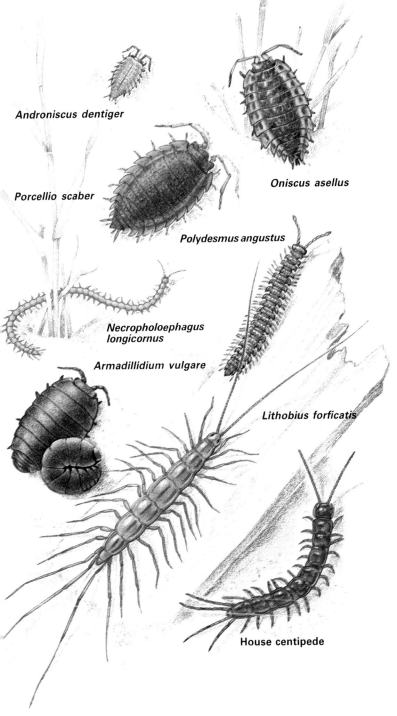

Androniscus dentiger

Oniscus asellus

Porcellio scaber

Polydesmus angustus

Necropholoephagus longicornus

Armadillidium vulgare

Lithobius forficatis

House centipede

Molluscs   Slugs and Snails

Few people like these animals. Some are serious pests, but several garden species perform a useful function by consuming vegetable waste. To identify the slugs mentioned here note position of breathing pore in relation to the mantle-shield (the flattened hump at the head end) and see whether the animal's back is keeled or rounded. In roundback slugs (Arionidae) the pore lies in the front half of the mantle; in keelback slugs (Limacidae) it is in the rear half. Lengths given are of extended animals.

Yellow Slug *Limax flavus*   Limacidae
75–100 mm. Yellow, with grey mottling; blue tentacles. Keel does not extend to the mantle. Closely associated with man, often found in cellars and outhouses, sometimes kitchens. Hides under logs, etc by day. Feeds on vegetable waste and fungi. T, ex Ic, No, Fi and most of Sw.

Netted Slug *Deroceras reticulatum*   Limacidae
35–50mm. Cream, brown or grey, usually with dark brown flecks and streaks; a white ring round breathing pore. Back with short keel. A serious pest. T.

Garden Slug *Arion hortensis* agg.   Arionidae
25–40mm. The name covers what have recently been found to be three separate but not easily distinguishable spp., two blue-black, one brownish. All three are slender and cylindrical, yellow or orange underneath, with body slime similarly coloured. Devour plants, above and below ground. T.

Large Black (or Red) Slug *Arion ater* agg.   Arionidae
100–150mm. May be black, brown, grey, brick red or cream; pale colours rare in N. A skirt-like feature touching the ground (the foot-fringe) is marked with transverse stripes). Internal anatomical differences suggest two spp. (named *A. ater* and *A. rufus*) but external appearances are no guide. Omnivorous; active on compost heaps. T; coastal in No; in greenhouses Fi.

In the following notes on snails H = height of shell, B = breadth, Wh = number of whorls. All the spp. occur in waste places as well as in gardens. The lime which they need to build their shells can be obtained from mortar.

Garden Snail *Helix aspersa*   Helicidae
Shell globular, H 25–35mm, B 25–40mm, Wh 4½–5. Distinctive markings. The largest snail normally found in towns, often crowding together under cover. B (mainly the S.) Ir, Fr, Be, Ne, west G.

Strawberry Snail *Trichia striolata*   Helicidae
Shell slightly flattened, with a slight keel. H 6–9mm, B 11–14mm, Wh 6. Variable; dark reddish to yellowish; hairy when young. A pest of strawberry beds. B, Ir, north-east Fr, Ne and south G.

Rounded Snail *Discus rotundatus*   Endodontidae
Shell flattened, H 2·5–3mm, B 5–7·5mm, Wh 6–7, tightly coiled and strongly ribbed. A wide hollow (umbilicus) on the underside. Found under stones, logs, etc. T, ex Ic and most of Fi; coastal in No.

Cellar Glass Snail *Oxychilus cellarius*   Zonitidae
Shell thin-walled and translucent, H 5–5·5mm, B 9–12 mm, Wh 5½–6, underside white. Inhabits damp places, including cellars and outbuildings. T, ex Ic, most of Fi and No.

arden Slug

Netted Slug

ellow Slug

Large Black Slug

Strawberry Snail

Garden Snail

Cellar Glass Snail

Rounded Snail

Miscellaneous Invertebrates   Aquatic Species

The following species occur in various freshwater habitats, and some of them provide an indication of pollution levels. As on p. 160, when describing shells, H, B and Wh stand respectively for 'height', 'breadth' and 'number of whorls'. Measurements for other species = body length.

Great Pond Snail *Lymnaea stagnalis*   Lymnaeidae
The largest European pond snail. Shell with pointed spire and roughly oval mouth; H 45–60mm, B 20–30mm, Wh 7–7½, the body whorl occupying two thirds of the height. Prefers hard water, slow or stagnant. Can be seen moving upside-down on the underside of the surface film, opening the respiratory pore to take in air. Consumes vegetable matter and carrion, and attacks other aquatic animals. T, ex Ic; rare in north, even in B.

Wandering Snail *Lymnaea peregra*   Lymnaeidae
Smaller and more compact than last sp. H 15–25mm, B 12–17mm, Wh 4–5. Variable; body whorl can be distended or not; mouth of shell pointed above in some forms but not others. Found in ponds, lakes, canals and slow-flowing rivers, in both hard and soft water; remarkably pollution tolerant. T.

The well-named **ramshorn snails** (Planorbidae) may also be encountered in weed-rich waters. Their shells are coiled in a flattish spiral. *Planorbis planorbis* is one of the commoner spp.

Zebra Mussel *Dreissena polymorpha*   Dreissenidae
An unmistakable bivalve mollusc, the brown and yellow bands suggesting its name; length normally 25–40mm, H 12–18mm, B 17–26mm. Anchors itself to solid objects with sticky threads. Zebra mussels occur in canals, docks, slow rivers and reservoirs; can choke water mains. Originally confined to S. Russia, but now spread over much of Europe (T, ex Ic, Ir, No.). They reached Surrey Commercial Docks, London in 1824, probably with imported timber, and spread throughout England. Also occurs in Scottish Lowlands.

Hog Louse or Water Slater *Asellus aquaticus*   Isopoda: Asellidae
8–12mm. A non-swimming freshwater crustacean resembling a woodlouse (to which it is related) but with longer legs and antennae. Found in ponds, lakes and slow-moving streams; most abundant in rather polluted waters, amongst the plants and especially common in 'blankets' of green algae. T.

Freshwater Shrimp *Gammarus pulex*   Amphipoda: Gammaridae
15 – 20mm. A laterally flattened crustacean which swims on its side. It resembles, and is related to, the sandhoppers found on the seashore. Occurs in shallow, well-oxygenated running water and is sensitive to pollution. Its reappearance in an urban stream indicates an improvement in water quality. T, ex Ic, No.

River Worm or Bloodworm *Tubifex tubifex*
Oligochaeta: Tubificidae
Up to 85mm. One of many red, segmented worms inhabiting polluted ponds and watercourses. Haemoglobin in their blood accounts for their colour and enables them to exploit what little oxygen is available. They protrude 'tail-first' from tubes they build in the mud; their vast numbers colour exposed mud banks pink. When the Thames in Central London was still polluted they were collected at low tide for sale to aquarists as fish food.

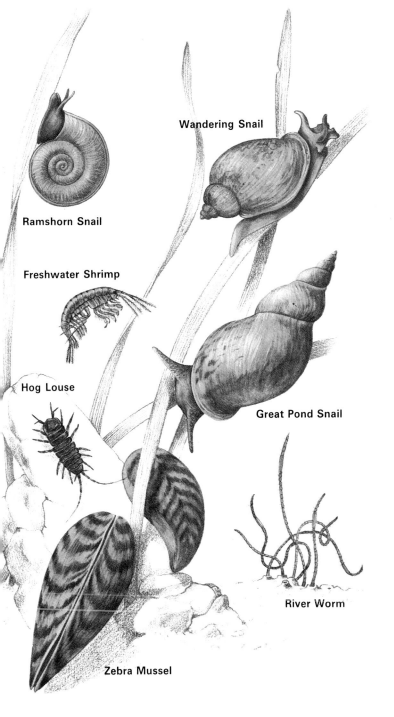

Wandering Snail

Ramshorn Snail

Freshwater Shrimp

Hog Louse

Great Pond Snail

River Worm

Zebra Mussel

Fish

Angling is a popular pastime with town-dwellers, and park lakes and urban reservoirs are often stocked with fish to meet this demand. The canals and the pools on industrial wasteland also support a fish population, and anti-pollution measures have enabled fish to return to rivers and streams which were, until recently, practically devoid of life. The remarkable improvement in the tidal reaches of the Thames is demonstrated by the fact that salmon *Salmo salar* can once again migrate through the heart of London. Fish grow throughout life and the lengths quoted below are often exceeded.

Roach *Rutilus rutilus*   Cyprinidae
10–25cm. Can be confused with **rudd** *Scardinius erythrophthalmus* but the position of the pelvic fins is diagnostic – directly below the front edge of dorsal fin in roach, slightly nearer the head in rudd. Roach are the fish most often introduced into park lakes and reservoirs. In 1971 the population in the Serpentine in London's Hyde Park was estimated at 50,000. Roach also occur in canals and pools on industrial wasteland. Fairly pollution tolerant. T, ex Ic.

Common Carp *Cyprinus carpio*   Cyprinidae
20–40cm at three-four years. Four barbels on upper lip and a long dorsal fin. A native of E. Europe and C. Asia originally introduced to W. Europe to be bred for food. Now widely redistributed for angling and present in park waters, canals and rivers. King carp, mirror carp and leather carp (varieties produced by selective breeding) also occur. T, ex Ic; an important food fish in F, G, (and E. Europe).

Perch *Perca fluviatilis*   Percidae
15–30cm. Distinctively striped; two greenish-grey dorsal fins, other fins red. Found in rivers, canals and industrial wasteland pools. Introduced into park lakes and reservoirs; an estimated 30,000 in London's Serpentine in 1971. T, ex Ic.

Rainbow Trout *Salmo gairdneri*   Salmonidae
25–50cm. A purple band along each side; dark spots from head to tail and on dorsal fin. A N. American fish extensively farmed for food; occasionally released or escapes into rivers, but usually fails to establish a wild breeding population. Has been introduced into reservoirs to provide fishing, notably around London. T.

Eel *Anguilla anguilla*   Anguillidae
30–100cm, females larger than males. Migratory fish, starting life in the Sargasso Sea and ascending the rivers of Europe as elvers. Adults change appearance before returning to the sea; head becomes more pointed, back colour darkens and yellow underparts turn silver. Eels occur in all urban wetland habitats; can travel short distances overland to reach garden ponds. Tolerant of quite serious pollution, but unable to survive in deoxygenated water. This prevents migration along grossly polluted rivers. T.

Three-spined Stickleback *Gasterosteus aculeatus*   Gasterosteidae
4–6cm. Easily recognised from its small size, three dorsal spines and the breeding colours of the male. Familiar to all town children with access to a pond, stream or canal. It is unable to tolerate serious pollution and its return to an urban watercourse indicates an increased level of dissolved oxygen. T.

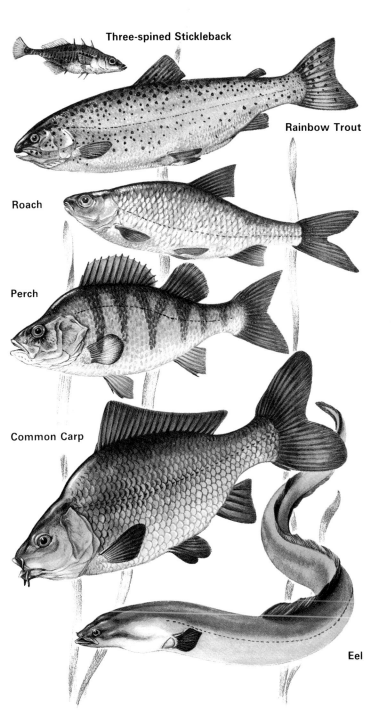

Three-spined Stickleback

Rainbow Trout

Roach

Perch

Common Carp

Eel

Amphibians and Reptiles

Northern Europe has fewer species of amphibians and reptiles than the Mediterranean countries and these cold-blooded animals are poorly represented in the British Isles. The amphibians considered here resort to water for spawning, and their offspring are aquatic, gill-breathing tadpoles. They breed, after hibernation.

Northern towns provide few habitats for reptiles. Of those mentioned below only the wall lizard is associated with buildings; the others occur on industrial wasteland and railway embankments.

Smooth Newt *Triturus vulgaris*   Salamandridae
Usually under 100mm. Smooth-skinned; male has orange belly with large dark spots; also spotted above during breeding season, when long dorsal crest is developed. Female has yellow belly with smaller spots. Breed mainly March-July, spending rest of time on land, concealed during day under logs, etc. Hibernating newts found under rockery stones are sometimes reported as lizards! T, ex Ic.

Great Crested Newt *Triturus cristatus*   Salamandridae
80–142mm. Dark brown, black-spotted, warty skin. Orange belly with black spots. Male has high, jagged dorsal crest in breeding season and whitish flash on tail. May be found in water in any month. T, ex Ic, Ir. Legally protected.

Common Toad *Bufo bufo*   Bufonidae
Usually under 90mm, males smaller than females. Brown warty skin; two large glands behind head. Breed soon after hibernation; spawn laid in strings. Tadpoles have more rounded tail tip than those of frogs. Many toads killed by road traffic when migrating to traditional breeding ponds. T, ex Ic, Ir.

Common (Grass) Frog *Rana temporaria*   Ranidae
Usually under 80mm. Smooth, damp skin; colour variable, often reddish. Hibernation sites include compost heaps. Spawn laid in clumps. Frogs have become scarce in intensively farmed areas, and town and garden ponds play an important part in their conservation. T, ex Ic.

Slow-worm *Anguis fragilis*   Anguidae
A legless lizard, usually under 400mm; old specimens usually have a blunt, regenerated tail. Young (born alive) golden above with black dorsal stripe and underside. Adult females usually retain stripe, dark underparts and flanks; males more uniformly coloured. Some have blue spots, usually males. Often found under corrugated iron and other rubbish. Feed on slugs and therefore to be welcomed by gardeners! T, ex Ic, Ir.

Common Lizard *Lacerta vivipara*   Lacertidae
Up to 180mm. Dark markings (variable in pattern) on a brown or olive background. Belly usually orange, spotted with black, in males; paler, sometimes whitish in females. Live-bearing normal; may lay eggs in S. Europe. T, ex Ic.

Common Wall Lizard *Podarcis muralis*   Lacertidae
Can exceed 200mm. More flattened than common lizard; larger head and limbs; colour extremely variable. Lays eggs. A skilled climber, frequenting walls and paved areas. F, Jersey, south Be and Ne. Occasionally introduced into En; colony present in London suburbs for over 20 years.

Common Wall Lizard

Common Lizard

Slow-worm

young

male

female

Common Frog

Common Toad

Great Crested Newt
breeding female

breeding male

Great Crested Newt

Smooth Newt

Grey Heron

Coot on nest

Great Crested Grebe

Birds   Grebes, Herons and Rails

Many birds can live well in urban surroundings, but success depends on human behaviour. Birds are still persecuted in some areas, and nests are vandalised. The symbolised distribution notes are not intended to indicate that a species is established in towns throughout its range. Measurements quoted are of length, bill-tip to tail-tip; acc = accidental visitor.

The following will frequent urban wetland sites if given protection.

Great Crested Grebe *Podiceps cristatus*   Podicipedidae
48cm. Unmistakable in summer; lacks ear-tufts in winter. Juv. striped on head and neck. Dives for fish. Once persecuted for its plumage but now breeding on some urban waters, including lakes in C. London used for various kinds of public recreation. Nests normally built of aquatic vegetation, but may consist more of twigs in town parks: paper sometimes used. Occasionally nests on concrete reservoir banks. T, acc Ic.

Little Grebe *Tachybaptus ruficollis*   Podicipedidae
27cm. Stocky, short-necked and 'blunt-ended'. Cheeks and throat brownish-buff in winter. Dives repeatedly. Utters a whinnying trill. Nest a floating raft of water plants anchored to submerged vegetation.

Breeds on undisturbed, well-vegetated waters with a good food supply – aquatic invertebrates, tadpoles and small fish. Industrial wasteland pools, disused docks, canal reservoirs and private lakes provide better conditions than conventional park waters, but has bred in C. London. More numerous on autumn passage, sometimes occurring in flocks; often frequents estuaries in winter. T, ex Ic, Fi; rare No.

Moorhen

Coot

Little Grebe

Moorhen chick

Grey Heron *Ardea cinerea*   Ardeidae

90cm. Long neck may be held in when bird at rest; always retracted in flight, when broad wings and projecting legs noticeable. Nests colonially, normally in trees but has nested on zoo aviaries containing breeding herons (London and Stockholm). Long established heronries in C. Amsterdam and London suburbs, and one in London's Regent's Park since 1968. Herons sometimes raid garden fish ponds; have taken fish from roof-garden of a Kensington department store. T, ex lc as breeding sp. Some Norwegian birds reach lc in winter. Herons are sometimes reported as 'storks'. **White storks** *Ciconia ciconia* do nest in the area (D, F, G, LC) sometimes on town buildings, but their numbers have seriously declined.

Coot *Fulica atra*   Rallidae (Rails)

38cm. Distinguished from moorhen by white frontal shield, all-black plumage and lobed toes. Juv. with whitish underparts. Dives for plants and grazes park lawns. Will eat bread. Usually nests away from bank, often making use of trees touching water. Fiercely territorial when nesting. Flocks outside breeding season. Of local occurrence as a town breeding bird. T, acc lc.

Moorhen *Gallinula chloropus*   Rallidae

33cm. Flirts white undertail coverts. Jerks head when swimming. Juv. brownish, with adults' white flank markings; lacks red frontal shield.

Commoner in towns than coot; on all wetland sites including small ponds. Nests in waterside vegetation, on structures in water; sometimes builds on nests of other species; nest materials can include paper. Omnivorous; readily accepts bread. T, acc lc.

Canada Goose

Mute Sw

female **Tufted Duck** male

Birds Waterfowl (Anatidae)

The popularity of waterfowl often prompts parks administrators to put domesticated ducks and geese on their lakes, and some authorities also introduce pinioned birds of species which live wild in Europe and elsewhere. These semi-captive waterfowl attract wild duck, which may sometimes stay to breed. Puzzling hybrids are occasionally produced, and mallard nearly always mate with the domesticated ducks.

Mallard *Anas platyrhynchos*
58cm. Male in 'eclipse' plumage (during summer moult) closely resembles female but has darker crown and yellow bill.

The commonest urban duck, but not found in every town. Most numerous where fed by public, males usually outnumbering females. Females sometimes injured when several pursuing males attempt mating. Can become very tame, feeding from the hand. In some cities (e.g. London, Copenhagen) will nest away from water; policemen hold up traffic to allow female and ducklings to cross streets. C. London nest-sites include roof-tops, hollow trees and boats moored on the Thames. Wild birds breeding with domesticated forms of mallard have strangely plumaged offspring, often showing much white. T.

Tufted Duck *Aythya fuligula*
43cm. Has compact shape of typical diving duck. Male's flanks pale brown in eclipse plumage. Females and imms. may have white patch at base of bill, causing confusion with female **scaup** *A. marila*, scaup are larger (with no tuft).

Not as widespread as mallard as urban breeding birds, but gaining ground. Large numbers in winter where not persecuted, on reservoirs, wasteland pools, dock basins and park lakes, especially in parks with introduced water-

Domesticated forms
of Mallard

Muscovy Duck

male **Mallard** female

fowl. Wintering birds ringed in St. James's Park, London found in Sweden, Finland and USSR. Will take bread, sometimes from the hand. T.

Muscovy Duck *Cairina moschata* domestic variety

Males *c.* 86cm; females considerably smaller. Heavy farmyard birds with variable plumage; bare red area on face in both sexes, grotesquely swollen at base of bill in male. Perches in trees. Descended from wild muscovy duck of C. and S. America and originally domesticated there. 'Muscovy' possibly a corruption of 'Muysca', the name of a Nicaraguan Indian tribe. Often seen in town parks – sometimes the only duck!

Canada Goose *Branta canadensis*

92–102cm, males larger than females. Recognisable by size alone; trumpet noisily in flight. Aggressively territorial when nesting, otherwise sociable, grazing together and flying in large skeins.

N. American birds, first brought to Europe (London) in 17th century. Spread aided by fresh introductions and redistribution of moulting birds while flightless. Free-flying populations in B (especially London and W. Midlands), Ir (e.g. Phoenix Park, Dublin), No (introduced Oslo, 1936), Sw, Fi and G; acc. Ic, Be.

Mute Swan *Cygnus olor*

152cm. Distinguished from other European swans by orange bill with black basal knob; curvature of neck also distinctive. Wings make throbbing sound in flight. Frequents lakes, rivers and estuaries. Can be aggressive when nesting, sometimes drowning flightless ducks. Has fared badly in towns recently; vandalism, high tension cables, oil spillage, nylon fishing lines and poisoning (from anglers' lead weights) have all taken their toll. T, ex Ic (but 'tame' birds sometimes kept in Reykjavik).

171

Birds   Gulls (Laridae)

Gulls were heavily persecuted in the last century and only visited inland towns in bad weather. They are now a familiar sight in urban areas, having benefited from greater protection and increased food supplies. Scavenging on rubbish tips is a common habit and birds may also be fed by the public. Thousands roost on reservoirs. Three species regularly nest on buildings. Juvenile and sub-adult birds have not been described because of limited space.

Black-headed Gull *Larus ridibundus*
35–38cm. Winter plumage acquired late summer; breeding plumage March, sometimes earlier. Red bill and legs; wing with white leading edge.

Mainly seen outside breeding season, but continue foraging in towns when nesting close by, e.g. on saltmarsh near an estuarine port. Scavenge on refuse tips, feed and rest on games pitches, take food from the hand in parks and even from the mouth in St. James's Park, London! Feed with pigeons in streets, and on window-sills and balconies. Perch on trees (regularly in Glasgow), street lamps, statues – even on human heads and open umbrellas in London. Birds ringed in London recovered in D, G, Ne, No, Sw and E. Europe. T.

Common Gull *Larus canus*
41cm. Usually with black-headed gulls; slightly larger, with darker grey wings, white- 'mirrored' black primaries, greenish-yellow legs and bill.

Behaviour and abundance variable. Bold and common in Edinburgh, competing for scraps with feral pigeons. Relatively scarce and shy in W. Midlands. Second commonest wintering gull in London parks; often large flocks on playing fields; adopts skua-like tactics to get food from black-headed gulls. A town bird in summer in Sweden; nests on buildings in Göteborg. T, but mainly in N.

Herring Gull *Larus argentatus*
56–66cm. Yellow bill with red spot on lower mandible; usually pink legs.

Commonest large gull, especially in coastal towns. Scavenges on beaches and rubbish tips. Less numerous in parks (but common in Dublin). Nests on buildings on coast in B and G (e.g. at Dover, Brixham, Bremerhaven, Wilhelmshaven) and sometimes inland in B (Merthyr Tydfil, Kilmarnock, London). Has also nested in parks in London. Steals fish from pelicans, etc. at London Zoo. T.

Lesser Black-backed Gull *Larus fuscus*
53–56cm. Slate-grey wings and back, but Scandinavian birds darker. Yellow legs when adult (the much larger **great black-backed gull** *L. marinus* has pink legs). Bill colour in both spp. as in herring gull. Migratory, but many winter in British Isles. Large flocks frequent games fields on autumn passage. Common town gull on W. side of B (e.g. Glasgow, Bristol, Cardiff). Nests in some towns; rooftops shared with herring gull in Cardiff. T.

Kittiwake *Rissa tridactyla*
41cm. Yellow bill, (normally) black legs, no white spots on wing tips. Name derived from call. A true 'seagull', normally coming to coast only to breed. Nests on warehouse window-sills at Dunbar, North Shields and (has done so) at Gateshead and Newcastle, *c.* 17 km up the R. Tyne; also nests on Lowestoft pier. T, ex Fi; coastal.

Kittiwake
1st winter

Black-headed Gull
1st winter

Kittiwake
Adult

Common Gull
1st winter

Common Gull
Adult, winter

Black-headed Gull
Adult, winter

Black-headed Gull
Adult, summer

Herring Gull
Adult

Herring Gull
Chicks

Herring Gull
Immature

Lesser Black-backed Gull
Adult

Birds   Pigeons (Columbidae)

Feral Rock Dove *Columba livia*
33cm. Colour and markings variable. Some birds resemble wild rock dove; blue-grey, with white rump and two black wing-bars. Others may be 'red', pied, blackish, or blue-grey with black chequering on wings. Dark birds are commonest.

The familiar street pigeons are descended from escaped dovecote birds – domesticated rock doves originally kept for food, later for pigeon-racing, trap-shooting and carrying messages. Feral populations are still joined by lost 'homers'. 'Fancy' breeds – pouters, tumblers, fantails, etc – do not establish themselves in the wild. In coastal towns feral pigeons may resort to cliffs once occupied by rock dove ancestors, but vast majority accept buildings as man-made substitutes. Exposed ledges may be used for nesting, but sites offering semi-darkness preferred, e.g. girders under railway bridges. Very dependent on man for food. Congregate at wharves and factories where grain etc is spilled, and where fed by public – parks, yards, precincts, streets and squares, sometimes becoming a tourist attraction, as in London's Trafalgar Square. Will enter railway stations to feed; have boarded trains on London's Circle Line! T, ex Ic.

Woodpigeon *Columba palumbus*
41cm. Largest of town pigeons. Adults and juvs reveal white wing-bar in flight. Juvs lack white neck patches. Cooing song of five syllables repeated several times and ending with an abrupt 'cuk'.

Not universally abundant in towns, e.g. quite scarce in northern B, even in well-wooded parks. Long established in London, Paris and Berlin, and common in Dutch cities. In C. London will feed from the hand, even perching on people who habitually feed them. Will nest in street trees and on occupied buildings. Sites in C. London include window-ledges, fire-escape landings, rainwater heads and scaffolding. Have used wire as nest material. Large flocks roost in park trees. T, acc Ic; summer only in FS.

Stock Dove *Columba oenas*
33cm. Smaller, darker and more compact than woodpigeon. Iridescent green neck patch noticeable at close quarters. In flight reveals pale grey area at centre of wing. Song a grunting double coo, accented on second note.

Nests in holes; therefore frequents town parks with hollow trees, but never numerous. A town bird in B in London, Birmingham, Leeds and almost certainly elsewhere; apt to be mistaken for feral rock dove and easily over-looked. Will nest in buildings in rural areas. T, acc Ic; summer only D, FS and east G.

Collared Dove *Streptopelia decaocto*
32cm. Greyish fawn; black and white on underside of tail; black half collar. Song a monotonous 'coo-cooo-cuk', often from rooftop or television aerial.

Has spread from SE. Europe since *c*. 1930, reaching F by 1950, B 1955 and Ic early 1970s. Frequents suburbs rather than city centres (is not yet estab-lished in C. London), but congregates in heavily built-up and industrialised areas where grain is available, e.g. mills, maltings, zoos and garden poultry pens. Normally nests in park, garden or churchyard trees, especially ever-greens, but occasionally on buildings. T, ex Fi.

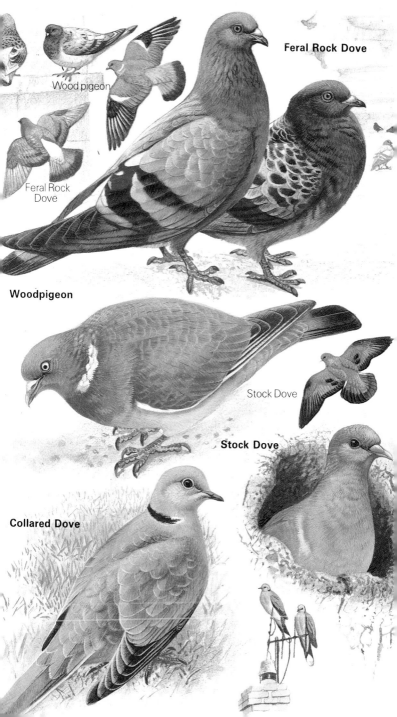

Feral Rock Dove

Wood pigeon

Feral Rock Dove

Woodpigeon

Stock Dove

Stock Dove

Collared Dove

Birds Raptors, Owls, Woodpeckers, Waxwing

Kestrel *Falco tinnunculus* Falconidae
32–35cm. Hovers over parks, waste ground, railway banks, road verges, etc. Wings narrow and pointed; wingspan 71–80cm. Male has blue-grey head, rump and tail. Female chestnut above with black barring. Sometimes mistaken for **sparrowhawk** *Accipiter nisus*, a woodland bird, less often in towns, darker coloured and with broad wings; does not hover.

Urban kestrels nest on church and cathedral towers, power stations, high-rise flats and other tall buildings, using ledges, holes and occasionally window-boxes. Preys mainly on house sparrows in British cities. Acc Ic, summer only Fi, No, most of Sw; otherwise T.

Black Kite *Milvus migrans* Accipitridae
55–60cm. Drab brown. Long, angled wings; wingspan 160–180cm. Long tail only slightly forked; can look almost straight-ended. Buoyant gliding flight on level-held wings. Gregarious.

Well-known scavenger of Asian and African settlements; less attracted to urban areas in NW. Europe, but nests in forests of Berlin. Frequents rubbish tips. Often seen over lakes and rivers. F, Be, G; has bred FS; acc B, D. Sixteenth century accounts (notably William Turner's) show that it was not this bird but the **red kite** *Milvus milvus* that once scavenged in London streets.

Tawny Owl *Strix aluco* Strigidae
38cm. Portly; ground colour varies from chestnut to grey; streaked breast. Shakespeare's 'Tu-whit, tu-who – a merry note' produced by two birds duetting, one uttering 'ke-wick', the other hooting.

Breeds in old trees in parks, gardens and squares, using same tree year after year. Will sit outside entrance hole in daylight, retreating inside if mobbed or alarmed. Hunts at night. Pellet analysis shows that C. London owls prey largely on birds, especially sparrows. T, ex Ic, Ir. The **long-eared owl** *Asio otus* occurs in Dublin and Belfast.

Great Spotted Woodpecker *Dendrocopos major* Picidae
23cm. Commonest of pied woodpeckers. Large white shoulder patches; red under tail-coverts. Male has red nape; juv has red nape and crown. Call-note 'tchick'; 'song' produced mechanically by drumming on dead wood or broken branch. Visits bird tables, especially when fat provided. Has been recorded opening milk bottles in Denmark, notably round Copenhagen. Nests in parks, even in city centres if old trees are retained, but removal of dead timber a limiting factor. Nest-holes sometimes taken over by starlings. Will break into nest-boxes occupied by other spp., devouring nestlings; even concrete boxes may be damaged. T, ex Ic, Ir.

Waxwing *Bombycilla garrulus* Bombycillidae
18cm. Unmistakable with its prominent crest, yellow-tipped tail and black-and-yellow wing-markings. Scarlet 'waxy' tips to secondaries less obvious in the female. Flight (and size) reminiscent of starling. Gregarious, acrobatic and often very tame.

A bird of northern forests which migrates SW. in winter. Attracted to berry-bearing shrubs in urban and suburban parks and gardens, showing marked fondness for *Cotoneaster* fruit. Some birds reported as far W. as Scotland and E. England in most years, but movements occasionally involve exceptional numbers and vagrants reach Ireland and Iceland.

Kestrel

Black Kite

Tawny Owl

Great Spotted
Woodpecker
female

Waxwing

Great Spotted
Woodpecker
male

Birds   Hoopoe, Swift and Hirundines

Hoopoe *Upupa epops*   Upupidae
The species illustrated here are summer vistors to NW. Europe. 28cm. Unmistakable, even when its crest is lowered – its usual position. Floppy, undulating flight; rounded wings with distinctive pied pattern. Name derived from call, a far-carrying 'hoop-hoop-hoop'.

Haunts human settlements in warmer parts of its world range, but in NW. Europe most likely to be seen in towns and suburbs on passage, briefly visiting parks, golf courses, garden lawns and rubbish tips. Breeds in rural areas, F, G; has bred Fi, Sw, southern En; acc Ic, No; elsewhere as passage migrant.

Swift *Apus apus*   Apodidae
16·5cm. Superbly fitted for aerial life. Wings longer than those of hirundines (swallows and martins) and always extended in flight; bird's outline suggests head of an anchor. Adults uniform dark brown, except for whitish chin, but look black when wheeling overhead. Emit piercing screams, especially when chasing one another. Cannot perch but can cling to wall surfaces.

More often seen over city centres in breeding season (May–July) than the hirundines; seek food at much higher altitudes. Built-up areas their main habitat, with colonies nesting under roofing tiles and in holes in buildings. In Berlin and other German towns suitable cavities have been deliberately built into apartment blocks. Nest-boxes used by the famous colony inhabiting the University Museum tower in Oxford. T as breeding sp. ex Ic, where acc.

Swallow *Hirundo rustica*   Hirundinidae
19cm including long tail streamers. Lacks white rump of house martin; forehead and throat chestnut-red. Perches on overhead wires. Has pleasant twittering song. Swallows are village and farmstead birds rather than urban, but pass through towns on migration, feeding over park lakes, playing fields, etc. May nest in porches, sheds, garages, boat-houses and similar structures on the outskirts and occasionally in inner areas, usually in places where livestock are kept, e.g. in stables, or shelters for deer, cattle or other animals in zoos and parks. T, normally ex Ic, but has bred there.

House Martin *Delichon urbica*   Hirundinidae
12·5cm. White rump; all white underparts; tail forked but without streamers. Colonial nester. Perches on wires, etc.

Regularly seen on migration in built-up areas. Breeds in greatest numbers in suburbs and small towns. More birds have colonised inner urban zones in recent years (e.g. Kensington, London), but a lack of mud for nest construction is a limiting factor. Nests normally built under eaves, but sometimes attached to arch soffits or sculptural detail (as in the Louvre cloisters, Paris). T as breeding sp. ex Ic, where acc.

Sand Martin *Riparia riparia*   Hirundinidae
12cm. Brown above, white below, with brown breast-band. A colonial nester, usually excavating nest-holes in sandy banks, often near water.

Urban expansion usually destroys usual nesting habitats; sand-pits filled in; sandy coastal cliffs subjected to 'improvements' to prevent erosion. Artificial sites, e.g. drain-pipes in walls, railway-, canal- and river-banks are often adopted and holes in brickwork and stonework occasionally used. T, ex Ic.

House Martin

Swift

Swallow

Sand Martin

Hoopoe

Birds Crows (Corvidae)

Rook *Corvus frugilegus*
46cm. Bare, whitish face distinguishes adults. Juvs have feathered faces like carrion crows but, like adults, have purple-glossed plumage and 'baggy' thigh feathers. Colonial nesters.

Town rookeries, mainly a British feature, can survive only when situated within easy flying distance of feeding grounds – farmland and, to a lesser extent, rubbish tips and beaches. Urban growth can eventually cause desertion; C. London lost its last rookery in 1916. Tree-felling (e.g. after Dutch elm disease) another cause of decline. Artificial sites rarely used; sometimes electricity pylons, occasionally buildings. T as breeding sp. ex lc, where acc; local in southern No and Sw; summer only in Fi.

Carrion Crow *Corvus corone corone* and
Hooded Crow *C. corone cornix*
47cm. Two races of same sp. Carrion crow all black with greenish gloss. B, D, F, LC, west G; rare vagrant Ir. Hooded crow has grey back and underparts. Ir, D, east G, FS, north and north-west Sco; acc lc. Two races will interbreed.

Less gregarious than rooks; solitary nesters, using park trees. Roost communally, often in large numbers in winter; 'hoodies' will roost on buildings on Continent. Scavenge at rubbish tips; London crows alight on river craft transporting refuse. Take eggs and young birds, including park ducklings. Normally wary, but will come for food in London parks. Perch freely on rooftops.

Jackdaw *Corvus monedula*
33cm. Noticeably smaller than other black crows. Adult has grey nape. Calls distinctive, especially high-pitched 'tchack'.

Prefers suburbs and small towns to heavily built-up areas, but may inhabit inner parks with old trees. A small colony known in London's Kensington Gardens in 1890s survived until 1969. Nests in hollow trees and (mainly old) buildings; causes annoyance by nesting in chimneys. Will perch on backs of grazing animals in parks and zoos, removing hair for lining nests. Visits bird-tables. T as breeding sp. ex lc, where acc.

Magpie *Pica pica*
46cm. Pied plumage and long (23cm), graduated tail. White primaries (with black tips) conspicuous in flight. Harsh rattling call. Nest is domed with twigs.

Well established in Dublin and many Continental towns, especially in No and Sw. Safer in British towns than in countryside, where regarded as 'vermin'. Nests in parks, gardens and sometimes street trees. Common in northern English towns, notably Manchester. Increased in London over last 40 years, but did not breed successfully in central parks until 1971. Known to take eggs from cartons delivered to suburban doorsteps. T, ex lc.

Jay *Garrulus glandarius*
34cm. Unmistakable. White rump the most obvious feature when flying away. Harsh alarm note, 'skaaah'. A woodland bird, particularly associated with oakwood and therefore only likely to become well established in the 'leafier' towns and suburbs. Prefers wooded open spaces, but frequents more open parks in C. London. Forages in park litter baskets. Nests in trees and bushes in parks and gardens, occasionally in squares and street trees, and sometimes on buildings. T as breeding sp. ex lc, where acc.

Rook

Carrion Crow

Hooded Crow

Jackdaw

Jay

Magpie

Birds   Thrushes (Turdidae)

Blackbird *Turdus merula*
25cm. Commonest and best known thrush. Juvs resemble females but more rufous and more heavily spotted. Rich, varied song, often delivered from buildings; town birds start singing (and breeding) earlier in year than country blackbirds.

Once avoided human settlements, now generally more abundant in gardens than in original woodland habitat and established in most European towns – except where human predation on small birds is still socially acceptable. Competition for nest-sites in C. London has prompted birds to build inside and outside buildings, on ledges, drain-pipes, girders, etc, on street lamps, and even traffic lights. T as breeding sp. except Ic, where occurs in winter.

Mistle Thrush *Turdus viscivorus*
27cm. Larger than blackbird and grey-brown above; has alert, upright stance. Like fieldfare, shows white underwing when flying. Flight action also similar – closes wings at regular intervals. Loud song; like inferior blackbird's with much repetition. Forms flocks in summer, feeding on rowan and other berries.

Not a universal European town bird but breeds in bleakest of British parks if a few trees present; usually builds in a fork. Even uses trees overhanging pavements or in middle of dual carriageways. C. London birds have also nested on scaffolding and stands erected for spectators of 1952 Coronation procession. T, ex Ic, where acc; summer only in Fi, No.

Song Thrush *Turdus philomelos*
23cm. Smaller than blackbird; has warmer brown upper-parts than mistle thrush. Shows buff under wings in flight. Loud clear song, with short phrases repeated; often delivered in twilight or under street lighting, giving rise to reports of 'nightingales'. Smashes snail shells on stone 'anvil'.

Outnumbered in towns by more adaptable blackbird. Frequents wilder urban open spaces, park and garden shrubberies; commonest in suburbs. Feeds on lawns. Severe winters seriously reduce population; C. and N. European birds migrate S. and W. T as breeding sp. ex Ic, but town birds mainly in B, F, G, Ir, Ne.

Redwing *Turdus iliacus*
21cm. Chestnut flanks, chestnut under wings and creamy eyebrow-stripe distinguish it from song thrush. Wintering birds scatter widely over ground when feeding in flocks. Possible to hear thin 'seeip' contact notes of nocturnal migrants flying over – when traffic noise permits.

Occurs T but over much of area as winter visitor; usually in urban parks during severe weather. Breeds FS (ex southern Sw), Ic, northern Sco; has bred Be, F, G. Nests in Norwegian and Icelandic towns, in parks, gardens, outbuildings and even (in Reykjavik cemetery) on graves.

Fieldfare *Turdus pilaris*
25·5cm. Size, stance, flight and underwing pattern reminiscent of mistle thrush, but chuckling 'chack-chack-chack' calls, chestnut back, grey head, nape and rump distinctive. T in winter; mainly hard weather visitors to built-up areas in S., but nest in Scandinavian towns; particularly well established in Swedish parks and gardens. Breeding range has long embraced FS and east G; now includes B (mostly Sco), D and west G. Has bred Ic, F, Ne.

Fieldfare

Mistle Thrush

Redwing

Song Thrush

female

Blackbird

male

Birds Park and Garden Species

The birds shown here are all found in town parks and gardens within the area covered by this book, but the park and garden birds of one country are not always found in those of another.

Robin *Erithacus rubecula* Turdidae
14cm. Only adults have the red breast and face; juvs are speckled with brown and buff. Sing throughout year, but relatively little mid-June to mid-July.

In British Isles a familiar suburban garden bird; less common as breeding species in inner city parks with little low cover; more widespread in winter. Normally nests in hollow in bank, but sites have included tins, bookshelves, old clothes, letter-boxes, vehicles and an unmade bed. Seeks human company and can become hand-tame.

Continental robins are shy woodland birds, less often seen in formal parks and gardens, even where they are unlikely to be persecuted, e.g. Scandinavia. Many northern birds, however, migrate S. in autumn to more hostile territory and learn to fear mankind. T as breeding sp. ex Ic, where occasional; overwinters south Sw and No coast, otherwise summer only FS.

Dunnock or Hedge Sparrow *Prunella modularis* Prunellidae
14·5cm. Not a sparrow. Thin bill, grey head, streaked flanks; characteristic shuffling gait, twitching wings. Usually feeds *under* bird-tables; an avian Autolycus, snapping up miniscule trifles. Warbles pleasant stereotyped song.

A shy woodland sp. in C. and N. Europe, but typical park and garden shrubbery bird in W., especially in suburbs. Rarely tame, but will forage between one's feet in Royal Botanic Garden, Edinburgh. T, ex Ic, as breeding bird; summer only Fi and most of Sw and No.

Wren *Troglodytes troglodytes* Troglodytidae
9·5cm. Barred, brown plumage; habitually cocked tail. Has incredibly loud trilling song for diminutive bird. Avoids densely built-up areas, except in winter when may seek food in backyards and waste sites, closely examining walls. May nest in town parks and gardens if low cover available; fares best in wooded open spaces, e.g. the Paris *bois*, Scheveningse Bosjes (The Hague), Holland Park (London). Will use next-boxes and holes in walls – also for roosting, sometimes large numbers sharing same cavity. Breeding female choses one of several nests built by male. T, but summer only Fi. **Iceland wren** *T. t. islandicus* is not an urban bird.

Spotted Flycatcher *Muscicapa striata* Muscicapidae
14cm. Upright stance; breast and crown streaked (not spotted!) Juvs have 'scaly' appearance. Catch insects in flight, usually returning to same perch, be it branch, fence or tennis net.

Summer visitor. Needs no ground cover, therefore more successful in town parks and gardens than most insectivorous migrants. Also frequents churchyards and squares. Usually nests on walls or tree-trunks, using shallow cavities, creepers and ledges. Accepts open-fronted nest-boxes. T, ex Ic.

Pied Flycatcher *Ficedula hypoleuca* Muscicapidae
13cm. Males resemble females after breeding season. Do not usually return to same perch when flycatching. Summer visitor, usually seen in towns on passage, but remarkably common in Swedish parks and gardens, using nest-boxes. T, ex Ic and Ir, where acc.

Spotted Flycatcher

Pied Flycatcher
female

Pied Flycatcher male

Dunnock

Robin

Wren

juvenile

Birds   Titmice and Their Associates

The typical titmice (paridae) are acrobatic, hole-nesting, woodland birds which readily adapt to life in parks and gardens. Those illustrated nest in holes in trees and walls, but also accept nest-boxes, drain-pipes, lamp standards and other hollow objects. Breeding success may be limited if suitable food for young (mainly caterpillars) not available. Bird-table provisions – fat, nuts, etc – while enabling adults to survive winter, are harmful to nestlings. Tits' habit of stealing cream from milk-bottles (first recorded near Southampton, 1921) noted in B, D, Ir, Ne, Sw. Often very tame; all three urban spp. take food from hand in Royal Botanic Garden, Edinburgh. Occasionally enter houses and indulge in 'paper-tearing', pulling at loose wallpaper, ripping newspapers etc; evidently a form of food-searching behaviour. Form mixed flocks after breeding season, often joined by treecreepers, nuthatches and goldcrests.

Blue Tit *Parus caeruleus*
11·5cm. Blue crown, wings and tail; yellow underparts. Commonest and most adaptable of urban titmice. More widespread in winter than in breeding season, even appearing at inner city waste sites and practically treeless recreation grounds. Sometimes roost inside street lamps. T, ex Ic.

Great Tit *Parus major*
14cm. Black crown and bib contrasting with white cheeks; black band down centre of yellow breast, broader in male than female. Has notoriously wide vocabulary; repetitive song usually composed of units of two notes, e.g. 'teacher, teacher . . .' Commoner in suburbs than in city centres. Unlike blue tit, obtains much of natural food from ground under trees; most parks too tidy to meet its needs. T as breeding sp. ex Ic, where acc.

Coal Tit *Parus ater*
11cm. Black crown and bib, white patch on nape, buff underparts. Song reminiscent of great tit's but less staccato. Closely associated with conifers; commonest in towns where these occur. Usually less numerous than great and blue tits. Tendency to nest near the ground possibly disadvantageous. T, ex Ic.

Goldcrest *Regulus regulus*   Sylviidae
9cm. Constantly searching for invertebrates in foliage. Black-bordered stripe on crown, yellow in female, orange in male; pale area round eye; two pale wing-bars. Thin, high-pitched calls.
   Associated with yews and typical conifers. Uncommon as urban breeding sp.; more often seen in parks, gardens and churchyards in autumn. T, ex Ic.

Nuthatch *Sitta europaea*   Sittidae
14cm. Shape unmistakable. Scandinavian birds have white underparts. Move jerkily over tree-trunks, *in any direction*. Loud whistling calls. Frequent wilder wooded parks and sometimes more formal open spaces with old trees. Modify nest-hole entrance with mud. Visit garden bird-tables. T, ex Ic, Ir, Sco.

Treecreeper *Certhia familiaris*   Certhiidae
12·5cm. Climbs upwards, supported by tail. Scarce as breeding bird in town parks and gardens. In British Isles roosts in cavities excavated in soft bark of wellingtonias *Sequoiadendron giganteum*. T, ex Ic, LC, western F, but mainly in mountain woodland S. of D. Replaced in lowland of F, LC and G by very similar **short-toed treecreeper** *C. brachydactyla*.

Coal Tit

Treecreeper

Great Tit

Blue Tit

Nuthatch

Goldcrest

male

female

Birds   Redstarts and Warblers

Redstart *Phoenicurus phoenicurus*   Turdidae
14cm. Name = 'red tail', the striking, constantly-twitching feature of all redstarts. Male unmistakable; female lighter brown above than female black redstart and buff below, not grey. Summer visitor. Breeds in Continental towns and suburbs; appropriately called Gartenrotschwanz (garden redtail) in Germany. Nests in holes in buildings and trees; readily uses nest-boxes in Swedish parks. Passes through British towns, rarely staying to nest and then generally in outer parks. Has bred Ir but usually bird of passage; otherwise T, ex Ic.

Black Redstart *Phoenicurus ochruros*   Turdidae
14cm. Young may lack whitish wing-patch. Song, usually from high building, includes sound like ball-bearings being shaken. A bird of rocky places which finds city centres a congenial substitute provided insect food and nest-sites (ledges and holes) obtainable. Is called Hausrotschwanz (house redtail) in Germany. Continental birds share garden habitat with redstart, filling what is the robin's ecological niche in Britain. Spread to England long before achieving fame by nesting on blitzed sites in London, Birmingham, Dover and elsewhere; has bred in London area since 1926. Now mainly in S. and SE. of country, usually at gasworks, power stations and other industrial sites. Summer visitor. Some winter in southern En, Ir, western F. Breeds D, En, F, Fi, G, LC, south No, south Sw; has bred Sco; acc Ic.

Warblers *(Sylviidae)* are, with few exceptions, only summer visitors to NW. Europe. Many spp. pass through towns, but they mostly need low cover for nesting. Intensively managed areas do not attract them.

Blackcap *Sylvia atricapilla*
14cm. Male with black cap; female and juv with red-brown cap. Experience needed to distinguish rich warbling song from that of **garden warbler** *S. borin!*
    Prefers the wilder, wooded open spaces (e.g. Bois de Boulogne, Paris) for nesting, but will breed in inner city parks like London's Kensington Gardens if sanctuary areas provided. Some birds winter in western F and British Isles. Visit gardens in latter area, feeding on berries and bird-table scraps. T, ex Ic.

Willow Warbler *Phylloscopus trochilus*
11cm. Closely resembles **chiffchaff** *P. collybita*. Best distinguished by sweet, descending song; chiffchaff monotonously repeats its name. Legs usually pale-coloured; chiffchaff's usually blackish – a somewhat unreliable guide to identity of silent birds seen on autumn passage. Fortunately, chiffchaffs often sing in autumn. Favours more open areas than the woodland-loving chiffchaff, therefore more likely to stay to breed, frequenting urban commons, waste ground, and even parks if sufficient ground cover left undisturbed. T, but Ic only on passage.

Icterine Warbler *Hippolais icterina*
13·5cm. A plump, long-billed, long-winged warbler with a pale wing-panel and a peaked crown. Song a repetitive torrent of sweet, harsh, and high, shrill notes, with some mimicry. Frequents parks and gardens on Continent. Habit of nesting in fork of tree or bush well above ground enables it to survive where breeding attempts of other warblers would be frustrated by 'tidying-up'. B, Ir on passage (has bred En at least once); otherwise T, ex Ic.

Black Redstart

Icterine Warbler

Redstart

Blackcap

male

female

Willow Warbler

Goldfinch

Juvenile

female

Bullfinch

Linnet
male

Birds   Finches (Fringillidae)

Seed-eating birds like finches do not find town life difficult. They feed on the seeds of waste ground weeds in autumn and winter, and several species inhabit parks and gardens – even the **hawfinch** *Coccothraustes coccothraustes* does so on the Continent. Some finches roost communally in towns, usually in trees and shrubberies, but the **twite** *Carduelis flavirostris* roosts on buildings in some German cities.

Bullfinch *Pyrrhula pyrrhula*
14·5–16cm. White rump obvious in flight; distinctive monosyllabic, low-pitched piping call. Juvs lack black cap of adults; underparts rather like those of female. Has spread from woodland and scrub into farmland and towns in recent years, especially in southern En. Damages fruit trees and various shrubs by eating buds, especially when ash trees fail to produce much seed. Visits bird-tables for seeds and fat in C. and N. Europe. T, ex Ic.

Serin *Serinus serinus*
11·5cm. Yellow-rumped, dark-streaked and stubby-billed. Male rather like diminutive male **yellowhammer** *Emberiza citrinella*; delivers rapid tinkling song from trees or overhead wires. Female duller, with less yellow. Frequents parks, gardens, churchyards and tree-lined roads; feeds on weed seeds at allotments, railway yards and other open areas. Has spread from Mediterranean area over last 200 years, but breeding in Britain so far confined to few places in S. England (first known case at Swanage, Dorset, 1967). Quite common in Paris. N. breeding limit south Sw and Fi; has appeared Ir, No, Sco.

Goldfinch *Carduelis carduelis*
12cm. Juvs ('greypates') lack colourful head markings but have the yellow wing-bars. For breeding habitat prefers suburban gardens and parks to city centres, but flocks ('charms') are attracted to seeding weeds (especially burdocks *Arctium* spp. and thistles) on inner urban waste sites. Have increased in Britain; commonest in S. but present in towns as far N. as Glasgow. Partial migrant. T, ex Ic, as breeding sp., but summer only FS.

Redpoll *Carduelis flammea*
12–14cm. Vary in size and colour according to geographical distribution. Larger and paler in N. than in S., but adults always recognisable as redpolls from crimson forehead, black chin and twittering flight-notes 'chuch-uch-uch'.
   Lesser redpoll (the British race) breeds in B, D, Ir and Ne. In B mainly found in parks and gardens from English Midlands northwards, but has nested in C. London. **Iceland redpoll** occurs in Reykjavik and Akureyri. On Continent redpolls are uncommon as town birds. Mainly nest outside area covered by this book, in northern FS and alpine C. Europe. More widespread in winter, when range includes northern F.

Linnet *Carduelis cannabina*
13cm. Female heavily streaked; male lacks red forehead and pink breast in winter. Nests on gorsy urban commons and industrial wasteland in B. Large flocks frequent playing fields in cold winters and on passage. Adoption of urban habitats in Finland and Sweden prompted by agricultural changes. Partial migrant. T, ex Ic, as breeding sp.; summer only Fi and most of southern No and Sw.

Birds   Finches and Sparrows

Greenfinch *Carduelis chloris*   Fringillidae
15cm. Stocky and stout-billed. Male olive-green with yellow rump, wing-patches and sides of tail. Utters nasal, buzzing call-note in breeding season and performs song-flight. Female duller and less yellow. Juvs streaked and with brown rump. Use evergreen shrubberies for nesting and communal roosting. In B now resident in city centre parks and regular at suburban bird-tables, especially where peanuts provided. Flocks gather to feed on weed seeds on waste ground and refuse tips in autumn. Garden visitors have developed habit of taking unripened berries of mezereon *Daphne mezereum* for their seeds. T as breeding sp., ex Ic, where acc.

Chaffinch *Fringilla coelebs*   Fringillidae
15cm. Both sexes have two white wing-bars and white-edged tail. Brownish-pink underparts and blue head distinguish male from pale yellowish-brown female. Loud rattling song usually ends with a flourish; subject to considerable regional variation. Commonest European finch. A normal inhabitant of suburban gardens and well-wooded parks, but can be scarce in heavily built-up areas. Shortage of suitable mosses and lichens for nest-building and insect food for nestlings may inhibit successful colonization. T as breeding sp., ex Ic, where acc; summer only Fi and much of southern Sw.

Sparrows (Passeridae), unlike finches, have an uncleft tail.

House Sparrow *Passer domesticus*
14·5cm. Sexes different. Females and juvs lack black bib, whitish cheeks, chestnut mantle and grey crown of male. Highly gregarious.

Associated with man the agriculturalist even before towns existed. Still primarily a seed-eater, but also takes insects, especially when feeding nestlings; sometimes picks flies off car radiators. Birds on urban fringes may resort to cornfields in summer, but large flocks of city centre sparrows 'harvest' seeds of grasses and various weeds found in parks, especially those of knotgrass. Readily accepts bread and other human food, sometimes taking it from the hand. Feeds on spillage from horses' nose-bags and undigested matter in horse dung; its population decline in town centres may be linked with change to motor transport. Enters buildings in search of food – factories, hospitals, cafés and even underground stations.

Nests in natural and artificial holes, and builds untidy domed nests in bushes and creepers, behind drain-pipes and occasionally in street lamps; will nest inside buildings as well as outside. Roosting habits vary according to season and latitude. Holes normally used, but in towns large communal roosts may occupy street trees, evergreens and creepers. T, ex Ic.

Tree Sparrow *Passer montanus*
14cm. Sexes alike. Mainly distinguished from male house sparrow by chestnut crown and black mark on each of its 'cleaner' white cheeks. Has more metallic chirp than house sparrow. Mainly associated with farmland in NW. Europe, but well established in Swedish towns, competing with redstarts and flycatchers for nest-boxes, mingling with house sparrows and adopting similar behaviour. In B small colonies can persist in the suburbs and 'wilder' open spaces, usually where there are old trees, and flocks may visit waste sites to feed on seeding weeds. T, ex south-west Fi, Ic.

House Sparrow

male

female

Tree Sparrow

male

Greenfinch
male

Chaffinch
female

Chaffinch
male

Grey Wagtail
adult, summer

Pied Wagtail
adult, summer

Birds   Starling, Wagtails, Crested Lark

Starling *Sturnus vulgaris*   Sturnidae
21·5cm. Shorter-tailed than the blackbird and other thrushes. Do not hop, but walk. Heavily spotted in winter; bill dark. Glossy plumage in breeding season, when bill yellow, with blue-grey base in males, dirty pink in females. Juvs brown. Gregarious. Frequent mown areas, probing soil for food, raid bird-tables, hawk flying ants, scavenge on refuse tips, and feed on invertebrates inhabiting filter beds at sewage works. Nest in holes in buildings and trees, wherever these are near food source. Thousands roost communally in city centres, especially in Britain, benefiting from warmth and absence of pred-ators; perform spectacular aerial manoeuvres. Use both trees and buildings. At some roosts maximum numbers in winter; in others (e.g. London) early summer, when juvs join adults. Birds have definite fly-lines to roost, with gathering points *en route*. Main London roost draws birds from 22km radius. Attempts to disperse birds have involved use of fireworks, electrified wiring, repellent substances on building ledges, amplified distress calls, stuffed owls and rubber snakes! T as breeding sp.; migratory on Continent – summer only Fi and much of No and Sw.

Pied/White Wagtail *Motacilla alba*   Motacillidae
18cm, including 9cm tail. Runs over ground, moving tail up and down. Bounding flight. Call-note 'chizzik'. Pied wagtail *M. a. yarrellii* (B, Ir and neigh-bouring Continental coast) can be confused with migrating birds of Continental race (white wagtail *M. a. alba*), especially in autumn; grey-mantled first summer female 'pieds' closely resemble 'whites'; the juvs (which lack black

194

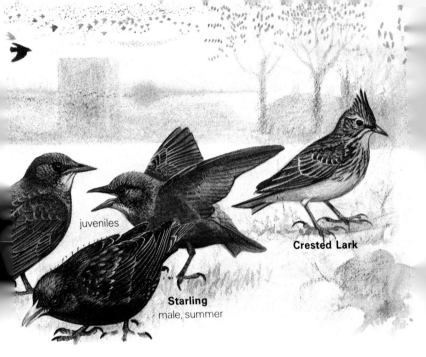

juveniles

Crested Lark

Starling
male, summer

crown) almost identical. But rump colour always black in pieds, grey in whites. Black bib and crown not joined in white wagtail; back never black as in male pied. Run and flutter after insects on mown lawns etc., waste ground, rooftops and roadways; not always near water. Nest in holes in walls and banks; also in sheds, abandoned cars, flower-pots, flower-beds, piles of wood, coal and builders' materials. Often roost in considerable numbers in city centres, occupying trees (as in Dublin), factory rooftops and cooling towers; also inside commercial greenhouses, but mainly in country. Breeds T, but white wagtail migratory and only in western F in winter.

Grey Wagtail *Motacilla cinerea* Motacillidae
18cm; tail *c.* 10·5cm. Male loses black throat and resembles female in winter, and underparts paler yellow, except under tail-coverts.

Frequents park waters and urban canals mainly after breeding season; also flat roofs, finding insects in rainwater puddles and blocked gutters. A few nest in towns, under bridges, in drain-pipes and holes in masonry, usually near water; canal locks often favoured. Communal roost reported in The Hague. Partially migrant; summer only south Sw. Has bred No; acc Fi, Ic; otherwise T.

Crested Lark *Galerida cristata* Alaudidae
17cm. Conspicuous erect crest. Short, tawny-edged tail. Rounded wings, orange-buff underneath. Sings on ground, from elevated perches and high in sky; climbs and descends silently.

Frequents wasteland, building sites, unmetalled tracks, railway yards and embankments on Continent. Acc B, Fi, Ic; otherwise T, but only in S. of No, Sw.

Mammals Badger, Fox, Mole and Hedgehog

Mammals often go unseen, but they leave numerous signs of their presence, only a few of which can be mentioned here.

The distribution notes given for each species do not necessarily mean it tolerates urban conditions throughout its range. HB = head and body.

Badger *Meles meles* Carnivora: Mustelidae
HB 61–88cm, tail 12–20cm; males larger than females. Unmistakable; striped head conspicuous even in poor light. Sett has large entrances; spoil heaps often contain old bedding. Hairs left where paths pass under barbed wire. Nocturnal. Usually avoids towns on Continent, but occurs in Copenhagen. In England mainly on suburban fringes, but setts may remain occupied for years in private grounds and 'wild' open spaces which have become isolated from countryside by urban growth. Also found on railway banks. Sometimes fed by householders and watched from their windows, T, ex Ic.

Red Fox *Vulpes vulpes* Carnivora: Canidae
HB 58–77cm, tail (brush) 32–48cm. Colour variable and brush often lacks white tip. Size and voice do not reliably indicate animal's sex. Strong characteristic smell. Mainly nocturnal. Established in suburbs of many English towns for past 30 years, inhabiting waste sites, parks, gardens, cemeteries, golf courses, building sites and refuse tips. Sometimes penetrate city centres, railway banks providing access routes – and sites for earths. Cubs also born under sheds, pavilions and occupied houses. Eat small mammals, birds (waterfowl taken from parks and zoos), earthworms, beetles, fruit, carrion and household scraps. Forage in dustbins and litter baskets; often fed by public in parks and gardens. Sunbathe on roofs in Bristol. In Ir occurs in Dublin, Belfast and Cork. Carries rabies on Continent. Not encouraged in built-up areas, but occurs in Copenhagen, Stockholm, Paris outskirts and some German towns – commoner in Essen than neighbouring countryside. T, ex Ic.

Mole *Talpa europaea* Insectivora: Talpidae
HB *c.* 11–16cm, tail 2–4cm. Rarely seen on surface. Existence indicated by molehills, which animal creates by pushing up soil from below with one of its spade-like forepaws; obvious on lawns and grass verges, less so in woodland.

Disliked by gardeners and rarely tolerated except in wilder open spaces (e.g. London's Hampstead Heath), but still occurs in Cardiff parks. May survive for a while in new suburbs but soon eliminated from formal areas. T, ex Ic, Ir, No.

Hedgehog *Erinaceus europaeus* Insectivora: Erinaceidae
HB 20–30cm, larger on Continent than in British Isles; tail inconspicuous, 2–3·5cm. Unlike any other mammal in area covered by this book. Rolls into spiny ball when alarmed. Nocturnal. Benefits from surburban growth; finds plenty of natural food (mostly invertebrates) in gardens and often receives additional food from householders; also finds hibernation sites – sheds, log piles, compost heaps and hedge bottoms. Risks involved in town life include being killed by traffic, poisoned by garden chemicals, drowned in sheer-sided pools, becoming entangled in netting and being burnt with garden rubbish. Can live in city centre parks, even in London. T, ex Ic.

Fox

Badger

Hedgehog
with young

Mole

Mammals   Lagomorphs and Rodents

Rabbits and hares (lagomorphs) differ from rodents in having two pairs of upper incisor teeth instead of one pair.

Rabbit *Oryctolagus cuniculus*   Lagomorpha: Leporidae
HB up to 40cm, tail (scut) 4–8cm. Smaller than brown hare *Lepus capensis* (sometimes found in suburban parks); greyer brown, with no black on ear-tips. White underside of scut noticeable when retreating. Seen in daytime but mainly crepuscular and nocturnal. Burrows usually obvious. Droppings spherical; not always distinguishable from hares'.
   Widely introduced (native of Mediterranean region); reached En 12th century. Arouse conflicting emotions; very destructive but disarmingly attractive – also good to eat! Normally confined to 'wild' suburban parks, commons and waste ground, but may reach inner areas (e.g. Princes Street Gardens, Edinburgh) via railway banks. Was unofficially introduced into some C. London parks. T, ex Ic, Fi; only in south Sw; local in No.

Red Squirrel *Sciurus vulgaris*   Rodentia: Sciuridae
Like grey squirrel, a diurnal, arboreal, non-hibernating rodent, but more associated with coniferous woodland than that sp. HB 18–28cm, tail 14–24cm. Ears tufted in winter. Some Continental animals almost black. Race indigenous to British Isles has whitish tail in summer. Stripped cones, split nutshells, etc are evidence of feeding. Nest (drey) usually built near tree-trunk. Occurs in Continental parks; sometimes hand-tame. Reintroduced into Ir from En in 19th century; found in Phoenix Park, Dublin. Hand-reared Scottish animals released in Regent's Park, London in 1984. T, ex Ic.

Grey Squirrel *Sciurus carolinensis*   Rodentia: Sciuridae
HB 23–30cm, tail 19–24cm. Chestnut flanks and limbs in summer, and yellowish-brown coloration on back and head sometimes prompt false reports of red squirrels and even red/grey hybrids! Food debris like that of red squirrel. Drey often built away from trunk; holes in trees also used.
   Several introductions from N. America into Britain (1876–1929) and Ireland (from England, 1913). Now occupies much of ground formerly frequented by red squirrel, especially in S. and C. England, and still spreading. Exterminated in C. London in early 1930s but had returned by late 1950s. Common in town parks and gardens; take food from the hand, and sometimes clamber over their benefactors! Cause annoyance by pillaging bird-tables, digging up bulbs and nesting in lofts. Cause serious damage to trees – as do red squirrels. B and Ir; absent from rest of Europe.

Field Vole or Short-tailed Vole *Microtus agrestis*
Rodentia: Cricetidae
HB 9–13cm, tail 2·5–4·5cm. Greyish brown; blunt muzzle (typical of voles); small ears and eyes; short tail. Inhabit rough grassland, waste ground and railways banks. Can be found under boards, metal sheeting and other rubbish; also their runs and nests. T, ex Ic, Ir. **Bank voles** *Clethrionomys glareolus* (reddish brown, with longer tail) prefer scrub and woodland.

Wood Mouse *Apodemus sylvaticus*   Rodentia: Muridae
HB 8–11cm, tail 7–11·5cm. Whitish underside, usually with yellowish streak on chest; large ears. Nocturnal. Frequents waste ground, railway banks, suburban parks and gardens, but has been found in Holland Park, C. London. Sometimes enters houses. T, ex Fi.

Red Squirrel

Grey Squirrel

Rabbit

Field Vole

Wood Mouse

Mammals   Inner City Dwellers

House Mouse *Mus musculus*   Rodentia: Muridae
HB up to *c.* 10cm; tail same length. Greyer than wood mouse, with smaller eyes and ears; usually only slightly paler below than above; characteristic 'mousy' smell.

Man's camp-follower since prehistoric times; probaly originated in SW. Asia, now world-wide. Infests buildings and outbuildings of all kinds; also refuse tips. Has been found nesting in frozen carcases in cold stores! Consumes and contaminates human food, attacks woodwork, shreds paper and other materials, and causes electrical faults by gnawing wiring. T.

Ship Rat or Black Rat *Rattus rattus*   Rodentia: Muridae
HB up to 24cm; tail same length or longer, thinner than common rat's and uniformly coloured. Ears relatively large (*cf.* common rat). Colour variable; can be all black, but also grey-brown with grey or creamy underparts. Common rat can also be black! Droppings smaller and proportionately thinner than those of common rat; usually rounded at both ends. Greasy fur (of both spp.) leaves dark smears on walls and 'loop smears' under joists. Loop smears of ship rat tend to be discontinuous, unlike those of common rat.

Mainly found indoors in cooler temperate countries, therefore easier to eliminate than common rat. A skilled climber, occupying upper floors of buildings, but has been found in sewers, where common rat more usual. Does not burrow. Original home probably SE. Asia. Followed trade routes across the world, and recently shown to have reached Britain by the Roman period. Its fleas can carry plague; the rat-borne Black Death of 1346–9 destroyed about half the population of Europe. Intensified control measures and vigilance at ports have reduced numbers and range. T, ex Ic, Fi, No; local in Sw; mainly in seaports in B, Ir.

Common or Brown Rat *Rattus norvegicus*   Rodentia: Muridae
HB 20 – 28cm; tail shorter, usually dark above, pale beneath. Blunter muzzle and smaller, thicker ears than ship rat (*q.v.*). Normally brown, sometimes black. Droppings often pointed at one or both ends.

Ubiquitous, indoors and outdoors, causing damage to stored products and materials of all kinds, including non-edible substances like lead piping, earthenware and plastics. Eats both animal and vegetable matter, and even candles and soap. Takes eggs of park waterfowl. Partly responsible for decline of less adaptable ship rat. Originated in Asia, reaching Copenhagen from Russia in 1716, other European countries later in century. Arrived En *c.* 1728, but not in No until 1762 – no justification for name *norvegicus*. Now T.

Feral Domestic Cat *Felis catus*   Carnivora: Felidae
The domestic cat is too well known to warrant description. Free-living, owner-less cats exhibit same variety of coat colour as household pets.

Breeding colonies now inhabit urban sites over much of Britain and Conti-⸳ nent, including parks, hospital and factory grounds, dockyards and waste ground. Prey on birds, including park waterfowl, and rodents, but much of food scavenged or provided by public. Shelter in heating ducts, whereby their fleas invade heated rooms. Destruction or removal of animals and use of oral contraceptives prove less satisfactory control methods than neutering the cats and returning to site.

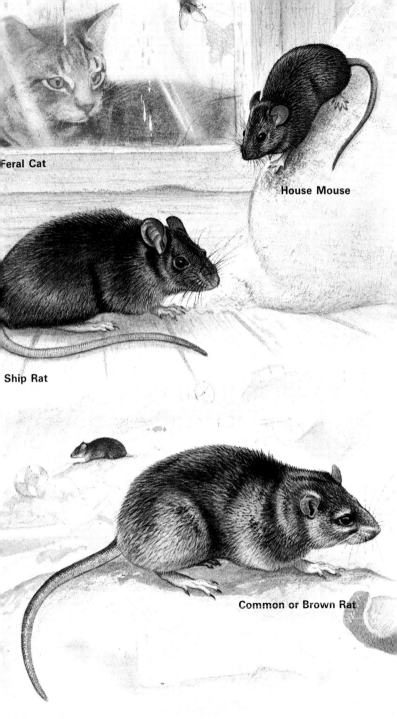

Feral Cat

House Mouse

Ship Rat

Common or Brown Rat

Mammals   Bats (Chiroptera)

The only mammals with powers of true flight. Crepuscular and nocturnal, but may also fly during day. European species feed on moths, beetles and other flying insects; also snatch insects and spiders from trees. Feed over parks and gardens, often over water; also round street lamps. Roost, breed and hibernate in tree holes and buildings, therefore at risk in towns – hollow trees often felled; building maintenance involves blocking holes used as entrances, and insecticides used to prevent beetle and fungus damage. Now illegal to harm bats or bat roosts in United Kingdom; bats are protected in all European countries. Bats are harmless, useful and maligned animals – and do not get entangled in human hair! They deserve sympathy and understanding.

Identification mainly based on features which cannot be seen while animal is flying, such as dentition, and the shape of skin lobe (tragus) arising from base of ear. It should be left to those legally authorised to handle these animals. More species occur in urban areas than are shown here. Small bats seen are not necessarily pipistrelles and large bats need not be noctules! WS = wingspan.

Pipistrelle *Pipistrellus pipistrellus*   Vespertilionidae
WS 19–25cm. Fur light, dark, reddish- or blackish-brown. Short, rounded ears; short blunt tragus. Projecting membraneous lobe on outside of calcar (cartilaginous heel-spur bordering tail membrane).

Smallest and commonest European bat; occurs in city centre parks. Emerges just after sunset. Often occupies space between slates and roofing felt. Nursing colonies of up to 300 or even 1,000 females congregate in buildings in summer. In France will roost behind window-shutters which are left fastened back. T, ex Fi, Ic.

Noctule *Nyctalus noctula*   Vespertilionidae
WS 32–39cm. Fur entirely golden-brown. Short, rounded ears; tragus short, kidney-shaped, wider at tip than at base. Glandular swellings on muzzle. Tail membrane has post-calcarial lobes. (See pipistrelle).

Breed and roost in tree holes in numbers of up to 1,000, occasionally audible during day. Emerge early, sometimes feeding with swifts and hirundines. Frequent city centre parks; hunt over refuse tips, taking house crickets *Acheta domesticus*. Hibernate in trees and buildings. T, ex Fi, Ic, Ir, No; no recent Scottish records.

Leisler's Bat *Nyctalus leisleri*   Vespertilionidae
WS 28–34cm. Resembles small noctule but darker in colour, with hair blackish at base.

Uses tree holes, but also buildings in England and Ireland. Distribution and habits poorly documented but certainly occurs in C. London and Belfast (fairly common in Ir). Be, En, F, G, Ir.

Brown Long-eared Bat *Plecotus auritus*   Vespertilionidae
Formerly common long-eared bat WS 23–28·5cm. Extraordinarily long ears (up to 38mm). Bat sleeps with ears folded under wings, and tapering ear-like features which remain visible are actually the traguses; tragus is nearly half length of ear!.

Most likely to occur in wooded parks. Roosts in trees and buildings. T, ex Ic. Can be confused with very similar **grey long-eared bat** *P. austriacus*, more often found in towns on Continent than *auritus*; rare in southern En.

Pipistrelle

Noctule

Brown Long-eared Bat

Leisler's Bat

Gazetteer – organisations and areas of wildlife interest within urban boundaries

National and regional organisations

There are many national and regional organisations concerned with nature conservation and wildlife. Most of their sites and reserves are either in the countryside or on the urban fringes. This part of the gazetteer consists only of those major organisations which have direct involvement in areas within urban boundries with wildlife interest, either owning or managing their own sites or being involved with the development and management of sites in conjunction with other bodies such as local councils.

Avon Wildlife Trust
209 Redland Road,
Bristol BS6 6YU
Tel: Bristol 603076
An active trust with particular interest in managing urban reserves and sites, mainly in the Bristol area.

British Trust for Conservation Volunteers (BTCV)
36 St. Mary's Street,
Wallingford,
Oxon. OX10 0EU.
Tel: Wallingford 39766
Runs training courses and projects designed for schools, groups or individuals wanting to carry out practical conservation work, and has published several useful handbooks. It has twelve regional offices and over 300 affiliated local groups.

Council for Environmental Conservation (CoEnCo)
Zoological Gardens
Regent's Park,
London, NW1 4RY
Tel: 01 722 7111
Provides an enquiry service on all aspects of wildlife conservation including urban wildlife.

Ecological Parks Trust
c/o The Linnean Society,
Burlington House, Piccadilly,
London W1V 0CQ
Tel: 01 734 5170
Offers advice in setting up ecological parks and problems related to urban ecology. Manages three sites in London.

Friends of the Earth
377 City Road,
London EC1V 1NA
Tel: 01 837 0731
Campaigns to protect wildlife areas.

Glasgow Urban Wildlife Group
8 Kirklee Road
Glasgow G12 0TP
Is involved in urban wildlife sites in the Glasgow area.

London Wildlife Trust
80 York Way
King's Cross
London N1
One of the liveliest organisations campaigning for the conservation of urban wildlife sites. Manages a number of its own sites within Greater London and is involved in numerous others. Publishes useful information on setting up sites.

London may seem a concrete jungle on the ground but a bird's eye view reveals a patchwork of green parks, secret gardens and treelined roads, bustling with wildlife.

Nature Conservancy Council (NCC)

The official Government-funded body responsible for nature conservation throughout Great Britain. Responsible for the establishment and maintenance of National Nature Reserves and the notification of Sites of Special Scientific Interest (SSSIs).

Great Britain and England HQ
Northminster House,
Northminster,
Peterborough PE1 1UA
Tel: Peterborough 70345
Scotland HQ
12 Hope Terrace,
Edinburgh EH9 2AS
Tel: 031 447 4784
Wales HQ
Plas Penrhos,
Ffordd Penrhos,
Bangor,
Gwynedd LL57 2LQ
Tel: Bangor 355141

Nature Reserves Committee for Northern Ireland

Hut 6, Castle Grounds,
Stormont,
Belfast BT4 3SS
Tel: Belfast 768716
Similar responsibilities to NCC

Plymouth Urban Wildlife Group

David Curry, Dept. of Natural History, City Museum,
Drake Circus,
Plymouth PL4 8AJ
Group of professional naturalists with a supporting scheme which anyone can join.

Royal Society for Nature Conservation (RSNC)

22 The Green,
Nettleham,
Lincoln LN2 2NR
Tel: Lincoln 752326
National umbrella organisation for the local County Conservation and Wildlife Trusts. It is directly involved with urban wildlife survey projects – particularly through its junior branch WATCH which is sponsored by *The Sunday Times*.

Royal Society for the Protection of Birds (RSPB) (and Young Ornithologists' Club)

National organisation with many local urban members' groups. Dedicated to the conservation of wild birds and the enforcement of protective legislation. Undertakes research and manages many reserves, some in an urban setting. Provides information through films, lectures and publications.
National HQ
The Lodge,
Sandy,
Beds SG19 2DL
Tel: Sandy 80551
Wales HQ
Frolic Street,
Newtown,
Powys SY16 1AP
Tel: Newtown 26678
Scotland HQ
17 Regent Terrace,
Edinburgh EH7 5BN
Tel: 031 556 5624
Northern Ireland HQ
Belvoir Park Forest,
Belfast BT8 4QT
Tel: Belfast 692547

Rural Preservation Association (RPA)

The Old Police Station,
Lark Lane,
Liverpool L17 8UU
Tel: 051 728 7011
A national conservation organisation based in Liverpool, but covering the whole of the British Isles, with branches in Leeds, Lancaster, St. Helen's and Greater Manchester. Organised the 'Greensight' project in Liverpool, using native vegetation to restore derelict sites.

Scottish Wildlife Trust
25 Johnston Terrace,
Edinburgh, EH10
The national organisation of Scotland
concerned with all aspects of wildlife
conservation including urban wildlife.
It liaises with the government and
landowners on wildlife issues and
arranges lectures for public information. It runs over 40 nature
reserves.

Urban Wildlife Group
11 Albert Street,
Birmingham B4 7UA
Tel: 021 236 3626
Promotes nature conservation in the
urban West Midlands, carries out
valuable survey work and campaigns
to protect existing wildlife sites and
improve others.

Wildlife sites within urban boundaries

The following abbreviations have been used:

AWT	Avon Wildlife Trust
BTCV	British Trust for Conservation Volunteers
CP	Country Park
EPT	Ecological Parks Trust
LNR	Local Nature Reserve
LWT	London Wildlife Trust
NCC	Nature Conservancy Council
NHS	Natural History Society
NNR	National Nature Reserve
RPA	Rural Preservation Association
RSPB	Royal Society for the Protection of Birds
SSSI	Site of Special Scientific Interest
SWT	Scottish Wildlife Trust
TNC	(after name of county) Trust for Nature Conservation
UWG	Urban Wildlife Group
WARNACT	Warwicks Conservation Trust

Where species are mentioned without Latin names, descriptions can be found in the field guide.

No-one has ever published a compre-
hensive list of nature reserves found
within urban boundaries in the British
Isles, or catalogued the many open
spaces and other features of our
towns and cities that have attracted
the attention of naturalists. Almost
every street has near it a patch of
waste ground, a grass verge, derelict
house, overgrown garden, park or
pond – these are what we usually
regard as the 'real' urban wildlife
habitats, areas which harbour many
of the plants and animals discussed
in this book. Obviously it is imposs-
ible to catalogue sites of this sort.

The following list covers sites within
urban boundaries which possess
general wildlife interest. All of these
sites contain 'urban wildlife' but
many are reserves which also attract
or sustain species which are not
usually found within towns and cities.
   Sites on the urban fringe are
usually given a brief mention but not
those that are close to the limits of
the built-up area but are nevertheless
outside it. Nor can details be given of
coastal peninsulas which have
escaped urban development but are
completely cut off by it on the land-
ward side, e.g. Hengistbury Head,

Bournemouth (SZ 175905) and the localities of outstanding botanical importance, Berry Head, Brixham (SX 945566) and the Great Orme's Head, Llandudno (SH 770830). The localities listed have been grouped under regions. Addresses and/or National grid references are given to help the visitor to find the site. (The National Grid is a referencing system that applies to all maps of Britain. The two letters identify the 100 kilometre grid square. The numbers that follow pin point the position of the reserve, usually its centre. The first three (or four) numbers are across the square, the second three (or four) up the square.)

Greater London

London is fortunate in having many large open spaces, not only in its suburbs, but at its centre. Most of London's parks have been managed on formal lines but some of its commons have retained something of their original vegetation. A good deal of broad-leaved woodland has survived, especially in the south-east. The Thames, once heavily polluted, is now celebrated for its abundance of fish and for the large numbers of ducks and waders that frequent its lower reaches. London's reservoirs are also an important refuge for duck. Permits to visit some of these waters can be obtained by *bona fide* birdwatchers from the Thames Water Authority (see entries for Barn Elms and Walthamstow Reservoirs). Several of the larger reservoirs which may be visited lie on the outer fringes of London — only those situated within the built-up area are included in this Gazetteer.

Central London and the inner suburbs. Birds have adapted very well to the inner city environment. Kestrels, herring gulls, mallard, woodpigeons and jays have nested on buildings. Black redstarts still breed, despite the fact that bomb sites, their

original stronghold, have now been largely built over. Great crested grebes have colonised park lakes and there is a heronry in Regent's Park.

Public open spaces

Alexandra Park, Wood Green, N22 (TQ 298900). An area of woodland and scrub has been developed and a pond dug to support waterfowl, wetland plants and insects. Racecourse now managed as a meadow. Information Centre.

Barnes Common, Rocks Lane, Barnes, SW13 (TQ 225757). Relatively wild acid grassland and scrub. SSSI.

Battersea Park, SW11 (TQ 280771). Wildfowl collection attracts wild birds, including remarkable numbers of shoveler (*Anas clypeata*). Pochard (*Aythya ferina*), tufted duck and great crested grebe breed and grey herons visit.

Greenwich Park, Greenwich, SE10 (TQ 390775). Royal Park with many old trees, wooded sanctuary enclosures (no access) in paddock for fallow deer (*Dama dama*) — 'The Wilderness'. Small lake with wildfowl collection. Park adjoins games pitches of **Blackheath, SE3 (TQ 95765)**, frequented by migrating wheatears (*Oenanthe oenanthe*) and large flocks of gulls.

Hampstead Heath, NW3, NW5 and N6 (TQ 277–870). Mostly open grassland but West Heath more wooded. A small area, Ken Wood with near-by grassland and *Sphagnum* bog, is an SSSI. Several ponds.

Highgate Wood (TQ 283885) and Queen's Wood (TQ 288885), Muswell Hill Road, N6. Ancient woodland; dominant trees common oak and hornbeam (*Carpinus betulus*). Parkland Walk links the area with Finsbury Park.

Holland Park, Kensington (TQ 247797), entered from Holland Walk, W8. Northern end is wooded.

Hyde Park, W1, W2 and SW1 (TQ

275805) and Kensington Gardens W2 and SW7 (TQ 265803). Royal Parks sharing a lake called the Serpentine in Hyde Park and the Long Water in Kensington Gardens. Long Water is flanked by narrow wooded sanctuary; bank suitable for nesting kingfishers (*Alcedo atthis*) constructed here by LWT in 1984. Tufted duck, great crested grebes and herring gulls breed.

Regent's Park, NW1 (TQ 280830). Royal Park with an important wildfowl collection. Heronry on an island in the lake. Great crested grebe, tufted duck, pochard and herring gull also nest, and passerine species breeding recently include goldcrest, blackcap, long-tailed tit, bullfinch and redpoll.

St James's Park, Westminster, SW1 (TQ 295798). Royal Park with celebrated waterfowl collection. Tufted duck, pochard, great crested grebe and herring gull nest; little grebe bred in 1983. Thousands of roosting starlings, May–November.

Walthamstow Marshes, Clapton, E5 (TQ 354875). Last of the Lee Valley marshes, rich in plant, bird and insect life. Managed by the Lee Valley Regional Park Authority. Proposed SSSI

Cemeteries

Some of London's oldest cemeteries have become wildlife sanctuaries. The most important are those of **Abney Park, Stoke Newington High Street, N16 (TQ 334867)** (see photo p.10); **Brompton, Fulham Road, SW10 (TQ 256776); Highgate, Swain's Lane, N6 (TQ 285870),** restricted access; **Kensal Green, Harrow Road, W10 (TQ 230825),** restricted access; **Nunhead, Linden Grove, SE26 (TQ 354755); Tower Hamlets, Southern Grove, E3 (TQ 354755).**

Reservoirs

Barn Elms, Castelnau, Barnes, SW13 (TQ 228770). Four reservoirs and a reedy pond, the latter with breeding reed warblers (*Acrocephalus scirpaceus*). SSSI. Permit from Thames Water Authority, New River Head, Rosebery Avenue, EC1 4TP.

Walthamstow, Ferry Lane, Tottenham, N17 (TQ 353893). Large group of reservoirs in Lee Valley with famous heronry. SSSI. Permit from Thames Water Authority, The Grange, Crossbrook Street, Waltham Cross, EN8 8LX.

Newly-developed habitats

These are but a few of the many sites where vacant land has been transformed into a place of wildlife interest.

Brookmill Road, Lewisham, SE8 (TQ 377763). Old railway embankment. Grassland flora and tree nursery. Visits by arrangement with LWT.

Camley Street, Camden, NW1 (TQ 300834). A new pond with marsh, reed-bed and the beginnings of woodland beside Regent's Canal. Classroom and reception centre. Managed by LWT.

Gillespie Road, Highbury, N5 (TQ 314861). Natural park created on old railway land. London Borough of Islington.

Lavender Pond, Rotherhithe Street, SE16 (TQ 363805). Tel. 01 232 0498. A wardened EPT wetland nature park on site of Lavender Dock. Mon–Fri, 10.00–18.00 (or dusk).

continued over

Longmoor pool, Sutton Park in the West Midlands surrounded by heathlands and marshes, shows how much of the area looked before urbanisation. Canada geese are a common sight in the area.

Although the construction of motorways wreaks havock with wildlife, once the bulldozers have left, a wide variety of plants and animals soon move back in, as here under Spaghetti Junction, Birmingham.

Outer London

Public open spaces

Barn Hill, Wembley, Middlesex (TQ 194874) and Fryent Way, NW9 (TQ 198875). Woodland, grassland and ponds.

Brent Reservoir (Welsh Harp), NW2, NW4 and NW9 (TQ 217873). Canal reservoir with adjoining grassland, oakwood and scrub. Attractive to ducks and grebes. Rafts for breeding common terns (*Sterna hirundo*) and 'scrapes' dug for waders, etc. Plants include flowering rush (*Butomus umbellatus*). SSSI.

Bushy Park (TQ 148697) and Hampton Court Park (TQ 165680), Hampton, Middlesex. Park grassland with ponds and (mainly) open woodland. Fringed water-lily (*Nymphoides peltata*) and remarkable growths of mistletoe (*Viscum album*). Deer at liberty, red deer (*Cervus elaphus*) in Bushy Park, fallow (*Dama dama*) in both parks.

Crane Park, Great Chertsey Road, Twickenham, Middlesex (TQ 128729). Woodland by River Crane.

Crofton Heath, Crofton Road, Orpington, Kent (TQ 437666). Oakwood with hazel (*Corylus avellana*). SSSI.

Croham Hurst, Upper Selsdon Road, South Croydon (TQ 338632). Oakwood with hazel and birch. Rich molluscan fauna. Badger setts. SSSI.

Epping Forest (TQ 420980). Southern end penetrates NE. London. Ancient oak, beech and hornbeam woodland, more open areas and pools. SSSI. Conservation Centre at High Beach. Fallow deer (*Dama dama*) occur to N. end, sightings of Muntjac deer (*Muntiacus reevesi*).

Hounslow Heath, Staines Road, Hounslow, Middlesex (TQ 118746). Grassland and scrub with a little heath vegetation surviving.

Lesnes Abbey Wood, New Road, Abbey Wood, SE2 (TQ 481786). Broad-leaved woodland with wild daffodils (*Narcissus pseudonarcissus*). An SSSI because of its geological interest.

Mitcham Common, Croydon Road, Mitcham (TQ 290680). Grass heath with pond and woodland. Has a few reminders of its former botanical richness, e.g. needle whin (*Genista anglica*). Stonechats (*Saxicola torquata*) breed.

Oxleas Wood, Shooter's Hill, SE18 and Welling Way, SE19 (TQ 445757). Ancient woodland; oak (two spp.), hornbeam, wild service tree (*Sorbus torminalis*) and hazel coppice. Rich in bird and insect life. Adjoins Shepherdeas Wood and Jack Wood. Proposed SSSI.

Richmond Park (TQ 730200). Royal Park. Acid grassland with bracken areas, plantations and ponds. Red and fallow deer (*Dama dama*) at liberty. Badger setts.

Riddlesdown, Kenley, Surrey (TQ 327604). Chalk grassland, scrub and yew wood. Urban fringe. SSSI.

Wimbledon Common, SW19 (TQ 225720). Grass heath, woodland, ponds and two small bogs. Rich in birds and insects. SSSI.

Other sites

Chiswick (or Gunnersbury) Triangle, Chiswick Park, W4 (TQ 200787). Birch and willow woodland on old railway land. LWT to plan public access.

Dulwich Upper Wood, Farquhar Road, Crystal Palace, SE19 (TQ 337713). Tel. 01 761 6230. Victorian gardens reverted to woodland. Managed and wardened by EPT. Open 10.00–18.00 (or dusk).

Perivale Wood, Selborne Gardens, Greenford, Middlesex (TQ 160837). Oakwood with hazel coppice, wild service trees and bluebells (*Hyacinthoides non-scripta*). Contact Selborne Society for access. SSSI and LNR.

Ruxley gravel pits, Foots Cray, Kent (TQ 474700). Open water and marsh. Grebes nest, water rail (*Rallus aquaticus*) occurs and kingfishers (*Alcedo* *atthis*) have bred. Urban fringe. SSSI. Managed in conjunction with Kent TNC. Access by permit.

Sydenham Hill Wood, Sydenham Hill, SE26 (TQ 346726). Ancient remnant of the Great North Wood, with bluebells and wood anemones (*Anemone nemorosa*). Managed by LWT.

Syon Park Marsh, Isleworth, Middlesex (TQ 176766). Unmodified Thames river bank with willows and reed-bed. Habitat of rare invertebrates. Frequented by herons and cormorants (*Phalacrocorax carbo*). No access but can be viewed from towpath on Kew Gardens side. SSSI.

Thameside Ecological Park, River Road, Barking, Essex (TQ 469822). Old power station site. Grassland, pools and marsh with orchids. LWT management and development. Unrestricted access.

Southern England

Bristol and Plymouth are noted for their limestone plants; several towns in Kent and Sussex have areas of chalk downland within their boundaries; Poole, Bournemouth and Southampton have remnants of heathland. The estuarine mud-flats of Poole, Gillingham (Kent) and Portsmouth offer opportunities for seeing waders, ducks and brent geese (*Branta bernicla*). Herring gulls nest in many towns from Kent to Cornwall, mostly on the coast; the habit is well developed in Broadstairs, Brixham, Dover, Folkestone and Hastings. Both herring gull and lesser black-backed gull have nested in Bath and Bristol.

Avonmouth Sewage works (ST 535795), administered by Wessex Water Authority. Wetland plants, including ragged robin (*Lychnis flos-cuculi*) and marsh bedstraw (*Galium palustre*) in a meadow dissected by two streams. Permit only.

Bournemouth. Built on lowland heath, but little of it remains. Sand martins nest on the cliffs. (**Hengistbury Head,** see introduction).

Brighton. Still has rookeries, but no longer in the centre. **Moulsecoomb Wild Park, Lewes Road (TQ 327080)** has unmown chalk grassland and scrub on slopes encircling its games pitches.

Bristol. Celebrated for the **Avon Gorge (ST 563740),** habitat of many rare plants, some, e.g. Bristol rockcress (*Arabis stricta*) peculiar to the district. City has a large starling roost, centred on **Temple Meads Station (ST 597725)** and a flourishing fox population. Sites of interest include: **Dundry Slopes, above Aldwick Ave., Hartcliffe BS13**. AWT reserve with grassland, scrub and stream in public open space on urban fringe. **Kings Weston Hill, Kings Weston Road, BS11 (ST 550779).** AWT site, limestone grassland flanked by wooded slopes. **Snuff Mills Park, River View, BS16 (ST 626765).** Steeply wooded valley of River Frome. Dippers (*Cinclus cinclus*) occur. Plants include small teasel (*Dipsacus pilosus*).

Brixham. (Berry Head, see introduction).

Chatham. Coney Banks, Walderslade Road (TQ 760657). Chalk downland and scrub. Public open space.

Cheltenham. Rooks nest in The Promenade (SO 948224).

Exeter. River Exe is an important wildlife corridor.

Hastings. Badger setts within the town. **Thorpe's Wood, Upper Park Road (TQ 805103)** has a rich ground flora, and Alexandra Park, which adjoins it, has a varied bird population, with unusually tame collared doves.

Oxford. Open spaces beside **River Cherwell** create a wildlife corridor, allowing birds like sedge warbler (*Acrocephalus schoenobaenus*) and reed bunting (*Emberiza schoeniclus*) to penetrate the city. Blackbirds have been intensively studied in the Botanic Gardens and swifts in the tower of the University Museum.

Plymouth. Untamed edges of **The Hoe (SX 477536)** are noted for the Plymouth thistle (*Carduus pycnocephalus*) and a wealth of limestone and maritime plants. **Woodland Wood, Crownhill Road, Honicknowle (SX 470593)** is broad-leaved woodland with a rich ground flora; public open space. **The Plym estuary (SX 505550)** attracts waders at low tide.

Poole. Remnants of lowland heath damaged by urban expansion, e.g. part of **Talbot Heath (SZ 070930)** and, on the urban fringe, remains of **Canford Heath (SZ 032965)**. Good views of waders and brent geese from **Shore Road, Sandbanks (SZ 048880)**.

Portsmouth. Wintering purple sandpipers (*Calidris maritima*) frequent rocks off **Southsea Castle (SZ 642980)**. Sea holly (*Eryngium maritimum*), yellow horned-poppy (*Glaucium flavum*) and other shingle plants at **Eastney Beach (SZ 675989)**.

Salisbury. Water voles (*Arvicola terrestris*) frequent the River Avon in the main city car park (SU 143303) and around this area sand martins nest in drain-pipes.

Southampton. Southampton Common (SU 415145) has woodland, ponds and patches of wet and dry heath. Species not usually found in towns include bog bush-cricket (*Metrioptera brachyptera*), meadow thistle (*Cirsium dissectum*) and alder buckthorn (*Frangula alnus*). Field Studies Centre (managed by Southampton Common Studies Centre Association) in Cemetery Road, SO1 10.00–17.00 weekdays.

Weymouth. Radipole Lake **(SY 675800)**. RSPB reserve and SSSI with open water, reed-beds, hides, nature trail and reception centre; no permit needed. Grebes, ducks, waders, terns and gulls; little gulls (*Larus minutus*) regular visitors. An attractive alien spider (*Argiope bruennichi*) occurs. **Lodmoor (SY 687813)**. RSPB reserve and SSSI with hides; no permit needed. Wet grassland, brackish marsh and pools attracting waders, ducks and herons. Cetti's warbler (*Cettia cetti*) and bearded tit (*Panurus biarmicus*) at both reserves. **Ferrybridge (SY 666759)**. Intertidal area with saltmarsh at south end of The Fleet, attracting waders and terns. Unrestricted access.

The Midlands

The canals and old industrial sites of the Black Country and the Potteries are of particular interest. Abandoned railways in Birmingham, Wolverhampton and Stoke-on-Trent now serve as walkways and linear nature reserves.

Birmingham. A large starling roost is concentrated on **New Street** and **St Philip's Cathedral (SP 070868)**. Canals penetrate the centre. Brooks form wildlife corridors through the suburbs; frequented by grey wagtails, kingfishers and water voles. Canada geese very common on park lakes. UWG has involved local residents in transforming neglected sites into community nature parks, e.g. on **River Rea at Mill Lane, Northfield, B31 (SP 020786)** and at **Plants Brook. Kendrick Road, Sutton Coldfield (SP 138922)**. Only a few other species-rich localities can be mentioned. **The Ackers, Small Heath, B10 (SP 1033845)**. Variety of habitats on wetland includes replanted woodland. Public open space. **Cannon Hill Park, Edgbaston Road, B12 (SP 065837)**. Intensively managed gardens, lawns, open woodland, lakes and ponds but with interesting bird population. **Edgbaston Park, Edgbaston, B15 (SP 055841)**. SSSI. Broad-leaved woodland and swamp-fringed lake (Edgbaston Pool), adjoining golf course. Breeding birds include little grebe, great crested grebe, tree sparrow, reed bunting. **Edgbaston (or Rotton Park) Reservoir, Reservoir Road, B16 (SP 043867)**. Canal reservoir in public park. Waterside vegetation includes flowering rush. **Moseley Bog, off Yardley Wood Road, playing field, B13 (SP 094821)**. SSSI and proposed LNR. Wet broad-leaved woodland with *Sphagnum* and abundance of wood horsetail (*Equisetum sylvaticum*).

Priory Fields, Yardley Wood, B14 (SP 100791). Grass and wetland by canal, managed by WARNACT. Restricted access. **Sutton Park, Sutton Coldfield (SP 100970)**. SSSI with oak, birch and alder woods, heathland, pools and marshes. Birds include woodcock (*Scolopax rusticola*), tree pipit (*Anthus trivialis*) and redstart. Grass of Parnassus (*Parnassia palustris*), butterwort (*Pinguicula vulgaris*) and cranberry (*Vaccinium oxycoccos*) are a few of the many unusual plants. **Plants Brook, Walmley, (SP 139922)**. Grassland, open water, marsh and willow carr, fringed by industry and housing. **The Vale, Edgbaston, B15 (SP 054840)**. Landscaped area with lake overlooked by University halls of residence. Attractive waterside plants; breeding great crested grebes.

Coventry. WARNACT manages conservation gardens and tree nurseries at **Bell Green (SP 360822) and Wellington Street (SP 342796)**. Access by arrangement. **Stoke Floods (SP 375785)**. Lake (caused by mining subsidence) and wet meadow in the Sowe Valley. WARNACT site. Unrestricted access. **Tilehill Wood (SP 279790)**. Oak woodland with *Sphagnum* bog, on urban fringe. SSSI. Access by arrangement with WARNACT and Coventry NHS. **Wyken Slough, Alderman's Green (SP 362832)**. Pool, marsh and grassland. Access by arrangement with WARNACT.

Dudley. Several canals and old industrial land of exceptional interest.

Wooded limestone outcrops at **Dudley Castle Hill (SO 945915)** and the NNRs of **Mons Hill (SO 935925)** and the internationally famous **Wren's Nest (SO 938917)**, which has a geological nature trail. Other sites include **Doulton's Claypit, Netherton (SO 935872)**, SSSI with rock exposures, woodland scrub and marsh; **Ham Dingle, Stourbridge (SO 915826)**, public open space with damp oakwood and stream; **Pensnett Chase (SO 915885)**, grassland and scrub around canal reservoirs (Brierley Hill Pools) and derelict canal; **Saltwells Wood, Netherton (SO 932871)**, ancient oakwood, an SSSI and LNR. **Sedgley Beacon, (SO 923945)**, calcareous grassland; partly in SSSI. No permits required for the above sites.

Leicester. Knighton Spinney, Knighton Park (SK 605008). Ash woodland with wood anemones. Managed by Leicester and Rutland TNC and Leicester City Council. Permit needed. **Watermeads Ecological Park, Oakland Avenue, off Melton Road.** Wet meadow, oak, ash, alder carr, willow scrub, new pond. Managed by City Wildlife Project. Access along footpath.

Nottingham. Martin's Pond (SK 526402). Aquatic and marsh vegetation on LNR managed by Nottingham City Council and wardened by Nottingham TNC. Boardwalks across marsh.

Sandwell. Haden Hill Park, Haden Cross (SO 958855); public park where wildlife is encouraged; gardens, woodland, lake and river bank; nature trail. **Holly Wood, Queslett Road, B43 (SP 054943)**; woodland managed by UWG; unrestricted access. **Sandwell Valley CP, West Bromwich**; created on derelict industrial site and farmland; nature trail with woodland and pools at SP 032927; new lake, entrance off Park.

Stoke-on-Trent. Restoration of industrial dereliction on a massive scale and conversion of railway tracks into 'greenways'. **Central Forest**

Children taking part in the Glasgow Urban Fringe Clean-up Project one of many such projects organised by the British Trust for Conservation Volunteers.

Priory Wood near Walton Cemetery, Liverpool, is an area of reclaimed woodland and pasture close to the site of the 1984 International Garden Festival.

Park, Hanley (SJ 875485); tree-planted colliery site with pool. **Westport Water Park, Longport** (SJ 855502); Westport Lake and specially created wetland nature study area along Fowlea Brook. **Parkhall CP** (SJ 927443); old quarries; urban fringe.

Walsall. Rough Wood, Short Heath (SJ 984010); public open space; naturally restored industrial wasteland with woodland, scrub and pools. **St. Margaret's Lakes, Great Barr, B43** (SP 055950); ornamental woodland and lakes in hospital grounds; managed by Staffordshire TNC; access by arrangement.

Wolverhampton. Peasecroft Wood, Bilston (SO 950970); woodland managed by Bilston Conservation Association; unrestricted access. **West Park, WV1** (SO 905990); intensively managed public park with waterfowl collection; tufted duck breed.

Eastern England.

This predominantly agricultural region has few large towns.

Cambridge. Provides the best habitat for woodland birds in Cambridgeshire. Cattle-grazed commons by River Cam have wetland plants and birds. Along the river, sand martins nest in drainpipes.

Colchester. Plants growing on ancient town walls include East Anglian speciality lesser calamint (*Calamintha nepeta*).

Southend-on-Sea. Belfairs Great Wood (Great Wood and Dodds Grove), Hadleigh (TQ 820877). Public open space and nature reserve SSSI; broad-leaved woodland rich in birds and butterflies. **Leigh NNR** (TQ 831858). Waders, ducks and brent geese on Thames estuary off Leigh Old Town.

North of England

Much industrial wasteland is of interest, as at Bolton, where several species of orchid have appeared on an alkali works site in the Irwell-Croal valley. Wildlife has benefited from numerous reclamation projects based on ecological principles, e.g. the restoration of the once-industrialised **Sankey Valley, St. Helen's** (SJ 527976 – 565948), and Birchwood, Warrington New Town's development on **Risley Royal Ordnance Factory site** (SJ 660920). The Mersey and Tees estuaries are frequented by large numbers of ducks and waders. Herring gulls nest in many towns on the north-east coast, with largest numbers in Scarborough, South Shields, Staithes and Whitby. Kittiwakes nest on a flour mill in Newcastle and on buildings by the Tyne ferry, North Shields. The largest starling roosts are in Bradford, Huddersfield, Liverpool, Manchester, South Shields and Sunderland.

Blaydon. Shibdon Pond, Shibdon Road, NE21 (NZ 195628). Pond, reedbed, marsh, scrub and nature trail managed by Durham County Conservation Trust.

Crosby. Seaforth Dock Pools, Seaforth (SJ 315970). Two pools, one saline, one freshwater, and seasonally flooded hollows on reclaimed land north of Seaforth Container Base. Attractive to birds. Permit from Lancashire TNC.

Darlington. Brinkburn Pond, Brinkburn Road, DL3. Pond, reedbed, marsh and scrub managed by Durham County Conservation Trust and Durham CC.

Doncaster. Potteric Carr, Carr Hill Industrial Estate. Mining subsidence with reed-fen, lake and small pools. Managed by Yorkshire Wildlife Trust. Access unrestricted in part; permit for rest from British Rail.

Eastham. Eastham Woods CP (SJ 363815). Woodland and foreshore on western side of Mersey estuary.

Formby. Town has coastal dunes and woods on west side with red squirrels in pinewood at SD 280082. Ainsdale NNR (non-urban) close to north-west of town.

Gateshead. Windy Nook, Albion Street, NE10 (NZ 275605). Public open space with wild area developed by BTCV (Gateshead).

Leeds. Roundhay Park (SE 335380). Public park with lakes and woods. Pied flycatcher has nested.

Liverpool. RPA has planted many small derelict sites with native species, especially to the south of the conventionally managed Sefton Park (SJ 365940), e.g. at 14 Linnet Lane (SJ 370880). Croxteth Park CP (SJ 409944). Parkland, ponds and woodland on urban fringe, with facilities for field studies. Walton Cemetery, Priory Road, L4 (SJ 365940). Unofficial 'nature reserve' with mature trees and scrub.

Manchester. Magpies are remarkably common; redpolls occur in parks. Numerous derelict reservoirs ('lodges') formerly supplying water for dye-works, e.g. at Lower Crumpsall (SD 855016), now rich in aquatic plants and animals. Extensive restoration of land adjacent to rivers and canals passing through city. Mersey Valley, from Manchester Ship Canal (SJ 727935) to Stockport (SJ 881903) is a recreational area managed by Mersey Valley Joint Committee; water parks at Sale and Chorlton, reed-beds, meadows, woodland and scrub; nature reserve at Chorlton Ees (SJ 805933). Heaton Park (SD 830045). Public open space with some wild areas, ponds and interpretative centre.

Newcastle-upon-Tyne. Benwell Nature Park, Atkinson Road, Benwell, NE4. Educational nature park with nature trails, created by local children. Jesmond Dene, Jesmond, NE2 (NZ 260665). Public park in rocky ravine with stream and waterfall, still partly wild; woodland birds.

Peterlee. Castle Eden Dene (NZ 437400), steeply wooded, botanically rich and entomologically famous valley forms southern boundary of the New Town. Red squirrels. Managed by local authority. Footpaths. SSSI.

South Shields. South Marine Park (NZ 373675). Kittiwakes bathe on lake.

Southport. Wildfowl visit the Marine Lake (SD 335180) and Hesketh Park (SD 348182): sea duck on the Marine Lake. (A National Wildfowl Refuge lies north-east of the town). Waders frequent mud by the pier.

Stalybridge. East Wood, Cheetham Park (SJ 972977). RSPB reserve. Access by arrangement with Warden, 12 Fir Tree Cresent, Dukinfield, SK16 5EH.

Sunderland. Hetton Staiths (NZ 392575). Derelict site beside River Wear reclaimed and planted as semi-wild public open space. Timber Beach (NZ 369584). Durham County Conservation Trust reserve by River Wear; Saltmarsh. Unrestricted access.

Whitley Bay. Marden Quarry, Marden Road South (NZ 355715). Public park; scrub, grassland, pond.

continued over

Wales

The only large conurbations are on the south coast. In the coal-mining region more or less continuous ribbon development has taken place along the mountain valleys. The built-up areas here are so narrow that the countryside is rarely more than a kilometre away. Both herring and lesser black-backed gulls have nested on buildings in Llandudno in North Wales, and in Cardiff, Newport and the inland towns of Hirwaun and Merthyr Tydfil in the south. Herring gulls have colonised several other towns.

Cardiff. Ravens (*Corvus corax*) have nested in the city. **Bute Park (SO 175775).** Public park by River Taff, forming a green corridor to city centre. Wild woodland and waterside vegetation as well as usual park features; rich in bird life. **Glamorganshire Canal Nature Reserve, Whitchurch (SO 143803).** Canal rich in aquatic plants; alder carr and bluebell wood. SSSI. Footpaths. **Roath Park (SO 184795).** Public park with some wild vegetation, mainly at north end. Large lake with introduced waterfowl which attracts wild duck frequenting Llanishen and Lisvane Reservoirs (SO 187820) where access is limited and by permit only.

Llandudno. (Great Orme's Head, see introduction.)

Swansea. Lower Swansea Valley (SS 665960). Classic example of industrial wasteland restoration, with lake, woodland, river bank and nature trails. Unrestricted access. **Singleton Park (SS 632924).** Public park; fine trees and pond; some wild vegetation.

Scotland

The main interest is centred on Glasgow and Edinburgh in the Central Lowlands. Both cities have starling roosts.

Edinburgh. Common gulls are particularly numerous in winter. Coastal roads between Cramond and Portobello afford views of large numbers of wintering duck on the Firth of Forth. **Bawsinch Wildlife Reserve, Duddingston (NT 286722).** SWT reserve with ponds, trees and goose-grazing area created on former rubbish tip. Adjoins Duddingston Loch. Access by arrangement. **Duddingston Loch (NT 283725).** Department of Environment bird sanctuary. Open water and reed-beds. Important wildfowl sanctuary, especially for pochard. Introduced greylag geese (*Anser anser*). No access but visible from Holyrood Park. **Holyrood Park (NT 275732).** Public park, dominated by Arthur's Seat. Of considerable geological interest and the more rugged parts have interesting vegetation. **Royal Botanic Garden, Inverleith Row (NT 246753).** Open daylight hours. Several species of bird feed from the hand.

Glasgow. Tree-planted walkways, notably by the Rivers Kelvin and Cart and along old railway track near Victoria Park. Scots pine, oak, birch and hazel planted around road inter-section north of **Kingston Bridge (NS 580654).** Indian balsam is common on river banks; large-flowered hemp-nettle (*Galeopsis speciosa*) occurs on wasteland. **Dawsholm Park (NS 553696);** oak/beech woods, bird sanctuary and nature trail. **Hogganfield Loch (NS 643672);** wildfowl collection attracts wild duck, cormorants and whooper swans (*Cygnus cygnus*). **Linn Park (NS 584590);** woodland and water-side nature trail and nature centre. **Pollok Park (NS 555625);** parkland, woodland, meadow and nature trail; roe deer (*Capreolus capreolus*) occur.

Nature trails in several other public parks. Possil Loch (NS 585701). SWT reserve on urban fringe. Loch and marsh near canal. Wintering birds include whooper swan. Access by arrangement.

Northern Ireland

Belfast. The BTCV is in the process of developing a network of sites throughout the inner city limits. **Beersbridge Nature Walk, Beersbridge Road (off Newtonard Road), East Belfast** is an old railway cutting. Scrub, marshland, badger setts and marsh plants.

Acknowledgements

The publishers would like to thank Bridget Daly, W. G. Teagle and the following people for their help in compiling the information in the gazetteer:

R. Barber, Rural Preservation Association

George Barker, Nature Conservancy Council

John Barnes and Clive Morgan, Glasgow Urban Wildlife Group

Brian Bar-Taylor, Southampton BTCV

Linda Blogg, West Yorkshire BTCV

Ian Collis, West Midlands County Council

Angela Cooper, Cleveland Nature Conservation Trust

Mike Crafer, Hertford County Council

Clive Davies, Midland BTCV

Tim Edwards, N. Ireland BTCV

Julie Gammar, Durham County Conservation Trust

Nigel Greenhalgh, East Anglia BTCV

D. Griffiths, Recreational Services Dept., Manchester

Elizabeth Holder, BTCV

Alison Johnson, Avon Wildlife Trust

Trevor Leadbitter, North East BTCV

M.E. Ben Monra and Barry Caldow, Liverpool City Council

John Newton and Chris Jordan, London Wildlife Trust

Graham Pinfield, Urban Wildlife Group, Birmingham

Annette Preece and Roger Broad, RSPB

Dr Franklyn Perring, RSNC

Tony Seymour, Northumberland Wildlife Trust

Roger Shaw, Yorkshire Wildlife Trust

Chris Shore, Nature Conservancy Council

Philip Steele

David Stevens

Margaret Wood, Warwickshire Conservation Trust

PHOTOGRAPHIC ACKNOWLEGEMENTS

AEROFILMS: 204; AQUILA PHOTOGRAPHICS, STUDLEY: Steve Downer 10 top, 63 left; J.V. and G.R. Harrison 10 bottom, 11; Michael Leach 30; E. Soothill 13; BIOFOTOS, FARNHAM: Heather Angel 22 top, 33 top, 37, 50, 210; MICHAEL CHINERY: 76; BCTV: 215 top; BRUCE COLEMAN, UXBRIDGE: 25, 33 right, 67; Joy Langsbury 33; Kim Taylor 73; BOB GIBBONS PHOTOGRAPHY, RINGWOOD: 42 bottom; BRIAN HAWKES 17 top; JACANA, PARIS: Bernhard Stieger 42; Varin 19; Volot 27; PETER LOUGHRAN: 63 right; NATURAL HISTORY PHOTOGRAPHIC AGENCY: L. Campbell 79; Steven Dalton 41 top; Michael Leach 6; NATURE PHOTOGRAPHERS LIMITED: 17; Andrew Cleare 60; Michael Leach 22 bottom; RICHARD PORTER: Title-Page, 14; PREMA PHOTOS: R.G. Preston-Mafham 5, 41 bottom; RURAL PRESERVATION ASSOCIATION: Tom Kemp 215 bottom; ZEFA: Hackmann 53; Dr David Corke, 55.

Glossary

Arthropods Invertebrate animals with segmented bodies and jointed legs, e.g. the insects, centipedes, millipedes, crustaceans, spiders, and their allies.

Awns The bristles which are sometimes a prominent feature of flowering and fruiting grasses, e.g. the 'beard' on an ear of wheat or barley.

Axil The angle between a leaf-stem and the plant stem from which it grows.

Barbels The fleshy, beard-like filaments drooping from a fish's mouth.

Bract A leaf-like feature which grows below a flower stalk.

Calcar The long, bony or cartilaginous spur projecting from the heel of a bat, which forms part of the outer margin of the tail membrane.

Chelicerae The biting jaws of spiders and other arachnids.

Cultivar A variety of a plant produced by cultivation.

Disc-floret One of the minute flowers which form the central feature of some composite flower-heads.

Eclipse The plumage ducks acquire in summer during which period the flight feathers are moulted and the males may resemble the females.

Elytra The hard, horny forewings of a beetle (sing. elytron).

Epiphytic From 'epiphyte', a non-parasitic plant which grows on another plant.

Foliose Leaf-like.

Node The point on a stem from which leaves grow.

Nutlet A small nut – a fruit with a hardened outer covering.

Pappus The hair-tuft that enables a tiny fruit (e.g. that of a dandelion) to be dispersed by the wind.

Parthenogenetic From 'parthenogenesis' (virgin birth).

Pinioned The term used to describe a bird which has been rendered flightless by the amputation of part of its wing.

Pinnate Composed of separate leaflets arranged in opposite pairs on either side of a leaf stalk, so that the whole (compound) leaf resembles a feather.

Prolegs The sucker-like legs on the hind end of a caterpillar or a sawfly larva.

Ray-floret One of the minute (usually) strap-shaped flowers which form the margin of a composite flower-head like that of the daisy.

Rhizome A creeping, underground stem which acts as a food store.

Sett The burrow system of a badger.

Spikelet A single grass flower or a group of grass flowers together with their enclosing bracts.

Stipules Scale-like or leaf-like appendages at the base of a leaf-stalk, usually paired.

Suckers Shoots growing directly from the underground stem of a tree or bush, often appearing at some distance from the parent plant.

Tendril A modified stem or leaf which enables certain plants to climb, usually by entwining.

Thallus A simple vegetative plant body which is not differentiated into root, stem and leaf.

Tragus A lobe of skin projecting from the base of the outer ear; particularly well developed in certain species of bats.

Umbel A more or less flat-topped inflorescence in which the flower-stalks arise from one point at the top of a stem – like the ribs of an umbrella.

Whorl (in plants) A circle of leaves or other structures radiating from the same level on a stem.

Whorl (in molluscs) A section of a coiled or spiral shell which forms a complete turn of the coil or spiral.

Selected Bibliography

Baines, C., *How to Make a Wildlife Garden*, Elm Tree Books, Hamish Hamilton, 1985

Baines, C., *Wildlife Garden Notebook*, The Oxford Illustrated Press, 1984

Baines, C., and Smart J., *A Guide to Habitat Creation*. Ecology Handbook No. 2. Greater London Council, 1984.

Bornkamm R., Lee J.A., and Seaward, M.R.D. (ed.),*Urban Ecology*, The Second European Ecological Symposium, Berlin, 8-12 September 1980. Blackwell Scientific Publications, Oxford, 1982.

Burton J.A., *Nature in the City*. The Danbury Press, London, 1976.

Burton R.M., *Flora of the London Area*. London Natural History Society, 1983.

Chinery M., *A Field Guide to the Insects of Britain and Northern Europe*. Collins, London, 1974.

Chinery M., *The Natural History of the Garden*. Collins, London, 1977.

Darlington A., *Ecology of Refuse Tips*. Heinemann Educational Books Ltd., London, 1969.

Darlington A., *Ecology of Walls*. Heinemann Educational, 1981.

Fitter R.S.R., *London's Natural History*. Collins New Naturalist, London, 1945.

Goodwin D., *Birds of Man's World*. British Museum (Natural History), London, 1978.

Hawksworth D.L., and Rose F., *Lichens as Pollution Monitors*. The Institute of Biology's Studies in Biology No. 66. Arnold, London, 1976.

Jones D., *The Country Life Guide to Spiders of Britain and Northern Europe*. Newnes Books, 1983.

Laurie I. (ed.), *Nature in Cities: The Natural Environment in the Design and Management of Urban Green Space*. Wiley, Chichester, 1979.

London Natural History Society, *The Birds of the London Area*. Revised edition. Rupert Hart-Davis, London, 1964.

Mabey R., *The Unofficial Countryside*. Collins, London, 1973.

Mabey R., *Street Flowers*. Kestrel Books, Harmondsworth, 1976

Mead C., *Robins*. Whittet Books, 1984.

Mitchell A., *A Field Guide to the Trees of Britain and Northern Europe*. Collins, 1974.

Morris P., *Hedgehogs*. Whittet Books, 1983.

Mourier H., and Winding O., and Sunesen E., *Collins Guide to Wild Life in House and Home*. London, 1977.

Murton R.K., *Man and Birds*. Collins New Naturalist, London, 1978.

Nadel I.B., and Oberlander C.H., *Trees in the City*. Pergamon, Oxford, 1977.

Owen D., *Towns and Gardens*. Ed. Ferguson-Lees J., and Campbell, B. Hodder and Stoughton, London, 1978.

Rose F., *The Wild Flower Key: British Isles and Northwest Europe*. Warne, 1981.

Ruff A., *Holland and the Ecological Landscapes – A Study of Recent Developments in the Approach to Urban Landscape*. Deanwater, London, 1979.

Salisbury, Sir Edward, *Weeds and Aliens*. Collins New Naturalist, London, 1961.

Simms E., *Birds of Town and Suburb*. Collins, London, 1975.

Simms E., *The Public Life of the Street Pigeon*. Hutchinson, 1979.

Soper T., *Wildlife Begins at Home*. David and Charles, 1975

Sukopp H., and Werner P., *Nature in Cities*. Council of Europe, Strasbourg, 1982.

Summers-Smith J.D., *The House Sparrow*. Collins New Naturalist, London, 1963.

Teagle W.G., *The Endless Village*. Nature Conservancy Council, 1978.

West Midlands County Council, *The Nature Conservation Strategy for the County of West Midlands*. West Midlands County Council, Birmingham, 1984.

Wheeler A., *The Tidal Thames: The History of a River and its Fishes*. Routledge and Kegan Paul, London 1979.

Index

Page numbers in **bold** indicate field guide entry.